To Kyle

To God Be All
the Glory!

Edwina
302 690 6679
Edwina-bell@yahoo.com
11/30/17

Be Blessed

AS IT WAS WRITT(I)N

By Edwina Bell, M.H.S.

FOUR-YEAR JOURNAL ENTRIES
OF A RECOVERING PERSON
DRUGS/ALCOHOL/MENTAL ILLNESS
CRIME/PROSTITUTION/MURDER
HOMELESSNESS...

As It Was Writt*(i)*n - Journal Entries

By: Edwina Bell, M.H.S.

Cover Design, Editing, Photography by: Leroy Grayson

Logo Designs by: Andre M. Saunders

Editor: Anelda L. Attaway

Co-Editor: Edwina Bell, M.H.S.

Images: Edwina Bell M.H.S., Leroy Grayson, whstatic.com

© 2015 Edwina Bell, M.H.S.

978-0-9916648-8-7

Library of Congress Control Number: 2015955753

FOREWORD

Mom went from Riches to Rags,

From having the most Swag to eating out of Trash Bags.

From Fame to Shame, she remained the only one to Blame.

Who was she before she became a Prostituting Whore?

She was an aspiring young woman, full of Goals and Perseverance,

But was looking in all the wrong places for Acceptance.

God bestowed on her the strong will to Survive, which

is why she is standing here today thanking Him that she is still Alive.

She still has a vision to accomplish her God-given Mission.

She is just Grateful she NO LONGER in that Demonic Disposition.

So from Rags back to Riches, to Eating off of fine Dishes.

Who is she we asked before – she is OUR MOTHER who WON the

Spiritual War only through the Grace of God!!!

Kenisha T. Dockery, CEO
Dwight K. Dockery II, Ed.D.

ACKNOWLEDGMENTS

To God be the Glory!!

Lord, *THANK YOU* for *EVERYTHING!*

Your Grace and Mercy brought me through, I'm living this moment because of You; I want to thank You and Praise You too, for it was Your Grace and Mercy that brought me through…!

Amazing Grace how sweet the sound that saved a wretch like me. I once was lost but now am found, was blind and now I see…!

I'm not a natural being having a spiritual experience; I'm a spiritual being living this natural experience!

Song by Donald Lawrence

Lord, my present mind-set
And my present attitude
Is displayed in my present behavior.
Lord, help me to remain humble and teachable
Until my purpose has been fulfilled on this earthly journey!

DEDICATIONS

These journal entries are dedicated to:

Those who have a *"Made Up Mind"* to recover;

Those who pray to have a *"Made Up Mind"*
To recover from all addictions;

Those who are on the fence of having a *"Made Up Mind"*
To recover from all addictions;

Those who have a *"Made Up Mind"*
To learn from their mistakes *and* the mistakes of others;

Those who have a *"Made Up Mind"*
To ask for help and use it; and

Those who have a *"Made Up Mind"*
To accept and experience the joy of a *spiritual rebirth*!

TABLE OF CONTENTS

TABLE OF CONTENTS

TABLE OF CONTENTS

APPENDIX- AS IT WAS WRITT*IN* *(FOR REFERENCE)*

INTRODUCTION

The purpose of this book is to share with other recovering persons and those who provide treatment plans for them, the importance of keeping a daily journal of events, feelings, situations, and circumstances as they occur during the process of recovery from the disease of addiction. The rewards of journalizing are beneficial in so many ways to one's spiritual growth, in spite of not knowing the correct spelling, grammar or punctuation at the time of recording. I am a recovering person who have sustained from all mood altering substances since February 23, 1990, one day at a time.

As a former substance abuser, I feel compelled to share my experience, strength and hope with others. I hope to prevent someone from picking up a drug for the first time, inspire someone to choose a new way of life from drugs, and encourage those who have chosen a new way of life to reach back and help others to recover.

I was introduced to alcohol at a young age. To help make ends meet, my mother had parties where alcohol and food were sold. At one of those parties, I remember lurking in the background watching the adults drinking, eating and smoking while playing cards, and seemingly having fun. Once when my mother's back was turned, I grabbed a cup off the table and drank what was in it. It tasted nasty and made me gag. Nevertheless, I drank all of it.

Shortly thereafter, I felt giggly and began dancing in the middle of the floor. The grown-ups surrounded me saying, *"Ah, isn't she cute, just look at her."* What I remember most was the *attention* I received from others. However, I did not realize the behavior I was exhibiting was a result of the alcohol I drank. From that moment, *I associated drinking with having fun and being the center of attention.*

At age eight, I secretly began smoking cigarettes. By age 10, I began hanging out with girlfriends whose parents kept plenty of liquor in their homes. I experienced my first drunk at age 12 while visiting one of those friends. I decided, with encouragement from my friends, to taste all the different liquors stored in the cabinet. Shortly thereafter, while at the local recreation center, I fell down a flight of stairs, felt sick to my stomach and vomited all over the place. I was unaware how I got home. *But again, I remember having fun and being the center of attention.*

By 14, my friends had introduced me to marijuana. At 18, I was introduced to angel dust and black beauties (speed pills). By 20, I was snorting cocaine, and at 25 I began smoking crack. By 28, I had become a full-blown crack addict. I lost jobs, material things, family ties and, most of all I felt I had lost my mind. I had reached the point where I did anything to get drugs or money to buy them. I would have sold my soul if someone had offered to buy it.

I have been raped, beaten, set up, spit on and called all kinds of names. I have had guns put to my head and knives to my throat. By the grace of God, I escaped death many times. However, there were others who were not as fortunate.

I became a disgrace to myself, my family and to society. My physical hygiene was nonexistent. I was emotionally and spiritually dead. Eventually, I became homeless, felt helpless, and wanted to die. I attempted suicide twice. The last time I used drugs I was consumed with self-loathing, shame, guilt, despair and fear. During one of the most humiliating encounters of my addiction, I had a split second of sanity–I hollered out a desperate cry to a God I heard about but did not know asking him to, *"Take me out of this life NOW or show me a better way!"*

The journey began when He spared my life that early morning while underneath a parked car in the streets of Philadelphia. After being summoned by the police to come from beneath the car, I was taken home to a disgusted and frustrated husband. He asked a question I'm sure I heard many times, but this time it was different. He asked, "Edwina, what are YOU going to do now?" For the first time, I heard the word YOU!

I proceeded to get off the couch, made my way to the phone, called the first rehab I had went to several years ago and said to them, *"I not only need help, I want help!* They asked how soon I could come and I told them NOW! If I had to walk there, I would have. My husband took me there and I knew then somehow that I was going all the way or not at all. Through a power unknown to me, I had a *MADE UP MIND!* Thus began my journey of spiritual recovery 25 years ago!

It was suggested that I go to long term treatment because 30, 60, and even 90 days was not good for me. The rehab recommended that I take a year to build a foundation of recovery. I accepted. On March 7, 1990, I was taken by my husband to a recovery community in the mountains of Williamsport, Pennsylvania, and lived with 12 other women in a Recovery House. It was here that the foundation of recovery was etched in stone.

For the next couple of months, I did what was suggested majority of the time. I'm so glad I did! Within a short period of time, I faced three situations that could have sent me back: 1) I was diagnosed with cervical cancer; 2) one of the ladies' sucker-punched me twice over a pair of hot curlers; and 3) my youngest brother who I turned on to crack tried to commit suicide back home in Philadelphia.

It wasn't until the middle of April 1990 that I asked someone to be my temporary sponsor. The rest is history as you will see on the following pages. Just by taking simple suggestions put me on a spiritual journey with 12-spiritual principles from a 12-Step Program and incredible encounters with a God I did not even know.

To God be the Glory!!!

MAY 7, 1990

AT THE FORK IN THE ROAD

My first actual journal, to begin this given moment. I am on direction from my sponsor to keep a daily journal of my feelings.

Here goes!

I feel free enough to write about the newly found freedom. Freedom of expressions, without fear of expressing them. For the first time, I can truly say and feel as if I am finding a new way of life and of living a more positive and purposeful life. The new, and quite different, experiences I'm going through are met with a faith stronger than I realized. I am able to be challenged by big and small obstacles, but I feel this is nothing compared to what I experienced in my addiction. Being sober and learning to learn how to deal with life on life's terms is a very spiritual enlightenment and awareness.

I am finding out that following the advice and suggestions of my sponsor, and other significant others, are becoming more easily understood and acceptable. For a long while, I believed that no one else could possibly know what's best for me. But being an addict, I should know quite the opposite. I really don't know, any longer, what's best for me. I must begin to grow in all areas all over again. What I thought I knew got me into this predicament of not realizing the extent of the damage I have done to myself. It has only been by the direction of my Higher Power that I am exactly where my self-willed personality and by God given direction that I…

(Incomplete)*

MAY 8, 1990

My day started out with my usual meditation time and prayer.

I've been feeling rather undecided about the move I'm about to take. And after gathering feedback and opinions, and really soul searching, I decided the best move at this time was to go the "Y".

Going to meetings, after following direction, enables me to attempt to find the validity in them. I don't know what's best for me at all, especially in recovery, and relying on outside constructive opinions, I feel more comfortable taking them.

I was able to learn about my house manager; a little of the human side. We had a white book meeting and I was able to direct certain feelings and observations about her. At just by having that meeting, I learned a lot about myself through others. We all have our suppressed fears and knowing and sharing those of others is giving me the chance to recognize the masks of myself and of others. I'm really attempting to seek out the good and positive in others. I'm getting to realize that my disease has so many disguises that it takes others to help point them out. *I'm growing tremendously, even by taking the time out to do this. And I'm glad I am. For somewhere down the line, I want to be able to replay the tapes of my initial recovery.*

I'm truly grateful to my Higher Power and I'm beginning to see that slowly but surely, my prayers are being answered. I feel excited about my newly found faith in my Higher Power, the fellowship and people in general.

MAY 9, 1990

Woke up feeling pretty good and positive, thanking my Higher Power for all the blessings he has bestowed upon me.

Having went to bed feeling that all things can be taken care of through prayer and positive actions. It's funny how situations are not coincidental, but carefully mapped out by our Creator. Having talked with??? and getting to know her better, allowed me to believe that there is always hope for everyone, if given a chance.

After going to the morning meeting, I felt pretty damn good about the progress I seem to be making in all aspects of my life.

A very enlightening experience happened to me today. When I went to work at the Doctor's office, I found a note and a key for me at the door. I was there alone for two hours. I was amazed at the amount of trust that was placed upon me by the lady I worked for. I thanked my Higher Power immediately and said this was only possible in recovery. Things are beginning to piece together and not by my doing. I seem to be following the guidance of my Creator and the positive people he has placed into my life. I really, really felt trusted for the first time in my life. And the feeling was great. So great, that I came home in disbelief that what had taken place must have been a dream, but it wasn't, it was true. I feel so much alive and have so much to be grateful for, and I owe it all to my Higher Power direction; and am finally acknowledging that if I keep my hand out of it, all things are possible.

MAY 10, 1990

FIRST CHURCH IN RECOVERY

COVENANT-CENTRAL PRESBYTERIAN CHURCH

Having been aware of the blessings of my Higher Power and the amazing and uplifting feeling of someone entrusting me with sincere and unconditional trust, uplifted my spirit unbelievably. I shared the feelings with my sisters and others. It was truly an enlightening experience.

My day started out with prayer and meditation and reading of my literature. It always seem to fit some event of a previous thought or situation, which I find encouraging.

I did something quite differently this morning; I attended an aerobic class at the church. Sharing conversation and women talk before exercising was very pleasing and educational. For a sister and I were able to enlighten non-members on the growth of recovery and our outlook. We received praise, as well as an incentive to continue the growth we were able to share. I really found out that I'm really out of shape because I was tired out. But over all, it was fun, real fun.

After that, I was able to go to a meeting, and still following direction, I was able to listen once again. The topic was "Loyalty to the Group". It made me think of letting others down if I were to get high. And the friendships I have developed and the attachments I have developed make me aware of the hurt I would cause myself and others. It was a good topic.

I went to work at the church and I had asked my Pastor to write a "letter on my behalf" to help aid in me getting into the "Y". Well, I never really knew how much people were able to see and believe the potential in me. This letter I read was "one of the most" beautiful letters I have ever read about myself, even now tears of joy are flowing. Because I feel that God is truly working through me, to be able for others to see, as well as make comments of such positive and strong and sincere words and feelings about me. Another day of triumph!!, which I shall remember and put into the bank.

Thank you Higher Power!

MAY 11, 1990

Three o'clock am – woke up with "Get-up, get out the house – someone broke in – get out! Well, I froze for a minute and was scared and with uncertain feelings – as we panic a lot. But all that happened was someone threw a beer bottle in the window and we really found out that the house was really not safe. But, enough of that.

I want to express another miracle or reward in recover. One of the women whom I have the greatest admiration for called upon me to help her today. That person is Renee. I felt honored, privileged and special when she felt as though I was the one she chose to help her. Feelings of happiness, feelings of amazement and feelings of unbelief, but most of all, feelings of gratitude. This person is so special to me, I really believe she is filled with the Holy Spirit. I receive so much strength from her, for I can truly see the God-light shine through her.

I feel I'm depositing these rewards in the bank, for they are truly coming back to back.

MAY 13, 1990

Of all the days in my life, this was one of pure fulfillment. I awoke with the anticipation of sharing Mother's Day with my children. And oh what a day it was.

I did my usual daily prayer and meditation, called and wished "my Mommy" a very, very happy Mother's day.

I'm so grateful to be alive and sober today. I started preparing for church. I started early. By the time I was on my way out of the door, my children were parked and on their way out of the car. Oh! How I praised God. Oh! How I praised Him. Seeing my children in the light of sobriety and recovery was a feeling of complete wholeness.

We all went to church and the congregation was very attentive to me and shared a lot of affection and kind words on my behalf to my children. The feelings I was experiencing during service was so rewarding; holding my children hands, watching as they experienced something quite different – serving and praising Jesus among a 99% white congregation. It was kind of humorous at first, but the feelings of sharing this day with my children, "beginning" in the house of the Lord, made me feel total at one with my Creator. Giving thanks, gratitude and feelings of the utmost respect; for I have found that through it all "all things are possible" in the time "He" chooses. And I, glad this was my day of complete recognition of unity between the four of us, God, my children and myself. Thank you so, so, so much.

After service, we enjoyed a day of skating together and for the first time, I felt it was just me and my children enjoying the love, excitement and joy of being truly with one another. We snapped pictures, laughed,

laughed and laughed together. It was truly feelings that I can't even express. For so long I waited for this day because it gave me a chance to see what is truly important to me and my children and that is to enjoy and salvage each waking moment together. After skating, I took them to the movies. I let them enjoy a moment of independence. I, on the other hand, did something I wanted to do or should not have done. I went to see someone and was able to enjoy a close encounter, one that reopened feelings of the past. We were able to discuss our children in ways which proved to be beneficial as parents; it was as if I was among my real family. And I felt good. When we went to pick them up, we were late and I can imagine their first reaction. But it wasn't long before they saw the most important two people of their lives, their mom and dad. We played video games and I actually saw my family from a different view this time, being sober. I enjoyed every minute of it, I really, really did.

Afterwards, we came back to the house and ate and for a moment, we all sat together and prayed together. Well it was time for them to go and for the first time it was no ill feelings of ours that this was the last time because we all knew and wanted to do it again soon.

HAPPY MOTHERS DAY

THE FAMILY

MAY 15, 1990

Woke up this morning from a dream. A dream in which someone in my family was selling drugs at the house we lived in as children, 2642. It appeared that the neighbor knew about it but my family members were in denial. I knew it existed because I pretended to be a customer and found out that my nephew was selling caps; had a bundle; hid them under the couch, and saw and heard my family saying how the neighbors were talking. This is all I can remember now.

Got up and prayed and meditated and read my literature as usual. Feeling rather restless, for I go for the operation in two days. Entertaining thoughts of self-willing on a sexual tip. Attempting very hard not to feed into it.

I have feelings of concern for someone special, Renee, who is not feeling well at all. I prayed for her and asked God to have her call me if she needs me. Please God, please make her days as painless as possible; but fill her heart and soul with acceptance and endurance; uplift her spirits and bring forth moments of laughter, in Jesus name, I pray, Amen.

I finally came to realize, after talking with my counselor, the need to regain my independence from my husband. I felt strange at first by saying that because he is helping me financially. If I were to regain my financial status, how and what could he offer me? For all I ever wanted from any man was love and affection and the freedom to express it; as well as receive it. I feel I am gaining more and more insight each day. And I feel I am really keeping my focus on recovery and working this program. Overall, I feel I'm just starting a new way of life.

MAY 16, 1990

Thoughts of tomorrow are getting strong. Was able to pray and meditate as usual. Today was one of "facing fears" and getting feedback and support from others.

My day was basically busy, in attempt to keep myself from drifting afar. Feelings of faith prevailing.

Went to my morning meeting. Afterwards checked on the "Y" residency; was told to check back in a few days. Was able to gather information regarding camp for when my son arrives.

Worked at the church for a few hours; came home and relaxed until my meeting at 7:30/AA. I am chairperson and I feel more at ease and comfortable about not sharing at meetings, but even having to read material or the format proved to be satisfying. The step we read and shared on was Step 1. And by being directed by my sponsor to begin reading Step 1, gave me a chance to hear others share on this step.

I am really beginning to feel as though I am a "part of" the fellowship and the footwork I'm doing continues to give me the incentive to keep on.

I know the other night we had a house meeting among the women and the subject was gratitude. And it was interesting how my description of gratitude continues to change as I grow in my recovery. I'll soon have 90 days clean and feel as if I just climbed up one of the highest mountains. It feels damn good and I owe it all to my Higher Power. For He has worked through me and have sent people in my path to aid me with their faith, hope and strength.

I talked with someone whom I was involved with and because of "nipping things in the bud" we both acknowledged the fact that this should be a turning point of growth in our newly developed friendship. Before either one of us became emotionally involved, he took the initiative to say and show me a lot of things, habits, signs and behaviors about myself. In the end, I must say it was another growing experience in my life.

MAY 17, 1990

This was a day of triumph for me. I awoke after having a nice dream of my children. I did my usual prayer and meditation but noticed how quiet and withdrawn I was as the morning progressed. I was feeling nervous but attempted to try to not dwell on what was about to happen later on. It was hard for me to get up and I almost didn't. So I got dressed, did my hair and went to the meeting. I really wasn't there, so I decided to leave and as I started to go to the church, I stopped at Sue's and talked about tomorrow, as far as the modeling. And I also told her how I was really feeling. After I left here, I did decide to come home and rest my mind and my body until about 12:30.

Thea and I prepared ourselves to go to the hospital. Mike was nice enough to let me use my car. The feelings of anxiety and anxiousness prevailed and I continued asking for God's comfort, love and strength to help me make it through without too much discomfort. We went to lunch first and it was very comforting to know that someone was there with me. Before the time grew closer, I felt I needed to talk to my mom – just to hear her say "everything is going to be alright". I miss the comfort of my mother's arms at times and it does me good to be able to call on her, while we are both still alive. It's just a miracle that the relationship between my mom and me, that we have a spiritual connection and know it.

Thea was able to go into the room with me, holding my hand, laying her head on my shoulders during the process was a closeness with another human being I had never felt before. We held hands and talked about camping; I was even laughing for a while there and the peace and serenity we felt was God-given. For it was over in no time. I just thank God for the relief of not running away from my fears. For with faith, God does intervene.

Thank you Lord, I love you.

MAY 18, 1990

MODEL

Waking up and giving gratitude to my God always start my day. And reflecting on yesterday was a rewarding experience.

I felt pretty good and not trying to anticipate any discomfort. I reflected back on feelings of not wanting to use and how situations can be a challenge as far as running with things. I felt proud of myself in the way my Higher Power and the fellowship and sponsor and counselor has been able to restore faith in me in learning how to get thru situations and not wanting or desiring to use.

I was able to focus on recreation activities and enjoyed preparing myself for modeling tonite at Ladies Night. I get a real sense of self-esteem when doing this for me.

I somehow wanted to share this joy with Paul and decided to call him.

Boy, what a mistake! The whole conversation could have been a big trigger for me and if I haven't learned by now, I never will. I just decided to stop calling on a regular basis and just call maybe twice a week to say I love you and just a mere Hi.

I got a feeling that I am going to prepare myself from depending on him. Because if I get on my feet the right way, I won't need to depend on him financially and it scares me that I won't need him as much as I thought I did. *So mentally, I'm gonna prepare myself for independence.*

The show went well and I was surprised to see my counselor in the audience. And the praise I got from her was rewarding and uplifting. She even said I had a professional aura about me which felt damn good to hear. And to top it off, I actually got to see myself videoed – I was G-R-E-A-T. Boy, God's good!

MAY 19, 1990

Woke up feeling pretty good and continued by daily routine. By 8:30, my sponsor called and asked indirectly to use my car for the day and invited me to breakfast. We met up with two older members and was able to eat together. It was nice and quite different to sit and eat and talk with each other. I learned a lot and felt honored to be around three strong women, especially my sponsor. I am growing fond of my sponsor and our relationship. I can see a lifetime friendship being made in the mix. Her driving is not up to par at times and does make me feel a little uncomfortable. But with practice, she will get better.

I went skating afterwards with my play niece and boy did we have fun. I'm beginning to feel a lot of energy being exerted and a freedom of 'WOW"! *It feel so good to be clean and active.*

She picked me up and we went to a meeting, which was interesting. I'm finding out that regardless of how a meeting should go, I always hear a good message. And "patience" was the topic. I'm beginning to feel that at these meetings, I am able to put a puzzle together of advice, signs and growth. Especially, when a person with time shares. It helps summarizes a lot of recovery growth for me. Good meeting.

Spent the rest of the afternoon with my sponsor, and her sponsor, which felt like a sponsor of sponsees family and was a beautiful feeling. Even went to a small town's fair. It made me feel I was back in time.

The rest of the day I rested my mind, body and soul.

MAY 20, 1990

Woke up praying and meditating. I had to first rid myself of any anxiety, for I did not hear from my sponsor regarding the car. After calling her, I let her know it is necessary to call me to tell me her plans for the car or to return it after use at night. *It was funny, because I started out saying "I'm putting you on direction to return my car at night. My car don't spend the night out!"* I don't know, but my sponsor is a giving and sincere person; always ready to give of herself. I feel our relationship is growing and I'm glad.

After talking with her, I prepared for church, and oh what a big day it is for me. I am joining the church today. It is always a good feeling going to church, knowing I am blessed for ending and beginning my week with God at the center of it all. It really helps me to make a connection between all things. I just love it. I also am thrilled that some of my sisters are attending on a regular basis; and that I am also able to bring a new sister each time, whom always are glad at the end, that they went. It is a good feeling sharing the positive experiences with others.

Had a sponsee meeting and dinner at my sponsor's house. It was interesting having that meeting with most of the girls. But it was suggested I don't work from my sponsor. I feel somewhat undecided just how I'm gonna handle this situation. My primary purpose is to begin separating myself from my husband financially.

JANUARY 2, 1991

HAPPY! HAPPY! NEW YEAR!
THANK GOD I AM AN ALCOHOLIC AND DRUG ADDICT!!!

I can't even begin to express the feelings of growth I've encountered over these past ten months. Especially, reflecting back to the year before. For it was about a month and a half later I finally, finally surrendered to God, My Almighty God. I can remember quite clearly where I was during this time last year and boy, I'll never forget. No wonder God gave me enough pain and insight to realize how desperately I need His help.

As I look back on my early recovery, I can actually see and feel the difference in my new way of life. Boy, how I have grown. But it is only due to my Higher Power, the fellowship and to the people who really, really support me and those who want to see me succeed.

I've come a long way in such a short period of time. Now I can say that, looking back, for in the beginning I almost felt it would be forever. But having had the willingness to be taught by others in the fellowship, by my counselor, my family of church and by all means, my Savior, Jesus Christ. Oh God!, you can't image how I feel but then again I'm sure you do. For I feel the whole wide world is in your hands, and for the first time, I can actually believe, undoubtedly, that I am in your hands as well. *Oh, what a comfort to be a child of God. I love you.*

I haven't let up one bit on my responsibility to God, to the fellowship and my personal recovery. And the very act of me writing, at this moment, is a result of the perseverance I have acquired. I haven't wrote a daily diary for several months, as a matter of fact, it has been seven months. *I was able to keep one early on in recovery and I'm glad I did, for I can reflect back to the times of struggles, hope and faith.*

This New Year, I spent on my knees praying to God, who I owe all of my life to. I ended the year and started the year in prayer beside my husband. Which is another miracle of God, which I will discuss later.

All the footwork I've done, which includes service work to the fellowship, chairing, coffee commitments, etc., volunteer work in the church and at the hospitals, going to Sunday School, church and functions; helping other recovering alcoholics and addicts, and mainly, asking my Higher Power to continue to use me as His servant.

JANUARY 4, 1991

Today was an interesting day for me. I started my day feeling somewhat bothered by the dream I had last night. I got up and did my prayer and meditation and decided to map out our day.

I was about to tell my husband about my dream but halfway through, I stopped and realized it would have been useless to describe my dream, knowing I would have been judged and/or criticized. So I decided to go to a morning meeting. And I did, and I shared about my dream and was able to see why I dreamt it, and what I did. I have been reflecting back to a year ago and feeling the pain and remorse of where I was back then. I have been doing that for the last couple of days. *And my dream reflected back to where I was then in my addiction. I awoke, thanking God it was just a dream.* But I remember what I learned in the program and that was to share with other recovering addicts/alcoholics. Ironically, the meeting was on the 3rd tradition and it fit right in with what I was feeling. I felt better after I left the meeting.

The highlight of my day was seeing my mother, sister and nephew and talked on the phone to my father and another sister. I love my family and I know they love me. They are very supportive and loving. For when I think back on the relationship with my family, it was very, very close. The longer I stay clean and work my program and keep in contact with them, they are happy and glad. And it makes me feel good to see them that way.

My low for today was – well, I'm not going to even mention it. Because *I realize I don't have to feed into anyone else's misery, resentments or frustrations. I feel now that I am working my program when I choose the opposite of these feelings. For I'm beginning to realize that I have a choice today and I'm also learning not to allow anything or anyone to push my buttons to the point where I internalize it.*

This evening was very rewarding. My sponsor picked me up for a meeting, and I was able to share what my day was like and my feelings. It felt good to know that we share a lot of the same feelings; and she assured me that I'm not alone in the situations I go through. We were also able to share for the first time intimate feelings about our past and how we share some of the same feelings in our recovery. I believe we are beginning to really form a relationship. One that is honest, healthy and supportive. I'm glad I have her as a sponsor.

I'm beginning to feel that I no longer have to be the aggressive one in my relationship with others. I can allow others to be where they are, especially if it is based on negativity. I feel as though the tools I have learned and am applying makes all the difference in the world. I thank God for the wisdom, patience and understanding He has given me through this fellowship.

Thanks, God

THE FAMILY

JANUARY 5, 1991

Today was a day of revelation to me. I was able to feel the actual release of tension, anxiety and resentment as I shared at my morning meeting. And to really tip it off, I was able to do it while my husband was there. For the first time, without implicating him, I was at least able to share my true feelings in front of him and to him. Whether he really understood what I was sharing, I know my AA family knew exactly what I was talking about. And it felt damn good to share. I left the meeting feeling relieved of my burden and had a new attitude and feeling about myself. And it is only by the grace of God and this fellowship that I'm growing at a pace in which I allow God to direct.

One of my greatest accomplishments of the day was hearing Father Martin's tape on the 12 steps. My sponsor lent it to me and when I listened to it, stopping here and there, I was able to reflect back on the part I just heard and allowed what he said to penetrate into my very soul. I plan to listen to it several times again.

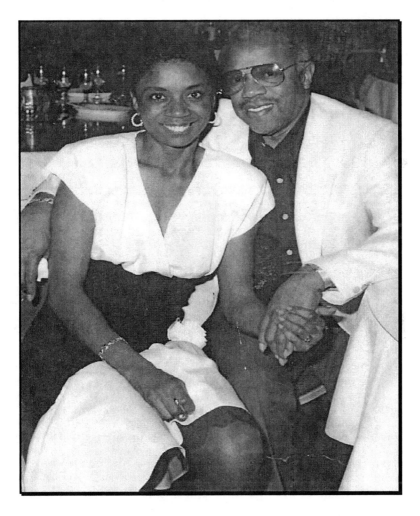

EDWINA & HUSBAND PAUL

JANUARY 7, 1991

Today was somewhat peaceful but also a little restless. My day started out with my morning reading and listening to my spiritual records.

In general, things have been pretty good, attitude wise, for the past couple of days. I'm still dedicated to my sobriety and was able to find a couple of new meeting places in the area. I continue to talk to my sponsor every other day and we have been attending some meetings together.

Today I went to my morning meeting and traveling in this type of weather was nothing compared to the weather I traveled through in my active addiction. If anything, I was determined to make my meetings. After coming home, I found myself somewhat restless. So I decided to eat, play, talk and sleep my afternoon and early evening away, as I'm planning to make my night meeting.

I was sitting back earlier today, watching the snow fall and it reminded me of a cleansing of self. And that includes a lot of things. And just to make myself see it in writing, I'm going to list a few of the things that are helping me to grow:

1) The patience to wait for God's will to be done. There are things that I may want to do or say, but I have to ask myself if it is not God's will then I'm learning to put it in its right perspective and to learn acceptance.

2) To make use of my idle time. Coming from Williamsport has been a big and challenging adjustment for me. When I was there I was involved with a lot of things, counseling, church, fellowship, functions and the very act of being surrounded by other recovering addicts/alcoholics, and for the nine months I was there, I was able

to gain my independence and learning how to keep my sobriety first. Not knowing that God had other plans for me, I was challenged to some new adjustments in my life. Now my life consist of a new residence – from Philadelphia, Williamsport and now Delaware. And my only connection to people in Delaware has been through the fellowship. I'm just as attentive to my meetings as I was in Williamsport, and thank God for that. I'm doing a lot more of entertaining myself by reading more literature; taking time out to pamper myself; learning to sit still; even the fact of starting a diary again. And this is helping me in a lot of respects. I've been able to open up in meetings, and in this short period of time, my sincerity and dedication to this program has been observed by others. I've also began taking on commitments, one of a coffee person, and chairing a meeting once or twice a month. I feel damn good about my continued growth and dedication to my sobriety. One thing I'm looking forward to is working on the steps with my sponsor and giving me the 12 step tapes is just the beginning of further growth.

I'm learning to deal effectively with not allowing others to have power over my feelings, emotions, attitude, etc. Having been in this fellowship, I have learned to identify others' attempts to trigger my buttons. I've learned to identify the little head games people try to play on me. And the amazing part about it is that when I look at it for what it is worth, is that people are losing the control I once allowed them to have on me. And when you have people close to you who are not recovering – it makes things easier to put in perspective because if not, it would allow me to have my self-esteem again in their hands. And I feel I have worked too hard on my self-esteem to give anyone the benefit to make me feel less than I am. And when I see things like this occurring, I'm able to 1) pray about it; 2) if it doesn't apply, let it fly; 3) and to see the obvious of what one is attempting to do to break my serenity; 4) and immediately begin to just keep the focus on myself. Once I see what really is going on, I remove myself from the situation. And things like this, I owe to the fellowship and my Higher Power. I thank God I have more control of myself and more insight so that I no longer have to ever go back to that other way of life. I'm finding that if I not allow anyone or anything to push me to the point of giving up, I find more strength and wisdom when I don't give in.

I actually got more motivated and determined to be patient with myself, my growth and most of all, with God. I'm glad I'm allowing God to direct my life and my path. I'm grateful to have the fellowship teach me new tools to deal effectively with life on life's terms. And most of all, I'm proud of myself and I just love the growth I'm experiencing without a drink or a drug. Well, I'm on my way to the meeting. Having returned after my meeting, I feel a lot better. By surprise, I got to chair the meeting and guess what my topic was? You got it! *My sobriety is my responsibility and must keep it in the forefront of my marriage, my family, my children. For if I ever lose my sobriety again, all else will fail.* I received some good feedback and it was listening to others and how they dealt with similar feelings. I came home feeling up; took my bath, perfumed down; washed my hair and am now doing my nightly meditation and writing. May God continue to direct my life with love, compassion, understanding, patience and willingness to be His servant. I Love You God, Good Night!

JANUARY 8, 1991, 6:00 AM

Today was a day of "whatever you make it." After last night's writing and after taking my bath and doing my reading, I finally decided to go to bed early and I did so in the other room, unintentionally. Woke up feeling as if I had to make the best of my day; I did. I tried not to carry over any feelings of yesterday. By 8:45 this morning, all of my house work was done. I find that when there is tension in my house, I choose to do something constructively and it makes me feel as though I have accomplished something and also to start out my day being productive. I decided to go to my morning meeting. And I'm glad I did. I was able to give some of my experience, strength and hope to a newcomer. And for a moment there I felt as though God connected us; as I saw a twinkle of tears in her eyes as I shared. Getting in touch with someone else's pain and to be able to convey hope is very rewarding. And that is what this program is teaching and that is the longer I stay in this program, ask God to direct my path and to use me as His servant, someone, somewhere, somehow, I will live to tell what God and this program is doing for me.

I asked Medaline for her number and yes, I called her this afternoon, just to let her know that the phone works if you use it and that I will be calling her again. I could hear in her voice that she was glad and surprised I called. But it made my day. Just to think of someone else's pain and to let them know someone cares. Thank God he is the God of us all.

The rest of my afternoon consisted of TV, eating, reading and an hours' sleep. I got up feeling somewhat restless but then I decided to go to the store, came back and curled my hair, which I dread doing; but I'm always satisfied with the results. Later on I decided to go downstairs after a few stones were thrown and begin to focus on myself and I listened to my spiritual records, sitting still for at least an half hour to forty-five minutes drinking a cup of tea. I felt better spiritually after listening to those records. I try and keep the focus on God's Will as often as I can and it does help me to do the right things, within my control. And I thank Him for that.

Well, my sponsor called and asked me to pick her up for the meeting. I actually performed my first true commitment in Newark. I am coffee person at the women's meeting and I'm elated about it. Well, I better start getting ready and will let you know what happens. Be back soon.

Well, I'm back from my meeting. And it was again fulfilling. When I leave home, I feel a part of the outside world, even if it is only AA. Taking the coffee commitment fulfilled a responsibility to others and makes me feel a part of it. I'm getting the support I need from the women, and most of all from my sponsor. And I feel our relationship will be that of a good one. Some of the other women suggested more things to do and how to ventilate myself more actively. Their support is real and sincere. I'm glad to see that this is all a process and I'm not nearly as anxious as I thought. Thank God for being with me at all times. Good God, I love you.

HUG OTHERS!

JANUARY 11, 1991

These past couple of days have been rewarding. I spent most of the two days in Philadelphia, mainly with my family. I got to see my mother two days in a row and that feels good. I also got to spend some quality time with my sister and my father. Oh, what a joy that was. Wednesday, I called my sister Deborah and asked her to spend the morning with me and she agreed. But the highlight of the day was the two of us attending a meeting together. She hadn't been to a meeting for a long time and she has slipped a few times. So it was God's will, I believe, that we got to spend this time together. And she agreed to go tomorrow with me also. And then on Thursday, I talked with my father about the good news he had received regarding his health and asked him to think about spending some time with me when I got to Philly. I was hoping and anxious that he would. And my dream came through. I called home and found out he was at the restaurant. And I went and met him and spent the most part of the day with him and later on my sister. And guess what, *we all went to my meeting together. You can't imagine how I felt to have my father, whom I love so very, very much and whom I care about deeply, to also have my sister, whom I am closest to, be together in my recovery and sharing my sobriety with them. Needless to say, what it did to my spirit and I thank God with all my heart and soul for uniting us together under these conditions.* We shared recovery tapes while driving. And the whole experience just made me think of the miracles of recovery. He later called me and said some touching things to me and the main thing he said was *"Welcome Back"* and how much he enjoyed seeing me in and around positive things. I only hope that he realized I did it for him, as well as for me. But God works in mysterious ways and I believe He will continue to work that way. And I pray God allows me to be His servant and I humbly and willingly obey.

As for me overall – I'm finding that it is by God's grace that I'm learning a lot about myself through this fellowship and through prayer and meditation. The literature and the meetings, as well as the tapes I've been listening to, have made me dream of the purpose my God is preparing me for. I believe that He wants to use me in a way that may touch the lives of others. *I have a dream and a vision to become a writer and a speaker. And just how that will come about, I don't know. But I'm sure through the life I have lived and the life I'm living now may be inspirational to one lost soul. And I pray to God that He allows this to happen, but only if it is His will.*

I went to a Step meeting this morning and we read Step 1. I am getting in touch with a lot of feelings regarding that Step. I truly believe I'm powerless over drugs/alcohol. But I'm finding out more and more how powerless I am over people especially those close to me; ones that I spend most of my time with. I'm realizing that I must not allow myself to fall into traps set by others, especially when one anticipates the outcome of my behavior. And when that happens now, I've learned more positive and constructive behavior to use. I cannot change anyone, nor do I have to prove anything to anyone. I'm learning that the change has to take place within me. And I have changed in the way I react to situations and to others. And I know that I must be willing to seek the productive means for me. I don't like feeling I'm on trial by anyone. And I don't like being treated as though I'm a bad person. God knows better than that and so do I. And I feel, as long as I'm doing the things that would please Him the best I can, I will continue to have a peace of mind, serenity and faith that, in time, all things will work out. I'm not longer trying to predict my future; I've learned to trust in God and find it to be a release from all the havoc I may encounter in a days' time.

I'm listening now to my spiritual records, and the song that is playing now "I've Come a Long Way, Since God Has Been on My Side". And I realize how good God has been to me. Looking back over the years, realizing how much He has done for me. I'm a miracle. I believe that with all my heart and soul. And I want to thank God Almighty for the life He has given me.

Mom & Me!

JANUARY 23, 1991

Wow! It has been over a week since I've last written in my journal. Well, one excuse is that I turned it over to my sponsor to read and review. I felt it would be a good idea if she read over the material I've written about since I've been into recovery. Our relationship is a good one, as we are building it very slowly, but consistently. We go to meetings together and I contact her by phone at least 3-4 times a week. After she reviewed my writing, she expressed feelings of support and encouragement and told me I have a good concept of the first 3 Steps. I'm looking forward to going through the other steps with her. I'm just beginning to start Step 4 and asked her advice and she gave me instructions to read upon Step 4 before I begin it. So that is my plan to do so.

I'm really feeling excited about my 11 months and I attended two meetings today. I even got to chair a meeting, unexpectedly.

MONDAY, JULY 13, 1992

Daughter's Letter of Expressions of Feelings

Just to let you know that I understand what kind of person you are about and the kind of female you are; but you have to understand that I am not your type of person you are to spend and give for non-important things and then turn around and ask for other people's money. Now when you told me at lunch break today that sense I work know I don't help you out when needed and you help me out, but listen to this <u>mother</u> when I didn't have a job last Summer did you mind spending <u>your money</u> on me <u>NO</u>; but know you to want to go on mouthing about I don't respond to your needs; you know what me and my father would say to that *BS*. While my father takes care of me and D.J. before and know, how do you think he feels when you don't respond to his needs when you don't give him SUGAR-HONEY-ICE-TEA. And he's been taking care of us, feeding, clothing, and educating us longer than we've been alive so far and you the one complaining about me giving you money, you've got a harsh nerve. Like when you come down to Philly to see us over our father's house you ask him for money and <u>you</u> never offered to help pay the bills just for him to spend some money on us because you never hardly do, and he wants to take us around the world like he has but he can't because of you being stuck up for money and I'm starting to hate you for that.

But let me just tell you something; and I'm going to tell you my feelings straight up; won't you go ask your wanna be boyfriends some money and not ask me for my little paycheck of a hundred something when they have mo money and stop pounding me O.K. because you're at my job; so just leave me along. On the third page I'm just going to give you a little message, me and my father has been planning to do; and the plan is that if you keep pounding me about giving you money, my father says that if he have to buy me a $60.00 train ticket to go to work in the morning and to come home after I get off of work then it will be for every week I come to work. And another thing my father said I can tell you and he would tell you to and he told me to tell you is that you can kiss both of our asses. And he said when you take D.J. that ain't doing or make it better for him because he will still have the bills forever and ever and ever because of you, not me because of you, being truly selfish. So just stop making me look like a heartless person and think of about what you say and tell me mother, because all that gas for the car, the bills, food, and personal needs is your RESPONSIBILITY for the last time saying it. You drive the same distance and use the same amount of gas to go back and forth home and to work, and the thing about it is that you've been paying the same amount of money for gas before I even started to work; and another thing why did you want me to have this job; no I know why so I can support your needs (NEVER THAT) so be on.

Signed,

Kenisha T. Dockery

P.S. Life sucks when it comes to stuff like this especially when it comes to you.

MOTHER & DAUGHTER

AUGUST 5, 1992, 5:05 AM

Good morning Lord, it is a blessing once again that I have returned to my writing. Thank you Lord for waking me up to another brand new day. Thank you Lord for keeping me safe and sound thus far.

Lord, I don't know where to begin as it has been a while since I have written to you, but, nevertheless I know you were patiently waiting as you always are.

Lord, as I look back over the readings I have written about, I can see gained wisdom and understanding in a lot of areas. First, the talk about the faith and trust I have acquired. Lord, there were situations like unmanageability in the area of my immediate responsibilities such as paying my bills, having food on the table, keeping a roof over the heads of myself and my children, and in general, just things like this which affected my serenity and given me the impression of being overwhelmed.

But Lord, oh Lord, by allowing the spirit to guide me and by me being obedient to the Spirit, I was able and willing to be humble enough to ask for help, guidance and direction in these areas. And Lord, guess what? You know! I got the help, guidance and direction I needed, and abundantly. And not only that Lord, I could see your workings in all of this and that truly, truly amazes me. But I guess you're saying, "Just what did you expect, for I am who I am." And it is making me realize more and more that there is "no failure in God." For with you Lord, all things and more are possible. And now that my immediate situation is a lot more manageable, I pray to you Lord that you keep me aware that regardless of how situations may appear that having the faith and trust in Thee lets me know the true reality. That thou art with me and thou will never leave me.

Thank you Lord for being who you are to me as well as who you are to all. "Our heavenly Father."

Another area Lord that I have experienced difficulty in is the area of relating honestly and openly with my children, mainly my daughter Kenisha. Lord, you know the pain of both our hearts. And you know the adjustment and transitions that we are both experiencing. God, I pray that you give us both the direction and guidance we need to open the lines of communication with understanding, patience, love and willingness. Lord, there are times when I feel confused and know not what to do. But Lord, you have brought me a long way out of darkness into the light. And I must continue to rely on Thee for guidance and direction. Lord, when things are not right within me I feel it and it has been necessary for me to set some boundaries where my daughter is concerned. The need for us both to express our feelings has been painful, but yet rewarding. For the reality is Lord is that we must bridge the gap that has separated us due to my addiction and me not being there for her. Lord I can't go back and undo what has been done emotionally physically or spiritually. And Lord, you know the guilt I have experienced and still experience at times. But Lord, you have shown me in many ways that the past cannot be changed but it can be used as an example of what need not be repeated. Lord our relationship is beginning to heal and with all my being I want it to continue to heal. Lord grant me the serenity to accept the things I cannot change courage to change the things I can and the wisdom to know the difference. Lord, help me to understand my children's emotional and spiritual needs as you have helped me to understand my own. Lord, grant me the patience and tolerance I need to effectively deal with these transitions. Lord, allow me to hear and recognize the pain of my children so that with you Lord I will be able to give comfort and love of a mother. Lord, help me to recognize Satan and his manipulative ways used through my children. Lord help me to look to Thee for the strength and guidance that will be needed for me to be a mother to my children in all areas of their life, a mother that has you as her leader.

The relationship we have is a really good one. I believe for we can share many things joy, laughter, sadness and the like. But Lord you have blessed us both. For the past few weeks, we have attended Bible study together and Lord you can imagine what that has done and will continue to do first and our relationship with you and then in our relationship with each other. We also plan to go to counseling together; and Lord I pray that Thee go before us and pave the way. And Lord, no matter how painful and uncomfortable things might get, Lord I ask that these times be the lessons we need to love, respect and understand each other better.

In Jesus Name, I pray Amen.

SEPTEMBER 14, 1992, 5:45 AM

Good morning Lord, I love you. Thank you Lord for waking me up to a brand new day, a day which holds the lessons of life I need just for today. Thank you Lord for being so patient and so willing to receive me with open arms now and forever.

Lord, I don't have to tell you all that has been going on in my life, as you already know. But as usual, it is helpful for me to express myself to you in writing. I have been negligent in my writing, for reasons that are unjustified. You promised Lord that you would never leave me and I sincerely believe that more and more each day. I need to honestly and sincerely and willingly establish my relationship with you Lord, for it is I that has become side tracked. I have been willingly exhibiting behaviors that are sinful in nature, and which are unpleasing to Thee. Lord, little by little, I have been shown as well as told what things are unhealthy to my spiritual growth. And even with this awareness, I still allow myself to fall short. And when this happens, I become distant from Thee. I stop writing, I start feeling the closeness of the Holy Spirit, and I believe that the spirit of Satan begins to try and rekindle the relationship we had; we Lord, you and I, have been building and preparing for me to do the work thou has planned for me.

As I look back over the last few months, I am not pleased at all with the behavior I've been allowing myself to partake in. I have been self-willing; and Lord, I continue to pray for strength and courage to change.

OCTOBER 15, 1992, 4:15 AM

Good morning my Heavenly Father. Oh what a beautiful day it is to wake up this early in the morning. I realized that it is by your grace that I have this very moment. Thank you Lord!

Lord, as I reflect back over the past 11 months after the death of my husband, I noticed the emotional roller coaster I am on. There has been tremendous growth within and around me; and yet, there are still some areas where my growth is needed.

SATURDAY, OCTOBER 24, 1992, 2:29 PM

Good afternoon my Heavenly Father. Thank you Lord for giving me a new day once again. Lord, I am sitting here in a room to which I come to be rejuvenated by thy will, and by thy grace, and to ask Thee to help me redirect my attitude, my behavior and my faith toward Thee.

Lord, it has been 11 months and 3 days since the death of my husband and I am feeling a lot of things during this time as I reflect back over that period of time. On one side of the coin, I am truly amazed and at awe at the way Thou have kept me and provided for me. For the way you have revealed things to me, things that have increased my faith and my trust in you. The opportunity to share with other Christians and with other alcoholics and addicts has been more than overwhelming, just the very way Thou has waken me up and has provided all of my needs, for this I'm truly blessed. But God, you have touched me even more where it really counts, in the spiritual realm. I have learned to seek Thee in the mist of sorrow and joy, and it each case, it was by Thy Grace that I have come this far on my spiritual journey. When in doubt and in fear, I reveal them to Thee in prayer, conversations, and writing. And you Lord, have made ways out of no way; you have turned my fears and doubts into faith and trust; you have proven to me more and more the deliverance from darkness and into the light. You have made known to me that you are with me and will never ever leave me, and Lord that is the most amazing feeling I have, especially now, which brings me to the other side of the coin.

Because I know that you are always available, I need to, once again, ask for help in the areas that still hinder my spiritual growth. And Lord, I pray that the Holy Spirit convicts me even more into doing the right thing. Lord, I have a great fear that goes deep, real deep; it is the fear of total commitment to Thee and thy will. I know that fear exists because and some areas of my life I still want to be in control. And I ask myself "In control of what?" I still have that manipulative and seductive behavior that gives me a high for the moment, but which also keeps me spiritually sick. Lord, there is still that need in me to conquer and I'm back asking myself, "Conquer what?" Why do I feel the need to be accepted in the flesh? Why do I fear being rejected and abandoned by others if I don't feed them with the flesh? Then I realize sometimes that it is the spirit of Satan in me and in them that allows the feeling and the act of submission to take place.

And Lord, why is it that I seek those that are unavailable for me. It seems that need to conquer and subdue is more prevalent than other situations. And the act of this type of situation is more intense. But then I realize it is a useless battle, but I still forge ahead, why? And this is where that commitment comes into play again. I fear commitment and in turn, I see that very few are committed when it comes to the flesh. But, I realize this is an area that only Thee can help me with and I need to make a conscious and sincere effort to change. You see Lord, as I look back just over the last few months, I have put more effort into doing the wrong thing, instead of the right thing. And it has made me "feel" distance to Thee, but yet the Holy Spirit continues to talk to me and I ignore it. Help me Lord, help me!

Lord, I ask you on a daily basis to mold me and shape me into thy image; I ask that thy continue to put me on the road to righteousness; I ask

Thee to let me touch and be touched by another sick and suffering soul; and I ask to make me thy servant to be used to share the works of the Lord. And Lord, in some areas of my life, my prayers are being answered, and I am useful to Thee; but I don't feel that I am totally useful to Thee until I get better with the dark side of my attitude and behavior. For God, it is darkness, total darkness.

Lord, you have shown me what unconditional love is through the Fellowship and through my fellow Christians. Why is it on a personal level that I can't love myself unconditionally? and others as well?

SUNDAY, OCTOBER 25, 1992, 10:52 AM

Good morning, good morning, good morning Lord, oh how I thank Thee for the insight Thy has given me to start this new day once again. I woke up this morning compelled to write on the sixth and seven steps, as well as letting my sponsor know what really has been going on the last few months. I really feel the need to lay the cards down on the table and admit to God, and another human being the exact nature of my wrongs.

One of the main themes that come from Step 6 is "any person capable of enough willingness and honesty to try repeatedly Step 6 on all areas of his faults without any reservations whatever, has indeed come a long way spiritually, and is therefore entitled to be called, a man who is sincerely trying to grow in the image and likeness of his own creator."

Just as God removed the obsession and reservation from alcohol and drugs, it is apparent that He can remove from me every other difficulty or defect as well. You know Lord, after doing my 4th and 5th Steps, it was revealed to me certain patterns that cause me a lot of pain and grief, and that were really self-seeking motives. And it was the pattern of seeking attention and affection through seductive and manipulative behavior from the opposite sex; starting from my childhood with my father. This pattern has been a part of my whole life and became a way of life for me before, during and after my addiction. Before, it was done automatically, but now I realize that I'm doing it by choice as well, and that scares me. It scares me because at any given moment that switch goes off in my head and I'm off to the races. The idea is premeditated long before the act is committed, rather consciously or subconsciously. And then the play begins.

I noticed first my non-verbal body language where I exhibit body movements that I know bring attention; the eye contact when I'm saying more than I verbalized. Then, the gestures of the invitation and you know what God, this is insane, but I get a thrill from this, it is a high of its own. If I look at this pattern as I did with my pattern of drinking and drugging, it brings back the realization of a false high, which I imagine starts out being and feeling good, but which also ends in despair, guilt and emptiness, all on a spiritual level. And I find myself asking the same questions I did in my addiction, "Why am I doing this?" I look back over the situation beginning to end, and I find that the answer is always the same, doing the same thing, expecting different results, and the results are always the same. I allow myself to be seen and used as an object and feel and use other people the same way. Lord, I'm tired of living like this, I am tired Lord. Step 6 reminds me that whatever character defects or sin that get in the way of my Creator to utilize me and the need to better my character, I need to get rid of it. And that is where I am at with this. I feel that I'm living a lie, a dark big lie, and I'm not fooling anyone but myself. I feel distant and not whole with my Creator and it causes me to withdraw from the very essence I want to belong and that is closer to my God. I realize I can't continue on this way because if I do, I will once again be lost into darkness; and that scares me to.

SUNDAY, OCTOBER 25, 1992, 11:52 AM

Lord, I have returned to this very same room tonight; but it's different from when I left earlier. Conversations have taken place where the light of truth was related. It was finally acknowledged what must be done in order for you to continue to use me successfully. I finally realized that it was "self" that wanted to hold on to the ways of destruction, selfishness, self-centeredness and egotism at the expense of myself and of others. And you revealed through the conversations what must be done in order to be delivered from this darkness. And that was to let the person go, and I mean let go. So that whatever it is that has blocked me in the past can be, first turned over to you, and then for us to make a real, real sincere and honest effort to change accordingly, for the good of us all.

Lord, once again, you have made the truth be seen for what it is. I no longer want to ignore it or suppress it. I do want to go on with my life and be set on a righteous path. I do yearn to do thy will, and to be prepared to do thy work. I want to be committed to Thee and to Thee only. And the only way I can, is to stop the bullshit now, and I mean really stop.

I've learned a lot about the traps and setups that make me fall short time and time again. I've learned when the "self" is at hand, and doing its thing. I learned if I don't continue to strive for progress I will regress and back to which I came. And Lord, you know that deep down inside my soul that is the last place I will want to return.

And if I am to be honest Lord, I have been setting myself up for the old patterns for which I have become accustomed to in the past. And if I don't attempt to alter this pattern, it will only repeat itself time and time again. And then, what? Who knows, but you Lord, and I know now that it will only lead to death, a spiritual death. And for once in my life, I don't ever want to die another spiritual death.

So Lord, I'm asking that Thy go before me and make straight my journey and go before me and clean house. To instill in me the need to be committed to Thee and to thy will.

Lord, I ask these things in the name of your Son,

Jesus Christ. Amen!

Good night Lord, sweet dreams.

SUNDAY, OCTOBER 25, 1992, 9:29 PM

Well Lord, things are really moving ahead. I just love my sponsor and shared with her all that I have been feeling and doing over the past months. And Lord once again, the burden was lifted from me, the burden of not being honest and open so that I can grow and seek direction & suggestions from others. I was able to confide in her the relationships I've had and their impact on my spirituality. I came away feeling that I am on the right track again, as long as I follow the suggestions she gave me. She suggested that I end the relationships that are causing me problems and she also suggested 4 things to do when the temptation arises again. She suggested that I first tell God that I have this desire and then to tell someone else, go to a meeting, and write about it. Hopefully, I will commit myself to doing these things, so I won't have to fall into the same set up or traps.

MONDAY, OCTOBER 26, 1992, 9:00 PM

Good evening Lord. I'm here in bed now winding down a very restful and insightful weekend. I'm so glad I allowed myself to rest and take the three days to do some soul-searching and internal housecleaning. I made two meetings today and shared about the experiences of this weekend and it helped me to realize that it was the best medicine I could have given myself. Being away in a room for the weekend availed a great opportunity for me to put things back into perspective and to come out committed to change something, mainly my behavior. It also gave me the opportunity to be totally honest with my sponsor, as I have not in the past, and that also kept me spiritually sick, for I thought I was keeping a big secret, but the secret itself was ugly and unhealthy for my spiritual well-being.

I have even committed myself to drop down on my knees, which I have failed to do for several months. And I realized that when I stopped humbling myself, the "self" got bigger. I can remember in the past when I did all the things I was supposed to do and had the willingness to do it; I felt whole; I felt I was being spiritually molded. But I thank God for the lessons I am learning now because it makes me appreciate life and myself and others with more understanding. I pray that the Lord continues to reveal things to me that will lead to a better and more useful servant for Thee.

Thank you Lord for spending this weekend with me and giving me the guidance and direction I need to start a new.

Love You, Lord, Amen!

SUNDAY, NOVEMBER 1, 1992, 6:35 PM

Thank you Lord for giving me the strength and courage I needed today and to allow the Holy Spirit to direct my thoughts and my actions.

Lord, this weekend was one of the most rewarding and yet painful weekend I have ever experienced. I needed and did come to terms with and about a few things that were stifling my spiritual growth. I committed myself to do certain things after talking with my sponsor this weekend and after having prayed and meditated over the situations.

One day, and if needed, one minute at a time I have to stop the impulsive behaviors; and when the thought or urge falls upon me, I must pray and tell God; then I must call someone, maybe my sponsor; and then I must write about it. I sincerely want to fulfill this commitment. I also must stop the phone calls, visits and daydreaming, or should I say fantasy about being and having someone that is not meant for me that way. But most importantly, I must do these things because my recovery is on the line, not necessarily drinking or drugging, but striving for growth and progress. And, recognizing that my recovery is on the line has made me more willing to get back on track. I promised myself early in recovery that I would not allow anyone or any situation to come before my recovery. And they both have. So I must regain my senses and my composure to restart this recovery process again.

SATURDAY, NOVEMBER 7, 1992, 7:06 PM

Good evening Lord, thank you for a marvelous and beautiful day. Lord, it has been very hard this week dealing with the emotions of letting go of someone I feel an emotional and loving bond towards. And the reality of letting go of someone you love has enlightened me even more spiritually. I know this whole thing is a process and at this point of the process is the physical withdrawal. There are times when I want to call, but I know I can't; there are times when I want to reach out and touch and hug; but I know I can't; there are times when the words "I love you and I want you" comes to my lips, but I know I can't say it; there are times when I want to give up this process and pay the consequences; but I realize I will die a spiritual death. And Lord, you must go before me and intervene. I must sit quietly and meditate before reacting. But sometimes that impulsiveness overwhelms me and I must seek your strength and courage to withstand the temptation. For the first time Lord, I love someone that I feel can fulfill all my needs, but then I come to realize that it is only you who could possibly do that. I struggle with trying to understand rather than to just accept. I believe your will for me and he is to grow and bind more closer to Thee so that the work you have for us to do can be done. I realize that it is "self" that gets in the way of us doing the right thing. The pain I am experiencing now is great, but I also realize that the pain of not doing it will be greater. Lord, help me to keep that in the forefront of my mind and soul. Help me to realize that it will take time and that the healing process will soon be realized; but for right now, Lord, it hurts - it hurts real bad. But I need to remind myself Lord that, "This too shall pass."

Love You Lord.

TUESDAY, NOVEMBER 17, 1992, 5:50 AM

Good morning my Heavenly Father!! Lord, thank you for touching me with the gift of life this morning. Lord, you still never ceased to amaze me. Your love and strength is once again being manifested, especially during some of the painful, yet amazing times of my life. For it is then that I truly experience your amazing grace.

This past week has been emotionally interesting to me, for I am experiencing feelings I never experienced before, sober or healthy. I am grieving like I never grieved before for my husband Paul. The kids have been coming and going. But yet Lord, I feel such a sense of closeness to Thee, but I have never experienced before either. You have revealed to my soul that you are here and that I can and should willingly, always depend on you. You have brought me a mighty long way, Lord, and for this I am eternally grateful. And Lord, I want to show and share my gratitude with you and others.

Lord, as I embark upon this journey, I ask that you pull away the layers of sin and temptation so that you may utilize me and a miraculous way, to become a witness for you to be shared with the world at large. For Lord, I know that you have no limitations and that you can make all things possible.

Lord, I continue to seek your will in my life, and pray that you continue to mold and shape me into your image. For the image I have learned and can see; the magnificent image is beyond my wildest dreams.

For when I am going through the molding and shaping, I am learning more and more to keep the focus on you Lord. I must keep the focus on you. I want to keep the focus on you.

WEDNESDAY NIGHT, NOVEMBER 25, 1992, 6:48 PM

Lord, this is the perfect opportunity for me to take the time I need to reflect over the past year, with much faith and gratitude. Lord, O Lord, you have bought me a mighty long way. And often times I have to pinch myself to feel if it is real. And Lord, it is more than real, it is truly awesome. Regardless of the trials and tribulations, you have made more than a believer out of me. You have made me more willing to follow you. Lord, I can't fully explain how I feel, but I just know that it is by keeping the faith and looking up to Thee that thou has and is revealing things to me that our nurturing and nourishing my soul. And I guess the main thing I see is that by asking Thy will be done and allow myself to believe that whatever happens, continue to ask that Thy will be done. And the spiritual manifestations have far out-weighed the physical and material manifestation.

Lord, a while ago the Devil wanted me to believe that I could and would not make it, especially after Paul's death. He tried to tell me and show me how impossible it will be. He tried Lord to make me give up this newly found life and faith I have in you. Lord, he tried to tell me that the mountains were too high and that I wouldn't make it. Lord, he tried to tell me that it was all up to me and I would have to do it all alone. But Lord Oh Lord, what a liar he turned out to be. Hallelujah Jesus-Lord, the tears are now flowing, for I have found something in you that I have been searching for all my life, that feeling of belonging to someone that truly, truly, and I mean truly loves me, loves me with all of my shortcomings, but one who wants me to strive for progress in the spiritual realm of life. And I'm beginning to see and understand how the spiritual growth within manifest itself on the physical plane. Lord, I can see a glimpse of the molding and shaping of my spirit and believe that you are preparing me for the purpose that is destined for me. Lord, and little by little, bit by bit, you have peeled away the layers of temptation and the layers of sin, and Lord, I learn more and more because I feel so different when I acknowledge that transformation and rightly attribute it to you. And Lord, the tears are flowing again, I just can't seem to stop them, for when I think of you Lord and what you have done for me and how you are using me, I get so filled Lord, I get so filled...

Lord, people wonder why I'm so happy-go-lucky and smile and just seemed to be full of life. But Lord, they just don't know; do they Lord, do they? But Lord, when the time is right Lord, they will know and they will see as well as feel the Power of your Almighty Love.

FRIDAY NIGHT, NOVEMBER 25, 1992, 7:55 PM

You know Lord; I'm beginning to see that although you are using me, you must allow the process of shaping and molding to take place. And it is through the process that I must look to you for strength and courage, accompanied with faith and trust. And while going through the process growth, I have found that by asking, One Day At a Time Sweet Jesus, that's all I'm asking from you, one day at a time. And it's in that saying that I find the strength and courage to go forward with faith and belief in you. And that no matter what comes down the pike as I travel onward that it won't be anything that you and I can't handle, Lord, no matter what!!! Instead of focusing on the problem, I focus on the lessons to be learned, and Lord it all boils down to just trusting in you and believe everything is going to be all right. And it also boils down to patience, true patience. For I have noticed that as long as I reveal to you what is on my heart, whether it be good or bad, you Lord have already set the plan and the course; all that is ask of me is to be willing, Lord, I just need to be willing. And it is with that willingness that change takes place gradually. Lord, it has been my willingness that has made all the difference in the world. And that willingness goes deep Lord, it goes deep.

SUNDAY, DECEMBER 6, 1992

Good evening Lord! Thank you for all the blessings Thou has given me.

Lord, for the most part, I have found peace and serenity in Thee and feel that all things happen for a reason.

Over the past few months I have noticed a change in me, a change that was needed and guided by you. I no longer feel the compulsion and obsession I had when it comes to the opposite sex. I feel when I prayed that that obsession and compulsion be lifted, and when it was, I noticed it was a gradual process. I feel that as long as I ask for the help, it is given. Thank you Lord. And although the change is still happening, I feel comfortable with it and look forward to continued progress.

JANUARY 14, 1993

Lord, I thank you for the gift of life; the gift of learning; the gift of change; the gift of joy and the gift of pain. Lord, it has been a while since I have allowed myself to sit down and focus on my writing Lord; you know the desire I have to write and I must turn that desire over to you. For I know that whatever I turn over to you, you will take care of; you will prepare me and it will manifest. I have no doubt about that; in your time God, in your time.

For the most part, a lot of progress has been made in all areas of my life. But what I noticed the most is the spiritual serenity I am experiencing. I have a feeling that is calm and serene about my life and about life itself. The process of life is a rewarding one; one that I can see and feel, but most of all, one that I can accept. I no longer fight and I surrender daily the situations I can't handle. And Lord, it goes without saying that you have brought me a mighty long way. And I am truly grateful for your love and your grace.

Lord, you are revealing to me my purpose. When I am called to share my experience, strength and hope to other sick and suffering souls, the light and life of your existence prevails through me to others. Lord, just by giving up and surrendering willingly to you, I've seen the effect it has on others. You know Lord that I desire to be your servant, to use me as you wish. And Lord, it never fails that at least one seed is planted; one soul is uplifted; one heart begins to feel; one's ears began to open, and the rest is left up to you. Lord, many times I do not realize the impact of you using me has on other people. But I do see the results in other people's reaction. Their eyes, ears and heart began to open to the realization that you are a loving God, one that only wants us to acknowledge you willingly; one who wants to put us on a spiritual journey of growth and attainment; one who wants to utilize us to help and aid another lost soul. And Lord, if one soul is helped by you using me, then the glory and praise belongs to you, not me Lord, but you.

Lord, you have prepared me and are preparing me for a change, one that involves many feelings taken place within. For I know that you feel I am ready for this change, and you have given me the strength and courage and faith to continue to look up to you and move forward, one step at a time, one day at a time. You know Lord I will do this even though I may be going through feelings about this change, I still view it as a gift from you; for without the guidance and direction I sought from you, in which you provided, this change would not be taking place. Just like with all the changes I have faced since I willingly gave you my life, they have been changes of progress. Lord, you showed me that believing and trusting in you that I will overcome any and all circumstances and situations. But I must on a daily basis ask you to lead the way and trust that you are the one in control. And whatever it is you are preparing me to do, I seek the strength and courage to do it Lord.

These things I pray in Jesus name amen.

JANUARY 27, 1993

Good evening Lord. What a glorious day it has been Lord, I feel so at one with you, regardless of what is going on in my life. The feeling that "all is well" is stronger than it has ever been. I have been doing a lot of footwork lately, spiritually and physically. I started building my foundation in Wilmington. I have attended new meanings, have shared my story and have met new friends of the Fellowship. This move is not without feelings, but it is a move with a lot of faith. I guess I've learned and applied a lot of the tools I learned from you and the Fellowship, tools that have been and are vital to my sobriety. I thank you Lord. I thank you for the awareness of your presence. I thank you for the strength and courage you have given me. I thank you for all the wonderful people I have met. I thank you for the peace of mind I have acquired. I thank you for my family who is so supportive. I thank you for my children and the relationships we are rebuilding. Most of all Lord, I thank you for "You."

In Jesus name, I pray, AMEN.

FEBRUARY 1, 1993, 12:25 PM

Good afternoon Lord. Lord, I thank you for the gift of Life today. And I thank you for bringing me a mighty long way. I thank you for the strength and courage you have given me to press onward in Life's journey. Lord I thank you for being there each step of the way. Lord, know that I continue to seek and ask for Thy strength and courage, no matter what adversities or obstacles that may come my way. For I know that thou art with me and will never ever leave me. Lord, I must lay down my burdens at your feet. I must surrender to you that which I cannot handle. And Lord, I must lay down my will to you to do with as you please.

Right now, Lord, I'm feeling financially burdened, and I need to turn this burden over to you. I'm about to move and financially I am not able to meet all that is required of me financially. You know Lord that I will take care of what is in front of me. The rest Lord is up to you. Lord, I pray that your Will be done. I pray that I may exercise faith and trust during this time and transition.

Lord, help me to put this in its proper perspective and help me to keep the focus on others rather than myself. Lord, continue to use me as Thy servant to be able to display the true meaning of humility and submission to Thee. Lord, keep me off the pity pot and put me on the road to more continued awareness of your love, patience and grace. For I realize now that if it is meant to be, it will, but only by your Will, not mine.

And Lord, when the Devil is ever so busy, help me to withstand the temptation he tempts me with. Help me to realize and believe that if I just hold on Lord, all will be alright. Give me the strength to look to you, during those times. Lord, as I look back over my life, I see that it is by your Will and my willingness that all has worked out according to your plan.

Lord, I love you and I thank you for being my Father.

In Jesus Name, I Pray

   AMEN!

FEBRUARY 3, 1993, 5:55 AM

Good morning Lord. Thank U! Thank U! Thank U! Lord, I dreamt last night that I was called to go to the podium. I had received several cards at this church, and among the cards was one that stood out the most. The card said "Your hour has come." It was written by a little girl and after reading all the cards, I selected the one the little girl wrote. Lord, in my dream I remember being distracted by the flesh, because the dream revealed to me that the people I was with, I should not have been with. And, I remember hiding from the crowd who was anxiously waiting for me. I also remember playing football, going back and forth between the goal line, never making it across. I remember being with my family and once again, prepared to go to the podium and I remember this man blocking me as I tried to go up the steps. Then after pushing him aside, I went upstairs and it seemed like I was playing in this room with my brother, waiting to be called.

TUESDAY, FEBRUARY 23, 1993, 3:20 AM

Good morning Lord. And Lord I praise your Holy name. Lord, I thank you for the gift of life this day. I thank you Lord for all the blessings you have bestowed upon me. Lord I thank you for being the Father of all creation, even a little creature like me. Lord I thank you for the opportunity to experience true humility in this very act of writing to you.

Lord, today especially marks our 3-year anniversary of sobriety. You continue to amaze me with your love, grace and mercy. I am truly grateful to you Lord and the fellowship you have provided for me. I am truly grateful for the strength and courage you have given me to continue onward on my spiritual journey. I am truly grateful for the humility you have given me to open up and express my fears and my doubts. I am truly grateful for the way you have guided my path and for the realization that without you Lord, I am nothing. But most of all Lord, I am truly grateful for the deliverance out of darkness into the light.

Lord, I can honestly say that I am grateful for the pain and for the joy; for the trials and tribulations; for the ups and downs; for the gift of life itself. I realize Lord that I need you and have always needed you. I realize that you are the captain of my ship and all I need to do is be willing.

Lord, the willingness I have is unbelievable and I pray that I continue to be willing. Being willing has brought me out of a lot of situations, where before I might have given up. The willingness to seek guidance from you and others has kept me from bondage of self. Lord, being willing have allowed me to express my true feelings and my desire to change. Being willing has allowed me to utilize tools of the fellowship to aid me in any situation. Being willing has allowed me to touch and be touched by other sick and suffering souls. But most of all Lord, being willing has allow you into my life.

I think back over the past three years and I see your love, grace and your mercy. I see your hand in your arms extended out to me. I visualize the times that I received them. And although somewhat afraid, I accepted them. I visualize myself in your arms against your bosom, being held and rocked like a baby in the arms of his mother. I visualize the love, warmth and security being there next to you. Lord, you have given me so much insight thus far of your loving power and then again, I realize it is just the tip of the iceberg of what you really have for me to see. All I need to continue to do is visualize more and more your endless love and mercy.

Lord, once again, I am in need of your guidance. I am in need of your strength and your courage. I am in need of acknowledgment of your Will for me. Lord, I need not tell you what is going on in my life for you already know. But Lord, you know me and you know that it is a need for me to write about the joys and the pain, the fears and the need for faith. Lord, recently I had to turn over completely to you the outcome of the house situation, and you know why. It is too much to handle, and I alone can no way endure the pressure. I feel the need of my spirit to be quiet and calm through this "storm." Only seeking strength and courage to endure this, no matter what the outcome.

For you know Lord, the enemy is hard at work and attempting to break my spirit. But Lord, I know if I rely totally on you, he don't have a chance. Lord, I pray at this very moment that your Will be done and for the acceptance of it. Although the way may seem dark, but I "visualize" the light at the end of the tunnel, and as long as I visualize the light, I know that that light is you.

Thank you Lord, in Jesus Name I pray. Amen.

I Love You Lord. Oh, Happy Anniversary!!!

ANNIVERSARY

MARCH 2, 1993, 4:49 AM

Good morning Lord. I love you. Thanks for waking me up this brand new day, one I've never witnessed before. Thank you for the gift of life. Thank you Lord for being my Father and my Comforter. For in seeking you, I have found peace and serenity in the midst of the storm. Lord, I ask that you go before me and continue to pave the way for me to be utilized by you.

It has been a week later that we celebrated over three years of sobriety. And although it is a joyous occasion, you continue to allow the seeds of faith and trust, love and joy and hope in the hearts of others. You know Lord, it always amazes me that when I ask you to utilize me to be helped and to help another sick and suffering soul, someone always feel a sense of hope in their lives by the testimony you have given me and my willingness to share it. I thank you Lord for using me. I truly thank you.

Lord at this time, I need to call on you again for strength and courage to keep the faith. I need to seek your guidance and your direction. Lord, you know the situation that is presently before me and only you Lord know the outcome. It becomes clearer to me more and more that regardless of any situation you have my best interest at heart, and you know all of my needs. I just pray for the acceptance and knowledge of your Will during and after the situation concerning the house. *Lord, what has helped me to minimize the situation has been the assignment of, "how Jesus prayed" from my Bible study class. And in no way does my situation compare to the intensity of the pain and suffering your Son experienced here on earth. And what has helped me the most is the realization that I must totally submit my will to you, and with that submission come total faith and trust in you. Lord, help me to remember that. For when I received the news yesterday that the bank would not approve my loan, for the first time Lord, I felt a sense of "okay," God is still and always will be in control, not I. And I even surprised myself by not feeling defeated in giving up all hope. For I realize that no matter what, I will be okay and all is well. I feel that deep within my spirit and I feel the need to be still and calm while you do your work Lord.*

Lord, I pray that you give me this chance to also face the health problems I am experiencing now. For signs of the cervical cancer are back and the need for treatment is at hand. But you know Lord I thank you for allowing me to be in my right frame of mind to make decisions regarding my health. I thank you Lord for having a job that offer benefits for me to get treatment; and most of all Lord, I thank you for my sobriety to go through this and any situation without giving up. But rather, rely on your love and strength to endure.

Lord, I pray that I continue to be humble and teachable; I pray for continued willingness to go onward on my spiritual journey; I pray that whatever is needed that you will provide; and most of all Lord, I pray for the knowledge and acceptance of your Will in my life and those just like me.

I love you Lord, in Jesus Name, I pray,

Amen.

THURSDAY, MARCH 4, 1993, 4:58 AM

Good morning Lord. How I thank Thee for the touch of life this morning. I thank you Lord for who you are and what you are to me in my life.

Lord, for some reason, the desire to commit myself to writing to you more on a daily basis is strong. And as you know Lord, the willingness to do so is there. It is strange that the feeling and desire is given to me during the early morning hours. It feels as if I'm starting my day with you. It feels so wonderful to keep a daily journal of my feelings and my thoughts. It also allows me to share with you how you are guiding and directing my life. For Lord you know I have no problem being honest with you about things that are troubling me and about things that I'm aware of that keeps me sick spiritually. And it is when I am honest and willing to change that You set the stage for that change to occur, gradually.

Lord, there is a step in my program that says "made a decision to turn my will and my life over to the care of God, as I understand Him." I truly believe in my heart that I have made that decision. For if I hadn't, then all that has happened and is happening to me would have felt it was just a coincidence or that "I" had everything to do with it. But Lord, I know better. For it is by your grace and mercy that I am here today. It is by your grace and mercy that I have weathered the storm. And has been by your grace and mercy that I am able to be touched and touch another sick & suffering soul. Lord, it is by your grace and mercy that allows me to be your servant, as well as an example of your divine love.

Lord, I desire wholeheartedly to turn my will and my life over to you on a continuous basis. For I realize that it is you who are in control, a loving control. For as I look back over these years, I can see your loving arms about me. Especially when I come to you with things I can't handle or even want to handle by myself. For I truly believe that if I sincerely and faithfully seek your strength and courage in whatever situation, that it comes forth from you.

A case and point recently, just two days ago I shared with you the pressure I felt I was under in the house situation and how when I totally surrendered to accept your Will the miracle happened. On the same day Lord I was presented a letter that said "gift" of $3443 to aid me in the purchase of this house - the same day Lord!!! And although I still am at your mercy as to the outcome, boy is this process and journey ever so enlightening of the work you are performing; and guess what, without me. Lord, it is situations like this and others that make me a believer that you and only you should I turn my will and my life over to.

Lord I Love You, In Jesus Name I pray,

Amen.

MARCH 8, 1993, 5:45 AM

Good morning Lord. Lord, I thank you for waking me up this morning with the breath of life. Lord I thank you again for the opportunity for another day I have never witnessed before. Lord, thank you for who you are and for what you are to me and all creation, our loving Heavenly Father.

Lord, last night I was feeling somewhat alone. Not in the sense of total aloneness, but experiencing feelings of not sharing intimately with someone special. But it was not long before you intervened Lord. For the phone rang several times and I was able to get off my pity pot and was there to listen and share with another sick and suffering soul that were somehow touched when you allowed our paths to cross. See Lord, this is what I'm talking about when I say to you, "Lord, use me as Thy servant to be touched and to touch another soul." I never know what seeds were planted when the opportunity to share with others that which you are totally responsible for. Lord, only you can receive the glory and the praise. For if it wasn't by your grace and mercy, these encounters would not be taking place. *And Lord, I thank you, I thank you, I thank you. I thank you for the way you have and are molding my life, as long as I am willing to seek your Will and your guidance; as long as I continue to do the footwork the rest is left up to you. And Lord, the many, many things you have revealed to me are only the tip of the iceberg. Lord, whatever it is you have in store for me, I know the journey and the process is the lesson in itself. I only pray that you continue to mold me and shape me, and to prepare me for the work you have set out for me to do. I pray that you use me as a seed planter, for already somewhere and somehow and in your time, those will begin to sprout.*

Lord, I just want to say, I love you and I love others, and I only pray that the light of your love continues that is within me shine bright so that it may attract other sick and suffering souls, so that they too may see an example of your mighty love grace and mercy.

In Jesus name!

Amen!

MARCH 12, 1993, 5:00 AM

Lord, How Great Thou Are!!! Lord, I praise you this morning and praise you throughout the day. For Lord, you are truly a mighty Lord. Lord, I thank you for touching me with the gift of life this morning and for the opportunity to live this day to the fullest. Beginning with my quiet time with you Lord, it never fails that when I begin my day acknowledging, praising and thanking you for all the blessings you have provided me gives me a feeling of awe when I think about you Lord.

Lord, another miracle has taken place in my life, for I already know that I am a miracle. *But Lord, when I talk and write to you about situations that are happening in my life that causes fear and doubt, I've learned the importance of sharing with you and others to help relieve and put into perspective that which hinders my spiritual growth. And Lord, each time I do this the practice and need to exercise faith in you has been rewarding and enlightening. Lord, it is evident that you have gone before me and did your thing.* For the rewards have been tenfold spiritually, and are being manifested by you Lord in providing me the things I need. You see Lord, the other day I wrote about the miracle of receiving a gift letter of $3443 for assistance needed in the purchase of this house. *Oh Lord, you know what happened! That letter went from $3443 to $5043; and not only that, Lord, we saw the approval forms and it is possible for me to become a homeowner, thanks to you Lord, thanks to you.* And Lord, you are also working in other areas of my life, by touching other souls to see and recognize that which dwelleth in me, and that is the light of you Lord that has been touching the souls of others, and better yet feeling a need to respond to that light in some way, shape, form or fashion. Lord, the seed you are planting through me, and unknowingly to me, has become more and more evident.

Lord, I pray that you continue to mold, shape and direct my life, for it is beyond my wildest dreams these things that are taking place in my life. And Lord, the credit and the glory go directly to you. Right at this moment Lord, I'm listening to a song, "Prayer Changes Things." And Lord, prayer does change things, as you well know.

In my Bible study class, we are doing a series on "prayer" and Lord, what an amazing feeling and understanding I am receiving. Lord, you have provided me with so much that I can't begin to tell you. But tell you I must, in my thoughts, in my actions, in my relationship with others, and in my service; but most importantly, in my communion and meditation with you Lord!!!

Lord, keep doing your thing, and I pray to continue to look up to you with love, love and more love.

In Jesus Name, I pray,

Amen.

SUNDAY, MARCH 21, 1993, 9:05 PM

Good evening Lord. Lord, I thank you for another day of life. I thank you for the blessings you have provided me. Lord I thank you for the many people you have placed in my life. But most of all Lord, I continue to thank you for the deliverance from darkness into the light.

Lord, first of all, let me share with you what is going on, as if you don't already know. But Lord, it seems when I write about things that are going on in my life at this time, I sometimes reflect back on my writing and I can see the growth, spiritual growth that is and has taken place. Lord, when it seems there is no way, you provide a way, especially talking about the miracle that took place just a few days ago when a check for $5043 was placed in my hands on 6th of March for settlement assistance on this brand new house. Lord, I had written just a few days earlier the need to turn this burden over to you to do as you will. And Lord, just look what happened. You provided every penny I needed. Lord I thank you, I thank you, I thank you. By this time next week I should be in our brand new house, thanks to you.

Lord, now to get to the real reason why I feel the need to write to you. I'm going through some changes regarding my personal life...

MARCH 24, 1993 4:45 AM

The feeling of being uncomfortable with my "normal behaviors." I'm feeling the need to disconnect myself from patterns which are unhealthy for me and in which are the same for others. Lord, you have brought me a mighty long way, even with my shortcomings and defects of character. Yet, you continue to provide all the things I need spiritually and physically. And the realization that it is only "You" that can provide the needs of my soul and my body that is being revealed to me more and more. The need to depend on you Lord is great. The need for the void in my life is being fulfilled by you and knowledge of you. Slowly, but surely, the need to depend on others in an unhealthy way is diminishing; and I'm very much aware of this. And I desire to keep on changing and getting better and stronger in areas where I am weak.

Lord, I need to focus on more important things now. I need this energy to be directed towards something more positive and useful to you. Lord, I need your guidance and direction at this time in my life. I want to be able to utilize the experiences in which you have bought me through. *I want to be able to give my testimony to as many souls that are in our reach. Only for the glorification of you Lord. Help me to put self aside and allow the spirit of you to flow through me.*

Lord, I do have a vision, a vision of sharing my story in writing and speaking publically. For I have received just a glimpse of my purpose. And that is Lord you have allowed other souls to be touched by sharing my experience, strength, and hope. Seeds have been planted and only you know Lord when they will sprout. But I pray that you continue to strength me in this area so that other seeds may be planted near and afar. But God, not as I will, but as Thy will.

In Jesus Name, I pray, Amen

TUESDAY, MARCH 30, 1993, 5:15 AM

Lord, I praise you this morning for who you are and what you are to me and all creation. For you Lord are a Mighty God. And it is more evident when I awake every morning given the touch of life just one more day Lord. I love you and I thank you for bringing me a mighty, mighty long way.

Lord, the time is nearing when I leave an old place to move into a new place. For Lord, the blessings of becoming a homeowner is about to take place because of you. You know, Lord, I shared at a meeting the other day how every change that has taken place since I surrendered my life to you has been a change for the good, a change up from the others. And Lord, I thank you. For each change that was presented did not come without feelings, but the reality of it all, is that there has been no change without your divine love and mercy. You have provided me with the strength, courage, faith and trust that I needed to make it through to the other side. And Lord, I have become more aware of your presence, which makes me seek your presence even more. In the morning, during our meditation; during the day, when I often say, "Lord, I love you" and especially when I reflect back over certain situations of my life and can see your loving hands extended out for me to take hold of and to hold on for dear life. And Lord, I have and will continue to. For I realize from where my strength to endure comes from. And often times I am at awe at how you perform the miracles that you do. For a lot of the times many things may appear to be hopeless or there seems to be no way out. But Lord, you reveal to me that if I but only seek you from the depths of my soul, you will and will always avail yourself to me. What a comfort that is to me. Lord, for there are times when I feel afraid, insecure, frightened, and alone. But in quieting my mind and closing my eyes, I can allow the Holy Spirit to direct my attention on where it needs to be. And Lord, it needs to be on you and your undying love for me and all of your children. But yes, I must seek in order to find; I must knock in order for the door to be opened; I must ask and it shall be given.

Lord, this brings me to the point of my writing that I need to humbly bow before Thee to ask for continued faith and trust in Thee to believe that you Lord will provide me with the things I need. Lord, at this very moment, the tears are flowing; for I realize Lord that it is only you that can and will provide if I only extend my arms to Thee. I'm listening to a song now, "Lord I stretch my hands to the, if you need something from the Lord today reach out and say I stretch my hands to Thee; no other help I know; if thy withdraw Thyself from me oh where would and shall I be."

Lord, you already know what I need and you already know how you are going to provide. And Lord, I need only to remind myself and remember that. No matter how things may appear on the surface, I sincerely believe in the depths of my soul, you will once again come on time.

Lord I Love You, and

Pray these things

In Jesus Name, Amen.

MARCH 31, 1993, 5:24 AM

Good morning Lord good morning. Lord, I thank you very, very much for allowing me to awake to a brand new day and touching me once again with the breath of life. For Lord, all days are a gift from you, especially today. What is today that we embark on another of your many, many miracles?

Lord, today at 2:30 pm, I will be at settlement for our brand new house. Lord, the feelings I am experiencing are many. But the one that outweighs the most is my feeling of amazement at how you have directed my life towards an event as big as this. Lord, I feel so overwhelmed by your love and your grace and it gives me feelings of happiness, enlightenment, amazement in the power of your undying love. Lord, I have expressed to you often in my writing the beginning and during struggles I have experienced in this process. And although the devil was extremely busy, you allowed your Will to be done. For I truly believe it has been your Will that has manifested in the lives of those who participate in this process. From those who helped me even initiate this whole idea, to those you have touched outside of my presence, and those you have touched to help me during this process. I had nothing at all to do with it, nor the outcome of it. All that was required of me was to strengthen my faith and trust in you; all that was required of me was to continue to do the footwork, willingly; all that was required of me was to seek Thy will, and for me to stay out of the way. And Lord, this whole experience adds to and enhances the testimony Thou has given me, to be able and willing to share with others your amazing grace and mercy. As I look back Lord, just over a year ago, I did not have a full-time job, but you provided the opportunity and I took advantage of it; I often wondered how I would keep up the bills and keep a roof over my head and food on the table, but you provided the opportunity and I took advantage of it; there were times when I fell short in my obedience to you, but you continued to forgive me and I took advantage of it by desiring to change and to get better; every situation that appeared to be negative, you showed me the positive and I was able to get to the other side.

Lord, you have revealed to me so much of your Almighty Power and I am still at awe about the way you have turned my life around. And all I had to do was just seek your Will and allow your Will to be done, and Lord, as I look at the outcome, I am filled with so much gratitude that at times I can only shake my head and say, Lord, I love you, I love you, I love you.

Lord, I pray that you continue to mold and shape the events of my life so that it may be useful to you and winning back to you the many lost souls of the world, whomever and wherever they are.

Thank you Lord, in Jesus Precious Name, I pray, Amen.

SATURDAY, APRIL 3, 1993, 7:09 AM

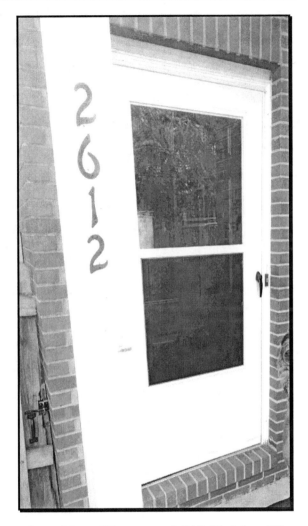

Our New Home at 2612 Zebley Place

Well, Lord, guess where I am, I am saying good morning Lord, good morning Lord, good morning Lord, thank you Lord, thank you Lord, thank you Lord for our new home at 2612 Zebley Place. Yes, Lord, we are here and I am here, by the grace of you, giving you the praise and the glory and the awe of your mighty, mighty love.

Lord, I'm sitting here writing to you as usual, but this time with continued faith and trust in you. Lord, I feel as though I am dreaming and the reality hasn't quite sunk in yet. But Lord, I'm seeing it with my own eyes; feeling it with my own hands; hearing it with my own ears; smelling it with my own nose, but still feel amazed and at awe. Lord, I truly, truly must thank you from the depths of my soul for permitting and allowing this miracle. For surely Lord, it is one of your many miracles you have provided for me like no one else ever has. You have given me the blessings that no human power can give. You have given me your abundant love, unconditionally and with such magnitude and manifestation.

Lord, it was just a year ago that the seed was planted and the possibility of me becoming a homeowner was availed to me. And Lord, all I did was the necessary footwork required to take advantage of this opportunity. The faith and courage was given from Thee; the strength and tolerance was given from Thee; I believe the Will of yours was done once again in my life and has increased the power of my testimony to share with others.

TUESDAY, APRIL 13, 1993, 6:00 AM

Good morning my Heavenly Father. Lord I thank you for the breath of life you have touched me with this very day. Lord, I thank you for all the blessings and miracles you have provided me. Lord I thank you for the opportunity to converse in writing to you the feelings, thoughts, gratitude and awareness of my inner self. Lord, I just thank you, praise you, and worship your mighty, mighty love.

Lord, it has been over a week now since I have taken the time to write to you, I am still floating on the natural and spiritual high of your mighty blessings. Becoming a homeowner has been so rewarding. The feeling of awe still comes from within. Many times I have to still look around and see; I have to actually touch it and feel it. For there are still times when I look around and I'm at disbelief, but reality tells me it is all so real. But more importantly, Lord, the feelings that come from within are of a spiritual nature, for I am able to see and witness your mighty and loving hand in it all. I am able to feel overwhelmed by the presence of your grace and mercy. Lord, although I have experienced other miracles you have provided, but it appears you are still providing more and more. *And Lord, I realize that these miracles and blessings only add to the testimony you have given me to be shared somehow with others and to make believers out of non-believers of your very existence.* Lord, I pray to you that you keep me humble; I pray to you that I remain grateful; I pray to you that I continue to seek and accept your will Lord; I pray for the continued strength and courage to continue on my spiritual journey; I pray Lord that whatever hinders my usefulness to you that it be minimized and taken away; Lord, I pray that you continue to peel away the layers of sin and temptation that binds my very soul; Lord, I pray that you will continue to lead my life toward the purpose you have for me, that I may somehow, somewhere, plant the seed of faith, love and hope in the hearts of others, only to give the glory to you. For you surely have more than turned my life around. *And Lord, the more I learn about you, the more I want to learn. I pray that I may thirst and hunger to the day I return to you for the knowledge and manifestation of your mighty Will. Love you Lord, just love you.*

All these things I pray in Jesus name,

Amen.

SUNDAY, APRIL 18, 1993, 6:30 AM

Lord, I thank you and I praise you. Lord, thank you once again for allowing me to be touched with the gift of life one more day. For Lord, I'm beginning to see and understand that life is a gift, a gift from you. For this, I truly, truly, thank you. And I pray that this day which you have given me can be used to be touched and to touch another sick and suffering soul, whomever and wherever they may be.

Lord, it is now day 18 since living in our new house. No Lord, the high and feeling of awe has not left me. For I still feel such feelings of gratitude that are hard to express. But Lord, I never forget, for one moment, that it is by your Mercy and your Grace that I am even experiencing this whole situation. It has been proven time and time again that you truly are directing and guiding my life. You have shown and proved to me that the results belong to you, for you already know what is for me and what is not. Lord, I continue to pray that I humble myself to you, and to continue to seek your guidance and your Will. I pray that you continue to strengthen me in areas where I am still weak. I pray Lord that you continue to peel away the layers of sin and temptation which keeps me detached from you. I pray Lord that you continue to give me the willingness I need to continue on the spiritual journey so that I may be utilized some way and somehow by you, that others may hear, see, feel and experience that which dwelleth within me, and Lord that is you.

Lord, one thing I am working on now is building my foundation for continued recovery here in Wilmington. I have started attending meetings and getting to know new people. Lord, you know, I have no problems whatsoever to do the necessary footwork. And in the short time that I have been here, people's situations have come about that needs the continued support from the fellowship and from you. Lord, as long as I continue to willingly put you first, the rest becomes easier. As long as I continue to open my mouth about the things that are in my heart, the fellowship is always there for me. Lord as long as I continue to do the things I should do, I will continue to get better. All these things Lord I owe to you. Thank you Lord, thank you for the deliverance from darkness into the marvelous light!!!

In Jesus Name, I pray, Amen.

FRIDAY, MAY 7, 1993, 7:20 AM

Good morning Lord! Good morning! Thank you Father for touching me, once again, with the gift of life. Oh what a gift it truly is Lord.

Lord, I come to you this morning with a humble heart and a desire to seek your Will today. Lord, there have been some changes going on in my life that I feel I must express to you. The Holy Spirit is truly working in my life and at times when it goes unnoticed, there is a sense of submission. *As I look back over the last few months, my behavior has taken on a different and more restraining awareness. I no longer dwell as much on physical and sexual fulfillment. I no longer close my eyes to behaviors that are unhealthy. I feel as though I am getting stronger in areas where I allow myself to be weak or to play into certain unhealthy roles I no longer feel comfortable. And I believe it is through the willingness I seek to change that the Spirit of your love and guidance has and is prevailing within my inner soul. And I believe it is due to the spiritual feedings I have been receiving from Your Word. I have a thirst and hunger about you and Your Will for me that won't stop. I desire more and more to learn about You. And the doors that have been opened and available to me, I have and am taking advantage of.*

The 12 STEPS & RELATED SCRIPTURES

THE TWELVE STEPS & RELATED SCRIPTURE

STEP ONE - We admitted we were powerless over alcohol -- that our lives had become unmanageable.

I know that nothing good lives in me, that is in my sinful nature. For I have the desire to do what is good, but I cannot carry it out. (Romans 7:18)

STEP TWO - Came to believe that a power greater than ourselves could restore us to sanity.

"O Lord my God, I pleaded with you, and you gave me my health again. You brought me back from the brink of the grave, from death itself, and here I am alive!" (Psalm 30:2-3)

STEP THREE - Made a decision to turn our will and our lives over to the care of God, as we understood Him.

"Acceptance with God comes by believing in Christ. I have been crucified with Christ; and I myself no longer live, but Christ lives in me. And the real life I now have within this body is a result of my trusting in the Son of God, who loved me and gave himself for me. (Galatians 2:19-20)

STEP FOUR - Made a searching and fearless moral inventory of ourselves.

Search me O God, and know my heart: try me, and know my thoughts: And see if there be any wicked way in me, and lead me in the way everlasting. (Psalm 139: 23,24)

STEP FIVE - Admitted to God, to ourselves, and to another human being the exact nature of our wrongs.

Therefore confess your sins to each other and pray for each other so that you may be healed. (James 5:16a)

STEP SIX - Were entirely ready to have God remove all these defects of character.

Humble yourselves before the Lord, and He will lift you up. (James 4:10)

STEP SEVEN - Humbly asked him to remove our shortcomings.

If we confess our sins, He is faithful and just and will forgive us our sins and purify us from all unrighteousness. (1 John 1:9)

STEP EIGHT - Made a list of all persons we had harmed and became willing to make amends to them all.

"Your heavenly Father will forgive you if you forgive those who sin against you; but if you refuse to forgive them, he will not forgive you." (Matthew 6:14, 15)

STEP NINE - Made direct amends to such people wherever possible, except when to do so would injure them or others.

Therefore, if you are offering your gift at the altar and there remember that your brother has something against you, leave your gift there in front of the altar. First go and be reconciled to your brother; then come and offer your gift. (Matthew 5:23-24)

STEP TEN - Continued to take personal inventory and when we were wrong promptly admitted it.

So, if you think you are standing firm, be careful that you don't fall. (1 Corinthians 10:12)

STEP ELEVEN - Sought though prayer and meditation to improve our conscious contact with God as we understood Him, praying only for the knowledge of His will for us and the power to carry that out.

"By our faith-the Holy Spirit helps us with our daily problems and in our praying. For we don't even know what we should pray for, nor how to pray as we should; but the Holy Spirit prays for us with such feeling that it cannot be expressed in words." Romans 8:26)

STEP TWELVE - Having had a spiritual awakening as a result of these steps, we tried to carry this message to others, and to practice these principles in all our affairs.

Brothers, if someone is caught in a sin, you who are spiritual should restore him gently. But watch yourself, or you also may be tempted. (Galatians 6:1)

Left - The First 12 Step Convention Held at Genetti Hotel

Top Right – First Home out of Rehab

Middle – Second Home in Recovery – YWCA

Bottom – First Year Anniversary held at the former Sheraton Hotel

ARTICLES OF MY VICTORY!!!

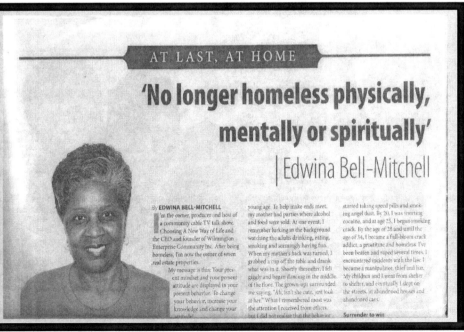

AT LAST, AT HOME

'No longer homeless physically, mentally or spiritually'

| Edwina Bell-Mitchell

By **EDWINA BELL-MITCHELL**

I'm the owner, producer and host of a community cable TV talk show, Choosing A New Way of Life and the CEO and founder of Wilmington Enterprise Community Inc. After being homeless, I'm now the owner of seven real estate properties.

My message is this: Your present mindset and your present attitude are displayed in your present behavior. To change your behavior, increase your knowledge and change your attitude.

young age. To help make ends meet, my mother had parties where alcohol and food were sold. At one event, I remember lurking in the background watching the adults drinking, eating, smoking and seemingly having fun. When my mother's back was turned, I grabbed a cup off the table and drank what was in it. Shortly thereafter, I felt giggly and began dancing in the middle of the floor. The grown-ups surrounded me saying, "Ah, isn't she cute, just look at her." What I remembered most was the attention I received from others, but I did not realize that the behavior

started taking speed pills and smoking angel dust. By 20, I was snorting cocaine, and at age 25, I began smoking crack. By the age of 28 and until the age of 34, I became a full-blown crack addict, a prostitute and homeless. I've been beaten and raped several times. I encountered incidents with the law. I became a manipulator, thief and liar. My children and I went from shelter to shelter, and eventually I slept on the streets, in abandoned houses and abandoned cars.

Surrender to win

With help, life's goals are attainable

Community View

Edwina Bell

Today, I will be graduating, with honors, from Lincoln University with a master's degree in human services. In my thesis, the first line of acknowledgment reads: "Your grace and mercy brought me through; I'm living this moment because of You; I want to thank You and praise You too; it was Your grace and mercy that brought me through."

If someone told me seven years ago I would be go back to school at the age of 39 and obtain a master's degree, I probably would have looked at them as if they were crazy. It was just seven years ago I surrendered to my disease of drug addiction. It was a surrender made out of utter desperation and hopelessness, after living 10 years in active addiction which nearly destroyed me mentally, physically, and spiritually. After countless attempts to overcome my drug addiction, I believed there was no human power available, not even my own, that could relieve the awesome pain and emptiness I felt during that time of my life. I finally realized and accepted that relief would have to come through divine intervention.

The last time I ever used drugs was Feb. 22, 1990. It was on that day I made a desperate plea to the divine spirit and asked that he take me out this life or show me a better way to live. By the grace of God, and only by the grace of God, was the obsession and compulsion to use drugs removed from my soul. With the help of individuals, addicts like myself, who found love and encouragement by attending 12-step support groups, I have been drug free for several years.

Learning to live life on life's terms without the use of drugs has not been easy, but it has been very rewarding. Since I've been in recovery and on this spiritual path, I've learned to face and walk through a number of self-imposed fears. For instance, I did not believe I could go through life without medicating myself with a mood altering chemical. I did not believe I could enjoy life and have fun without being high. I had many goals I wanted to obtain, but convinced myself they were unattainable. I have always wanted to own a home, but thought I would live in an apartment for the rest of my life. I had desires to go back to school to obtain a degree, but would talk myself out of it my saying I was too old and too dumb to even try.

Using the 12 steps

Utilizing the spiritual principles of the 12-step support groups, I have learned to enjoy life without the use of drugs. I have set and accomplished short term goals such as re-establishing my credit, becoming a homeowner, and being reunited with family members. In addition, I have learned to do the footwork necessary to set and accomplish long term goals such as going back to school to further my education.

When the opportunity presented itself to obtain a master's degree, I prayed on it, consulted the advice of others, then I went for it — head on. I truly believe this accomplishment was orchestrated by the Divine Spirit who provided me with the willingness to become his humble servant for the sole purpose of inspiring others to choose a new way of life, free from drugs. As I reflect back on my addiction, I remember asking myself how I got into this predicament. The only consolation I received for experiencing the devastating consequences of drug addiction was a deep belief and conviction that God had other plans for me.

Sharing with others

During my first few years of recovery, I volunteered for service work in the 12-step support groups. This service included sharing my experience, strength and hope with individuals who had substance abuse problems. I began sharing this information in detoxification and drug rehabilitation facilities, prisons, hospitals and institutions. I was amazed how attentive and receptive individuals were when I shared my story with them. I had no idea sharing my story with others would provide the opportunity for seeds of faith and hope to be planted in their lives. As time went on, I was prepared once again by the Divine Spirit and the support group to expand my horizon by sharing my story of recovery on a local radio station. A year later I was approached by a television producer, who had heard my story, and asked if I would be willing to share my story on a local cable community channel.

I now host a talk show entitled "Choosing a New Way of Life" aired every fourth Sunday on Cable Channel 28, at 3 p.m.

Having attained these accomplishments, I became convinced that with God all things are possible. In order to continue to inspire those who have substance abused problems, I have made plans to obtain my doctorate beginning in September 1997.

If I can do all this, believe me, you can do it too — with divine help.

▶ Edwina Bell of Wilmington works in the Wilmington Police Department and is a member of The News Journal Community Advisory Board.

Police prostitution sweep ends with a talk of hope

By TERRI SANGINITI
The News Journal

Ten women arrested in the New Castle area during a six-hour state police sweep Thursday got an unexpected pep talk to go along with their prostitution charges.

The suspects were the beneficiaries of some spontaneous outreach from someone who used to walk in their shoes and understood their plight.

When the 10 women were brought into Troop 2 to be charged with drug and prostitution offenses, Community Outreach Specialist Edwina Bell-Mitchell was there to greet them and offer some hope.

Bell-Mitchell, a motivational speaker and executive director of Wilmington Enterprise Community Inc., a nonprofit group that supports mothers and families who lost loved ones to violence, said she reached out to the women because she used to be where they are now.

"I'm a former prostitute, drug addict, alcoholic and rape victim," she said. "I told them when they're ready, people like me are here to help them."

State police Cpl. Jeff Whit-

> "I'm a former prostitute, drug addict, alcoholic and rape victim. I told them when they're ready, people like me are here to help them."
>
> **Edwina Bell-Mitchell,
> Community Outreach
> specialist**

marsh said his agency recognizes that merely arresting prostitutes does little to get them off the streets and into a productive life.

So, this time, they used a different tactic.

"Ms. Bell individually spoke with each arrestee in an attempt to assist them in addressing the many issues that have led them to a life of drugs and prostitution," Whitmarsh said.

He said the 10 suspects were arrested on a a total of 18 criminal charges.

"When they first came in, they thought it was a set-up," Bell-Mitchell said. "I let them know that I was trying to get them the help they needed. They were positive about that."

Bell-Mitchell said one woman said she had a 4-week-old baby and all she wanted was to get off crack.

"I used to be a crack addict," Bell-Mitchell said. "I told them the way I look now you, can look if you get your life together."

Bell-Mitchell said she gave each of the girls a hug to let them know she cared about them.

"One girl said all she wanted to hear was that someone cared," she said.

Before they left, they exchanged phone numbers.

"I told them it all starts with them wanting help," Bell-Mitchell said. "There's a difference between you needing it and you wanting it. When they're ready, I'll be there to hold their hands."

Whitmarsh said state police plan to continue working with Bell-Mitchell in the outreach effort.

Contact Terri Sanginiti at 324-2771 or tsanginiti@delawareonline.com

Comment

SEPT. 15, 1996 •• SUNDAY NEWS JOURNAL J3

Will can win over drug use

According to a government study, drug use among teen-agers is on the rise. It is unfortunate that many individuals, particularly youth, have resorted to drug use. Although the reasons for using drugs are many, the ability to stop or refrain from using them requires two main ingredients: a desire for a new way of life, and willingness to go to any length to accomplish it.

Community View

Edwina Bell

As a former substance abuser, I feel compelled to share my experience, strength and hope. I hope to prevent someone from picking up a drug for the first time, inspire someone to choose a way of life, and encourage those who have chosen a new life to reach back and help others.

I was introduced to alcohol at a young age. To help make ends meet, my mother had parties where alcohol and food were sold. At one, I remember lurking in the background watching the adults drinking, eating and smoking while playing cards, and seemingly having fun. When my mother's back was turned, I grabbed a cup and drank what was in it. It tasted nasty and made me gag. Nevertheless, I drank all of it.

Shortly thereafter, I felt giggly and began dancing in the middle of the floor. The grown-ups surrounded me, saying, "Ah, isn't she cute, just look at her." What I remember most was the attention I received from others. However, I did not realize the behavior was brought on by the alcohol I drank. From that point, I associated drinking with having fun and being the center of attention.

At age 8, I secretly began smoking cigarettes. By age 10, I began hanging out with girls whose parents had plenty of liquor in their homes. I experienced my first drunk at age 12, while visiting a friend. I decided, with encouragement from my friends, to taste all the different liquors stored in the cabinet. I fell down a flight of stairs, felt sick to my stomach and vomited all over the place. But again, I remember having fun and being cheered on by friends.

By 14, my friends had introduced me to marijuana. At 18, I was introduced to angel dust and black beauties — speed pills. By 20, I was snorting cocaine, and at 25 I began smoking crack. By 28, I had become a full-blown crack addict. I lost jobs, material things

and, most of all, I felt I had lost my mind. I had reached the point where I did anything to get drugs or money to buy them. I would have sold my soul if someone had offered to buy it.

I have been raped, beaten, set up, spit on and called all kinds of names. I have had guns and knives put to my head and throat. By the grace of God, I escaped death many times. However, there were others who were not as fortunate.

I became a disgrace to myself, my family and to society. My physical hygiene was nonexistent. I was emotionally numb and spiritually dead. Eventually I became homeless, was helpless and felt hopeless. I wanted to die.

The last time I used drugs I was consumed with self-loathing, shame, guilt, despair and fear. During a split second of sanity, I made a desperate cry to God, asking him, "Take me out of this life or show me a better way!"

God has shown me a better way. I have not touched any mood-altering chemicals since, and have been drug-free for nearly seven years, but one day at a time.

▶ **Edwina Bell is a civilian employee at the Wilmington Police Department and a member of The News Journal Community Advisory Board.**

Lincoln University

of The Commonwealth System of Higher Education
Upon the recommendation of the Faculty and under authority vested
in the Board of Trustees by the Commonwealth of Pennsylvania
hereby confers on

Edwina Clinton Hall-Bell

The Degree of

Master of Human Services

with all the rights, privileges, and perquisites pertaining to the
degree and in witness thereof presents this diploma.
Given under the seal of Lincoln University on this fourth day of May in
the year one thousand nine hundred and ninety-seven, A.D.

EDWINA BELL

3 West McCaulley Court - Wilmington, DE 19801 - (302) 690-6679 – edwina.bell@yahoo.com

PROFILE

Human Services Consultant with 25-years of broad record of accomplishments encompassing public, private, and community sectors. Adept at devising and implementing successful strategies to identify and meet the needs of client groups and agencies to develop realistic and obtainable goals in economic development, housing, workforce development, family, and community prosperity and empowerment. Utilize strong leadership and team building skills with technology to consistently achieve sustainable results. Expertise areas:

Organization Development/Strategic Planning	Recruitment/Public Relations/Marketing
Researcher/Needs Assessments Specialist	Youth/Adults/Seniors Wrap Around Services
Mental Health/Substance Abuse (ACT/ICM)	Inspirational Speaker/Trainer/Facilitator
Television Personality/Producer/Host/Author	Grant Writer/Monitor/Evaluator

PROFESSIONAL EXPERIENCES

DEVINE LIGHTS, INC. PHILADELPHIA, PA   FEBRUARY 2015 – PRESENT

Lecturer/Trainer/Facilitator/Inspirational Speaker (contract)

JEVS HUMAN SERVICES, WILMINGTON, DE   SEPTEMBER 2013 – PRESENT

Direct Home Care/Outreach Specialist (contract)

MOTHERS IN CHARGE, PHILADELPHIA, PA   MAY 2012 – PRESENT

Group Facilitator/Trainer/Motivational Speaker (contract)

WILMINGTON ENTERPRISE COMMUNITY, INC., WILMINGTON, DE   OCTOBER 2004 – JULY 2014

Executive Director (Collaboration of 200+ Agency Partnership/Network)

RESOURCES FOR HUMAN DEVELOPMENT, WILMINGTON, DE   MAY 2012 – JANUARY 2014

Mental Health/Substance Abuse Clinician/Trainer/Housing Specialist

CONNECTING GENERATIONS, INC., WILMINGTON, DE   SEPTEMBER 2010 – MAY 2012

Mentor Recruiter/Trainer Specialist (contract)

PEOPLE FOR PEOPLE, INC., PHILADELPHIA, PA   JULY 2010 – SEPTEMBER 2010

Mentor Support Coordinator/Trainer (contract)

PROFESSIONAL COUNSELING RESOURCES, INC., WILMINGTON, DE JUNE 2008 – MAY 2010

Marketing/Recruitment/Training Director (contract)

1212 CORPORATION, INC., WILMINGTON, DE   OCTOBER 2004 – FEBRUARY 2008

Executive Director (Recovery Safe Haven - contract)

EDWINA BELL
Page -2-

City of Wilmington, Wilmington, DE	**MAY 1990 – OCTOBER 2004**

Executive Director, Enterprise Community, Office of the Mayor	2000 – 2004
Program Manager, Enterprise Community, Office of the Mayor	1997 – 2000
Executive Assistant to Chief of Police, Wilmington Police Department	1995 – 1997
Data and Statistics Analyst/Clerk to Chief of Fire, Wilmington Fire Department	1993 – 1995
Word Processing Technician, Information Systems Division	1990 – 1993

EDUCATION

Ph.D. Candidate – New Calvary School of Ministry/DE   *M.H.S.* – Lincoln University/PA *('97 Graduate)*
  Focus: Biblical Studies   **Focus: Human Services/EAP Training Manual**

PUBLICATIONS

Published Articles:
- *"Will Can Win Over Drug Use"* Sunday News Journal, May 15, 1996 Edition, Wilmington, DE
- *"Ending Addiction Requires Real Desire"* Sunday News Journal, December 29, 1996 Edition, Wilmington, DE
- *"Never Too Late To Be A Role Model"* Sunday News Journal, March 5, 1997 Edition, Wilmington, DE
- *"With Help, Life's Goals Are Attainable"* Sunday News Journal, May 4, 1997 Edition, Wilmington, DE

Published Book:
- *A Training Program Manual For Employee Assistance Representatives*; City of Wilmington, Department of Personnel, May 1997

COMMUNITY SERVICE

May 1995 – Present: host/producer of a community-cable television talk show entitled, *"Choosing A New Way of Life,"* featured on the community cable Channel 28, with over 190,000 subscribers.

Show Featured in Articles:
- *"Former addict's story might help others"* News Journal-Our Readers' Views, 10/8/96, Wilm., DE
- *"People Are Listening To This Straight-Shooting Righteous Seed"* News Journal, 10/7/98 Edition, Wilm., DE
- *'Oprah' of DE: Edwina Bell, Host of Choosing A New Way of Life,"* SCOOP USA, 11/6/98 Edition, Phila., PA
- *"Talk Show Celebrity,"* Women's History Month, SCOOP U.S.A., 3/7/03 Edition, Phila., PA
- *"Staying clean one day at a time"* The News of Cumberland County, 9/20/10
- *"No longer homeless physically, mentally or spiritually"* One Step Away Newspaper/(R.H.D.), 4/11/12

TRAINING SESSIONS/SEMINARS/WORKSHOPS CURRICULUM

General Mentoring and Mentoring Children of Prisoners / Capacity Building & Organizational Development
Management/Leadership Skills Development / Workplace Culture Diversity / EAP Programs / Etiquettes
Youth and Their Issues, Concerns & Solutions / Thinking For A Change National Curriculum
Communication Skills & Techniques / Life Skills / Job Preparation and Education / Parent-Child Classes
Collaboration Building and Partnership Sustainability / Relationships – Personal, Professional & Spiritual
12-Step Recovery Programs/Drug/Alcohol Counseling / Mental Health Modules (ACT/ICM)
Staff Development & Team-Building / Anger Management/Problem Conflict & Resolution
Customized Training/Seminars Available Upon Request

ABOVE SERVICES PROVIDED TO THE FOLLOWING ORGANIZATIONS

YMCA/YWCA of DE – Crossroads of DE – City of Wilmington, DE – New Castle County – State of Delaware
DE Correctional Facilities – Homeless Shelters – Rehabilitation/Detoxification Facilities – Churches – Medical Facilities
Carson Valley School – Community Agencies - Elementary/Middle/High Schools – Hospitals & Institutions – Colleges

References Available Upon Request

EDWINA'S LOVED ONE'S

AUTHOR BIO - EDWINA BELL, M.H.S.

Edwina was born on December 16, 1955 and raised in Philadelphia, Pennsylvania. At the age of 15 and 17, mom and dad married and were teenage parents. By the age of 22 and 24 they had six children with three of them just 10 months apart (she is the 3rd child). Her dad was the provider, protector and disciplinarian, while her mom was the nurturer and home maker most of her and siblings' childhood years.

She was and still is a very active and energetic person. Edwina is a tomboy by nature, which is why she's not really the prancing type, but can "get down" if needed.

Edwina loves traveling, dancing, eating crabs, and enjoys spending quality time with her mom, children, grandchildren and other children as well.

Being in recovery for over 25 years has allowed the student within to be all so ready for any and every opportunity-opportunities that she often practice asking herself, "What is the lesson in this situation or from this encounter?" Edwina finds spiritual gratification and fulfillment when she utilizes the tools of the 12-spiritual principles and the Fruits of the Spirit.

Edwina truly believes that recovery is about being prepared for things and events yet to come. Therefore, she is adamant when she says, "When the student is ready, the teacher(s) will appear." Working with others in any forum is an opportunity to model and demonstrate the humility required to yield to the Spirit.

Edwina never thought in a million years she would: 1) take care of seven family members on hospice, 2) obtain a Ph.D. in Biblical Studies, 3) become a TV Talk Show Host, 4) leave the corporate world to work with those who suffer from substance abuse and mental illness, 5) have a son that is a Doctor of Education and a daughter that is owner of her own construction company, 6) be a part of a wonderful church family after being turned away from churches during her active addiction, and 7) have an awesome personal relationship with her Lord and Savior, Jesus Christ.

As a child, she always wanted to be a model. She was discouraged by family and friends. However, God had other intentions for her as a model – a model that would become, through His preparedness, a spiritual change agent for others.

APPENDIX A - AS IT WAS WRITT*(I)*N

September 14, 1992, 5:45 am

APPENDIX B - AS IT WAS WRITT*(I)*N

October 15, 1992, 4:15 am

10/15/92 4:15am

Good morning my Heavenly Father. Oh what a beautiful day it is to wake up this early in the morning. For I realize that it is by your Grace that I have this very moment. Thank you Lord!

Lord as I reflect back over the past 11 months after the death of my husband, I notice the emotional roller coaster I am on. There has been tremendous growth within and around me, and yet there are still some areas where more growth is needed.

APPENDIX C - AS IT WAS WRITT(I)N

Saturday, October 24, 1992, 2:29 pm

Sat. 10/24/92 2:29 pm.

Good Afternoon my Heavenly Father
I thank Lord for giving me a new day
once again.

Lord I am sitting here in a room to
which I came to be rejuvenated by Thy
Will and by Thy Grace and to
ask Thee to help me redirect my
attitude, my behavior and my faith
towards Thee.

Lord it has been 11 months and
3 days since the death of my husband
and I am feeling a lot of things
during this time as I reflect back
over that period of time.

On one side of the coin, I am
truly amazed and I am at the way
Thy has kept me and provided for
me. For the way you have revealed
things to me, things that have
increased my faith and my trust in Thee.
The opportunity to share with other
Christians and with other alcoholics &
addicts has been more than overwhelming.
I feel the very way Thy has woken me

up and has provided all of my needs,
for this I'm truly blessed. But God
you have touched me even more, where
it really counts, in the spiritual realm.
I have learned to seek Thee in
the midst of sorrow and joy and in
each case, it was by Thy Grace that
I have come this far on my spiritual
journey, when in doubt and in fear
I revealed to Thee in prayer, in
conversations and in writing. And you
Lord, have made a ways and of no
way, you have turned by
fears and doubts into faith and trust
you have proven to more and more
the deliverance from darkness and into
the light. You have made known
to me that you are with me and will
never ever leave me - and Lord that
is the most amazing feeling I have
especially now, which brings me
to the other side of the coin.

Because I know that you are always
available, I need to, once again,
ask for help in the area that I'll

under my spiritual ~~you~~ growth. And Lord I pray that the Holy Spirit convicts me even more into doing the right things ~~———~~ Lord, I have a great fear that goes deep, real deep. It is the fear of total commitment to Thee and to Thy Will. I know that fear exist because in some areas of my life, I still want to "be in control" and I ask myself "in control of what". I still have that manipulative and seductive behavior that gives me a high for the moment but which also keeps me spiritually sick. Lord there is still that need in me to conquer and I'm back asking myself "Conquer what". Why do I feel the need to be accepted in the flesh. Why do I fear being upheld and abandon by others if I don't feed them with the flesh. Then I realize sometime that it is the Spirit of Satan in me and in them that allows the feeling and the act of submission to take place.

And Lord, why is it that I seek those that are unavailable for me. It seems that need to conquer and subdue is more prevalent than other situations. And the act of this type of situation is more intense. But then I realize it is a useless battle but I still forge ahead, why. And this is where that ~~———~~ commitment comes into play again. I fear commitment and in turn I see that very few are committed when it comes to the flesh. But I realize this is an area that only She can help me with and I need to make a conscious and sincere effort to change. You see Lord, as I look back just over the last few months, I have put more effort into doing it wrong thing instead of the right thing. And it has made me feel ~~———~~ distant but then yet ~~———~~ the Holy Spirit continues to tug at me and I ignore it. Help me Lord, help me.

Lord, I ask you on a daily basis to mold me and shape me into thy image; I ask that Thy continue to put me on the road to righteousness; I ask Thee to let me touch and be touched by another sick & suffering soul; and I ask Jo make me Thy servant to be used to show the works of the Lord. And Lord, in some areas of my life my prayers and being answered and I am useful to thee; but I don't feel that I am totally useful to thee until I get better with the dark side of my attitude and behavior. For God it is darkness - total darkness.

Lord you have shown me what unconditional love is; through the fellowship and through my fellow Christians. Why is it on a personal level that I can't love myself unconditionally? and others as well?

APPENDIX D - AS IT WAS WRITT(I)N

Sunday, October 25, 1992, 10:52 am

Sun 10:52 am

Good Morning, Good Morning!
Good Morning Lord; Oh how I
thank thee for the insight thy
has given me to start this new
Day once again.
I woke up this morning compelled
to write on the Six and the Seventh Steps
as well as letting my sponsor know
what really has been going on these
past few months. I really feel the
need to lay the cards down on the
table and admit to God &, another
human being the exact nature of my
wrongs.
One of the many things that comes
from Step 6 is "Any person capable of
enough willingness & honesty to try
repeatedly Step 6 on all his faults —
without any reservations whatever — has
indeed come a long way spiritually, and
is therefore entitled to be called a "Man"
who is sincerely trying to grow in the
image and likeness of his own Creator.

Just as God removed the obsession
and reservation from alcohol & drugs — it is
apparent that He can remove from me
every other difficulty or defect as well.
You know Lord after doing my
4th & 5th Step it was revealed to
me certain patterns that caused me
a lot of pain and grief and that were
really self-seeking motives. And it
was the pattern of seeking attention
and affection through seductive and
manipulative behavior from the opposite
sex, starting from my childhood with
my father. This pattern has been a
part of my whole life and become a
way of life for me before, during and
after my addiction. Before it was
done automatically but now I realize
that I'm doing it by choice as well
and that scares me. It scares me because
at any given moment God switch goes
off in my head and I'm off to the races.
The idea is pre-meditated long before the
act is committed - rather consciously or subconsciously. And then the play begins

I noticed first with my non-verbal body language, where I exhibit body movements that I know brings attention; the eye contact where I'm saying more than I verbalize. Then comes the gestures of invitation, and you know what, God—this is insane but I get a thrill from this—it is a high of its own. If I look at this pattern as I did with my pattern of drinking and drugging it brings back the realization of a false high which I imagine starts out being and feeling good but which also ends in despair, guilt and emptiness—all on a spiritual level. And I find myself asking the same questions I did in my addiction, "Why am I doing this?" I look back over the situation beginning to end and I find that the answer is always the same—Doing the same thing, expecting different results. And the results are always the same. I allow myself to be seen and used as a object and feel and use other people the same way. Lord, I'm tired of living like this, I'm tired Lord

APPENDIX E - AS IT WAS WRITT*(I)*N

Sunday, October 25, 1992, 11:52 am

11:52 Am Sunday - Lord, I have returned to this very same room tonight, but it's different

from when I left earlier. Conversations have taken place where the light of truth was related. It was finally acknowledged what must be done in order for you to continue to use me, successfully. I finally realized that it was "Self" that wanted to hold on to the ways of destruction; Selfishness, self-centeredness and egotism - at the expense of myself and of others. And you revealed through the conversations what must be done in order to be delivered from this darkness. And that was to let the person go - and I be let go. So that whatever it is that has blocked me in the past - can be, first turned over to you and then for us to make a real real sincere and honest effort to change accordingly - for the good of us all.

Lord, once again you have made the truth be seen for what it is. I no longer want to ignore it or suppress it. I do want to go

on with my life and be out of a
righteous path. I do want to do Thy
will and to be prepared to do Thy
work. I want to be committed to Thee
and to Thee only – and the only way
I can is to stop the bullshit now,
and I mean really stop.

I've learned a lot about the
traps and set-ups that make me fail
short time and time again. I've learned
when the "self" is at hand and doing
it's thing. I've learned if I don't
continue to ~~strive~~ strive for progress
I will regress and back to which I
came. And Lord, you know that deep down
inside my soul, that is the last place
I ~~would~~ would want to return.

And if I am to be honest Lord, I have
been setting myself up for the old patterns
for which I have become ~~accustomed~~ accustomed
to in the past. And if I don't attempt
to alter this pattern, it will only repeat
itself time & time again. And then what?
Who knows – But you Lord – And
I know now that it will only lead to

death – spiritual death. And
for once in my life – I don't ever
want to ~~die~~ die another spiritual
death.

So Lord I'm asking that Thy
go before me and make straight
my journey. To go before me and
clear house. To instill in me
the need to be committed to
Thee & to Thy Will. Lord,
I ask these things in the name
of your Son, Jesus Christ. Amen!

Good Night Lord, sweet dreams.

APPENDIX F - AS IT WAS WRITT(*I*)N

Sunday, October 25, 1992, 9:29 pm

Sun 9:29 pm.

Well Lord, things are really moving ahead. I just left my sponsor and shared with her all that I have been feeling and doing over the past months. And Lord once again the burden was lifted from me. The burden of not being honest and open so that I can grow and seek direction & suggestions from others.

I was able to confide in her the relationships I have had and their impact on my spirituality. I came away feeling that I am on the right track again – as long as I follow the suggestions she gave me. She suggested that I end the relationships that are causing me problems and she also suggested 4 things to do when the temptation arises again. She suggested that I first tell God that I have this desire – and then to tell someone else – go to a meeting and write about it. Hopefully, I will commit myself to doing these things so I won't have to fall into the some set-ups or traps.

APPENDIX G - AS IT WAS WRITT(I)N

Monday, October 26, 1992, 9:00 pm

Monday: 9:00pm 10/26/92

Good Evening Lord. I here'm bed now winding down a very restful and insightive weekend. I'm so glad I allow myself to rest and take these 3 days to do some soul searching and house cleaning that is internal house cleaning.

I made two meetings today and shared about the experiences of this weekend and it helped me to realize that it was the best medicine I could have given myself. Being away in a room for the weekend availed a great opportunity for me to put things back into prospective and to come out committed to change some things, mainly my behavior. It also gave me the opportunity to be totally honest with my sponsors I have not in the past - and that also kept me spiritually sick - for I thought I was keeping a big secret - but the secret itself was ugly and unhealthy for my spiritual well being.

I have even committed myself to drop down on my knees - which I have failed to do for several long months. And I realize that when I stopped humbling myself - the "Self" got bigger I can remember in the past when I did all the things I was suppose to do and had the willingness to do it - I felt whole I felt I was being spiritually molded. But I thank God for the lessons I am _____ now because it makes me appreciate ~~the~~ life and myself and others with more understanding. I pray that the Lord continues to reveal things to me that will be led to a better and more useful servant for Thee.

I thank you Lord for spending this weekend with me and giving me the guidance and direction I need to start anew.

Love You Lord, Amen

APPENDIX H - AS IT WAS WRITT(I)N

Sunday, November 1, 1992, 6:35 pm

> Sunday: 6:35 pm.
>   Thank you Lord for giving me the strength and courage I needed today and to allow the Holy Spirit to direct my thoughts and my actions.
>   I said: This weekend was one of the most rewarding and yet painful weekend I have experienced. I needed and did come to terms with and about a few things that were stifling my spiritual growth. I committed myself to do certain things after talking with my sponsor this weekend and after having prayed and meditated over these situations.

> One day - and if needed - one minute at a time I have to stop the impulsive behavior; and when the thought or urge falls upon me - I must pray and tell God - then I must call someone - mainly my sponsor - and then I must write about it. I sincerely want to fulfill this commitment. I also must stop the phone calls, visits and day dreaming or should I say fantasy about being and having someone that is not meant for me that way. But most importantly I must do these things because my recovery is on the line - not necessarily drinking or drugging - but striving for growth and progress and recognizing that my recovery is on the line - has made me more willing to get back on track. I promised myself early in recovery that I would not allow anyone or any situation to come before my recovery, and they both have. So I must regain my sanity and my composure to restart this recovery process again.

APPENDIX I - AS IT WAS WRITT(I)N

Saturday, November 7, 1992, 7:06 pm

Sat. 7:06 pm

Good Evening Lord. Thank you for a marvelous and beautiful day. Lord it has been very hard this week dealing with the emotions of letting go someone I feel an emotional and loving bind towards. And the reality of letting go of someone I love has enlightened me even more spiritually. I know this whole thing is a process and at this point of the process is the physical withdrawal. There are times when I want to call but I know I can't; there are times when I want to reach out and touch and hug; but I know I can't; there are times when the words "I love you and I want you" comes to my lips, but I know I can't say it; there are times when I want to give up this process and pay the consequences; but I realize I would die a spiritual death. And Lord, you must go before me and intervene. I must sit quietly and meditate before reacting but some time that impulsiveness overwhelms me and I must seek your strength

to withstand the temptation. For the first time Lord, I love someone that I feel can fulfill all my needs but then I come to realize it is only You who could possibly do that. I struggle with trying to understand rather then to just accept. I believe you will for me and him is to grow and bind more closer to Thee so that the work you have for us to do can be done. I realize that it is "Self" that gets in the way of me doing the right thing. The pain I am experiencing now is great but I also realize that the pain of not doing it will be greater. Lord help me to keep that in the forefront of my mind and soul. Help me to realize that it will take time and that the healing process will soon be realized; but for right now, Lord it hurts - it hurts real bad. But I need to remind myself Lord "that this too shall pass."

Love Jan Lord.

- 120 -

APPENDIX J - AS IT WAS WRITT*(I)*N

Tuesday, November 17, 1992, 5:50 am

Tues 11/17/92 5:50 am

Good Morning my Heavenly Father!!
Lord thank you for touching me with
the gift of life this morning.

Lord you still never cease to amaze
me. Your Love and Strength is once again
being manifested, especially during some of
the painful, yet amazing times of my life.
For it is then that I truly experience
your amazing grace.

This past week has been
emotionally interesting to me. For
I am experiencing feelings I never
experienced before - some or healthy
I am grieving like I never grieved
before for my husband Paul. The
tears have been coming and going.
But yet Lord, I feel such a sense of
closeness to Thee - that I have
never experienced before either, you
have revealed to my soul that you
are here and that I can and should,
willingly, always depend on you.

You have brought me a mighty long
way Lord, and for this I am eternally
grateful. And Lord I want to show

APPENDIX K - AS IT WAS WRITT(I)N

Wednesday Night, November 25, 1992, 6:48 pm

11/25/92 6:48 Wed nite

Lord, this is the perfect opportunity for me to take the time I need to reflect over the past year with much faith and gratitude.

Lord, oh Lord, you have brought me a mighty long way. And after time I have to pinch myself to feel it is so real. And Lord, it is more than real - it is truly awesome. Regardless of the trials and tribulations, you have made more than a believer out of me - you have made me more willing to follow Thee. Lord I can't fully explain how I feel but I just know that it is by keeping the faith and looking up to Thee that Thy has and is revealing things to me that are nurturing and nourishing to my soul. And I guess the main thing I see is that by asking Thy will be done - and allowing myself to believe that what ever happens continue to ask that Thy will be done. And the spiritual manifestations have far out weighed the physical & material manifestations.

Lord, a while ago the Devil wanted me to believe that I could and would not make it especially after Paul's death. He tried to tell me and show me how impossible it will be. He tried hard to make me give up this newly found life and faith I have in thee. Lord he tried to tell that the mountains were too high and that I wouldn't make it. Lord he tried to tell me that it was all up to me and I would have to do it all alone. But Lord Oh Lord, what a lie He turned out to be - Hallelujah Jesus - Lord the tears are now flowing - for I have found something in I see that I've been reaching for all of my life that feeling of belonging to someone that truly, truly and I mean truly loves me - loves me with all of my shortcomings - but one who wants me to strive for progressive in the spiritual realm of life. And I'm beginning to see and understand how the spiritual growth rather

manifest itself on the physical plane.
Lord, I can see a glimpse of the
molding and shaping of my spirit and
I believe that they is preparing me
for the purpose that is destined for
me. Lord, little by little - but by bit
you have peeled away the layers of
temptation and the layers of sin and
Lord - I cease more and more because
I feel so different when I acknowledge
the transformation and rightly attribute
it to Thee. And Lord the tears are
flowing again - I just can't seem to
stop them - for when I think of
you Lord and what you have done
for me and how you are using me
I get so full Lord - I get so full.
      Lord, people wonder why I'm
so happy go lucky and smiling and
just seem to be full of life - But
Lord they just don't know - Do they
Lord - Do They just don't know.
But Lord when the time is right Lord -
they will know and they will see as well
as feel the Power of your almighty Love

APPENDIX L - AS IT WAS WRITT*I*N

Friday Night, November 25, 1992, 7:55 pm

FN 11/25/92 Fri Night

You know Lord, I'm beginning to see that although they are using me - they must allow the process of shaping and molding to take place. And it is through the process that I must look to Thee for strength and courage accompanied with faith and trust. And while going through the process growth I have found that by taking - one day at a time Sweet Jesus - that's all that I'm asking from you - One Day At a Time - and it's in that saying that I find the strength and courage to go forward with faith and belief in Thee. And that no matter what comes along the pike as I travel onward that it won't be anything that You and I can't handle - Lord no matter what - instead of focusing on the problem I focus on the lesson to be learned - and Lord it all boils down to just trusting in Thee and believing everything is going to be alright. And it also boils down to patience - true patience. For I have noticed that as long as I reveal to Thee what is on my heart whether it be good or bad, You just have already set the plan and the course - all that is ask of me is to be willing - Lord I

just need to be willing. And it is with that willingness that change takes place gradually. Lord it has been my willingness that has made all the difference in the world. And that willingness goes deep Lord, it goes deep.

APPENDIX M - AS IT WAS WRITT*(I)*N

Sunday, December 6, 1992

Sun 12/6/92

Good evening Lord! I thank you for all the blessings that [you] has given me!

Lord, for the most part, I have found peace and serenity in [thee] and feel that all things happen for a reason.

Over the past few months I have noticed a change in me. A change that was needed and guided by you. I no longer feel the compulsion and obsession I had when it comes to the opposite sex. I feel when I prayed that that obsession & compulsion be lifted, it was and I noticed it was a gradual process. I feel that as long as I ask for the help it is given, I thank you Lord. And although the change is still happening I feel comforted with it and look forward to continued progress.

APPENDIX N - AS IT WAS WRITT(I)N

January 14, 1993

Jan. 14, 1993

Lord I thank you for the gift of life, the gift of learning, the gift of change, the gift of joy and the gift of pain. Lord, it has been awhile since I have allowed myself to set down and focus on my writing. Lord, you know children I have to write and I must turn that desire over to you. For I know that what I write I turn over to you, you will take care of, you will perfect me and it will magnify. I have no doubt about that. In your time, Lord, in your time...

For the most part, a lot of progress has been in all areas of my life. But what I notice the most is the spiritual serenity I am experiencing. I have a feeling that is calm and sweet about my life and about life itself. The process of life is a rewarding one, one that I can see and feel but most of all, one that I can accept. I no longer fight and I surrender daily the situations I can't handle. And Lord, if you will hear saying, you have brought me a long, long way. And I am truly grateful for your favor and your grace.

Lord, you are revealing to me my purpose, for within I am called to share my experience, strength and hope to other people suffering souls. The light and life of your existence prevails through me to others. Lord, just by growing up and surrendering willingly to you - I've seen the effect it has on others. You know Lord that I desire to be your servant, to use me as you wish. And Lord I have faith that at least one seed is planted, one soul is uplifted, one head begins to quell, one heart begins to open - and the rest is left up to Thee. Lord, many times I do not value the impact of you using me on other people. But I do see the results on other people's reaction, their eyes and tears and heart begin to open to the realization that you are in them. Lord - one that only wants us to acknowledge thee willingly, one who wants to put us on a spiritual journey of growth and attainment, one who wants to always use to help and another lost soul. And Lord, if one soul is helped by you using me, then the glory and praise belongs to you - not me Lord but you.

APPENDIX O - AS IT WAS WRITT*(I)*N

January 27, 1993

Jan 27, 1993

Good evening Lord. What a glorious day it has been Lord, I feel so at one with you - irregardless of what is going on in my life. The feeling that "all is well" is stronger than it has ever been.

I have been doing a lot of footwork lately - spiritually and physically. I've started building my foundation in Wilmington. I have attended noon meetings - have shared my story and have met new friends of the fellowship. This move is not without feelings but it is a move with a lot of faith. I guess I've learned and applied a lot of the tools from you and the fellowship. Tools that have been and are vital to my sobriety, I thank you Lord. I thank for the awareness of your presence. I thank you for the strength and courage you have given me. I thank you for all the wonderful people I have met. I thank you for the peace of mind I have acquired. I thank you for my family who is so supportive. I thank you for my children and the relationship we are rebuilding. Most of all Lord I thank you for "You". In Jesus name, I pray Amen

APPENDIX P - AS IT WAS WRITT*(I)*N

February 1, 1993, 12:45 pm

APPENDIX Q - AS IT WAS WRITT*(I)*N

February 3, 1993, 5:55 am

2/3/93 5:55am

Good Morning Lord. Thank U. Thank U. Thank U. Lord I dreamed last night that I was called to go to the potem. I had received several cards at this church and among the cards was one that stood out the most. The card said "Your hour has come". It was written by a little girl And after reading all the cards. I selected the one the little girl wrote. Lord, in my dream I remember being distracted by the flesh because the dream revealed to me that the people I was with, I should not have been with. And I remember hiding from the crowd who was anxiously waiting for me. I also remember playing football, going back and forth between the goal line, never making it acrossed. I remember being with my family and once again preparing to go to the potem and I remember this man blocking me as I tried to go up the steps. Then after pushing him aside I went upstairs and it seemed like I was playing in this room with my brother, waiting to be called.

APPENDIX R - AS IT WAS WRITT*(I)*N

March 2, 1993, 4:49 am

Lord I pray that you give me the strength to also face the health problems I am experiencing now, for signs of the cervical cancer is back and the need for the treatment is at hand. But you know Lord I thank you for allowing me to be in my right frame of mind to make decisions regarding my health. I thank you Lord for having a job that offers benefits for me to get treatment and most of all Lord, I thank you for my sobriety to get through this and any situation without giving up. But rather to rely on your love and strength to endure.

Lord, I pray that I will continue to be humble and teachable, I pray for continued willingness to go onward on my spiritual journey; I pray that whatever is needed that you will provide; and most of all Lord I pray for the knowledge and acceptance of thy will in my life and those just like me.

I love you Lord, In Jesus Name, I pray

Amen.

APPENDIX S - AS IT WAS WRITT*(I)*N

Thursday, March 4, 1993, 4:58 am

Thurs. 4:58am 3/4/93

Good Morning Lord. How I thank Thee for the touch of life this morning. I thank you Lord for who you are and what you are to me in my life.

Lord for some reason the desire to commit myself to writing to you more and on a daily basis is strong. And as you know Lord the willingness to do so is there. It is strange that the feeling and desire is given to me during the early morning hours. It feels as if I'm starting my day with you. It it feels so wonderful to keep a daily journal of my feelings and my thoughts. It also allows me to share with you how you are guiding and directing my life. I as told you you know I have no problem being honest with you about things that are troubling me and about things that I'm aware of that keeps me sick spiritually. And it is when I am honest and willing to change, I/you set the stage for that change to occur, gradually.

Lord. there is a step in my program that says " Made a decision to turn my will and my life over to the care of God, as I understand Him". I truly believe within my heart that I have made that decision. For if I hasn't then all that has happened and is happening to me would have felt it was just a coincidence or that "I" had everything to do with it. But I said, I know better. For it is by your grace and mercy that I am here today. It is by your grace and mercy that I have weathered the storm. And has been by your grace and mercy that I am able to be touched and touch the sick & suffering souls. Lord, it is by your grace and mercy that allows me to be your servant, as well as an example of your desire love.

Lord, I desire wholeheartedly to turn my will and my life over to Thee on a continuous basis. For I realize that it is you who are in control, a loving control. For as I look back over these years, I can see your loving arms about me. Especially when I came to

you with things I can't handle or even
want to handle by myself. For I
truly believe that if I sincerely and
faithfully seek Thy strength and courage
in what ever situation, that it comes
forth from Thee.
A Case and point recently. Just two
days ago I shared with you the
pressure I felt I was under in this
house situation and how when I
totally surrendered to accept your
will, the miracle happened!
The same day Lord, I was presented
a letter that said "Gift" of $3,443.00
to would aid me in the purchase of
this house. The same day Lord!!! And
although I still at your mercy as to
the outcome, boy is this process and
journey is ever so enlightening of
the work you are performing, and
guess what, without me. Lord.
It is situations like this and others
that may me a believer that you
and only you should I turn my
will and my life over to.
Lord I Love You, In Jesus Name, I pray
Amen

APPENDIX T - AS IT WAS WRITT*(I)*N

March 12, 1993, 5:00 am

5:00 am March 12

Lord, How Great Thou Art!!! Lord, I praise you this morning and praise you throughout the day, for Lord you are truly a mighty Lord. Lord, I thank you for touching me with the gift of life this morning and for the opportunity to life this day to the fullest. Beginning with my quiet time with you Lord, it never fails that when I begin my day acknowledging and praising and thank you for all the blessings you have provided me - gives me a feeling of awe when I think about you Lord.

Lord, another miracle has taken place in my life - for I already know that I am a miracle. But Lord, when I talk and write to you about situations that are happening in my life that causes fear and doubts, I've learned the importance of sharing with you and others to help release and put into prospective that which hinders my spiritual growth. And Lord, each time I do this the practice and need to exercise faith in you has been rewarding and enlightening.

Lord it is evident that you have gone before me and did your thing. For the rewards have been twofold, spiritually and are being manifested by you Lord - in providing me the things I need. You see Lord the other day I wrote about the miracle of receiving a gift letter of 3,443 for association needed in the purchase of this house. Will Lord, you know what happened! That letter went from $3,443 to $5,043 and not only that Lord, We signed the approval forms and it is possible for me to become a homeowner, thanks to you Lord, thanks to you. And Lord you are also working in other areas of my life by touching other souls to see and recognize that which dwells in me and that is the light of you Lord that has been touching the souls of others. And better yet - feeling a need to respond to that light in some way, shape or form. Lord, the seeds you are planting through me, and unknowingly to me, has become more and more evident.

Lord, I pray dear that Thy continue to mold, shape and direct my life for it is beyond my wildest dreams these things that are taking place in my life. And Lord, the credit and the glory goes directly to you. Right at this moment Lord, I'm listening to a song "Prayer Changes Things". And Lord prayer does change things, as you well know.

In my Bible Study class, we are doing a series on "Prayer" and Lord what an amazing feeling and understanding I am receiving. Lord you have provided me with so much, I can't begin to tell you. But tell you I must; In my thoughts; in my action; in my relationship with others; in my service; and most importantly; in my communion and meditation with you Lord!!!

Lord, keep doing your thing – and I pray to continue to look up to Thee with Love, Love and more Love.

In Jesus Name, I pray
AMEN

APPENDIX U - AS IT WAS WRITT(I)N

Sunday, March 21, 1993, 9:05 pm

9:05 Pm Sunday 3/21/93

Good evening Lord. Lord I thank you for another day of life. I thank you for the blessings thy has provided me. Lord I thank you for the many people you have placed in my life. But most of all Lord I continue to thank you for the deliverance from darkness into the light.

Lord first of all let me share with you what is going on, as if you don't already know. But Lord it seems when I write about things that are going on in my life at this time, I sometimes reflect back on my writings and can see the growth, spiritual growth that is and have taken place. Lord when it seems there is no way, you provide a way. I'm especially talking about the miracle that took place just a few days ago. A check for $5,043.00 was placed in my hands on the 16th of March for settlement assistance on this brand new house. Lord, I had written just a few days earlier the need to turn this burden over to you to do as you will. And Lord, just look what happened! You provided every penny I needed. And I thank you, I thank you, I thank you. By the end of this week I should be in our brand new house, thanks to you.

Lord, now to get to the real reason why I feel the need to write to you. I'm going through some changes regarding my personal life

APPENDIX V - AS IT WAS WRITT*(I)*N

March 24, 1993, 4:45 am

APPENDIX W - AS IT WAS WRITT(*I*)N

Tuesday, March 31, 1993, 5:24 am

[handwritten journal entry, largely illegible]

... with so much gratitude that at this I can only state my need and say "Lord I love you, I love you, I love you.

Lord I pray that thy continue to mold me ... Freely ... be prayerful ...

... all.

Thank you Lord
In Jesus Precious Name
I pray ...

APPENDIX X - AS IT WAS WRITT(*I*)N

Saturday, April 3, 1993, 7:09 am

7:09 am Sat 4/3/93

Well Lord, guess where I am - I am saying Good Morning Lord - Good Morning Lord Good Morning - Thank you Lord - Thank you Lord - I thank you for from our new home at 2612 Zebley Place. Yes Lord, we are here and I am here, by the grace of you; giving you the praise the glory and the awe of your mighty mighty love!

Lord, I'm setting here writing to you as usual but this time with continued faith and trust in thee. Lord, I feel as though I am dreaming and the reality hasn't quite sunk in yet. But Lord, I'm seeing it with my own eyes, feeling it with my own hands, hearing it with my own ears, smelling it with my own nose but still feel amazed and ad awe. Lord, I truly truly must thank you from the depths of my soul for permitting and allowing this miracle. It is surely Lord it is one of your many miracles. You have provided for me like no one else ever has. You have given me the blessings that no human power can give. You have given me your abundant love, unconditionally and with such magnitude and manifestation.

Lord it was just a year ago that the seed was planted and the possibility of me becoming an home owner was availed to me. And Lord, all I did was the necessary

footwork required to take advantage of this opportunity; The faith and courage was given from thee; The strength and tolerance was given from thee; and I believe the will of yours is was done once again in my life and has increased the power of my testimony to share with others.

APPENDIX Y - AS IT WAS WRITT(*I*)N

Tuesday, April 13, 1993, 6:00 am

4/13/93 Tues 6:00am

Good morning my Heavenly Father. Lord
I thank you for the breath of life you
have touched me with this very day. Lord,
I thank you for all the blessings and
miracles you have provided me. Lord, I
thank you for the opportunity to commune
in writing to thee the feelings, thoughts,
gratitude and awareness of my inner
self. Lord, I just thank you, praise you
and worship your mighty mighty hand.
Lord it has been over a week
now since I have taken the time to
write to you. I am still floating on
the natural and spiritual high of your
mighty blessings. Becoming a home
owner has been so rewarding. The feelings
of awe still comes from within. Many
times I have to still look around
and see, I have to actually touch it
and feel it. For there are still times
when I look around and am in disbelief
but reality tells me it is all so
real. But more importantly Lord,
the feelings that come from within are
of a spiritual nature. For I am able
to see and witness your mighty and loving
hand in it all. I am able to feel
overwhelmed by the presence of your
grace and mercy. Lord, although I
have experienced other miracles you

have provided but it appears you are
still providing more and more. And Lord,
I realize that these miracles and blessings
only to add to the testimony that you
have given me ... to be shared somehow
with others and to make believers out
of non-believers of your very existence. Lord
I pray to thee that you keep me humble,
I pray to thee that I remain grateful,
I pray to thee that I continue to
seek and accept your will Lord; I pray
for the continued strength and courage to
continue on my spiritual journey; I pray
Lord that what ever hinders my usefulness
to you that if be minimized and
taken away; Lord I pray that you
continue to peel away the layers of
sin and temptation that binds my very
soul. Lord I pray that you will continue
to lead my life toward the purpose you
have for me, that I may somehow, somewhere
plant the seed of faith, love and hope
in the hearts of other, only to give the
glory to you. For you surely have more
than turned my life around. And Lord
the more I learn about you, the more
I want to learn. I pray that I may
thirst and hunger to the day I return
to you for the knowledge and manifestation
of your mighty will. I love you Lord, I just
love you. All these things I pray in
Jesus name, Amen

APPENDIX Z - AS IT WAS WRITT(*I*)N

Sunday, April 18, 1993, 6:30 am

Sun 6:30 am 4/18/93

Lord, I thank you and I praise you too, that you once again for allowing me to be touched with the gift of life one more day. Yes Lord, I'm beginning to see and truly understand that life is a gift — a gift from you. For this, I'm truly, truly thank you. And I pray that this day what you have given, me can be used to be touched and to touch another sick and suffering soul, whom ever and where ever they may be.

Lord it is now day 18 since living in our new house. No Lord, the high and feeling of awe has not left me, for I still feel such feelings of gratitude that just don't to express. But Lord, I never forget, for one moment, that it is by your mercy and your grace that I am even experiencing this whole situation. It has been proven time and time again that you truly are directing and guiding my life. You have shown and proved to me that the results belong to you — for you already know what is for me and what is not. Lord, I continue to pray that I humble myself to you and to continue to seek your guidance and your will. I pray that you continue to strengthen me in areas where I am still weak. I pray Lord that you continue to peel away the layers of sin and temptation what

keeps me detached from you. I pray Lord that you continue to give me the willingness I need to continue on this spiritual journey so that I may be utilized someway and somehow by you that others may hear, see, feel and experience that what dwelleth with me — and Lord, that is you.

Lord, one thing I am working on now is building my foundation for continued recovery here in Washington. I have started attending new meetings and on getting to know new people. Lord, you know I have no problems, whatsoever, to do the necessary footwork. And in the short time that I have been here, people and situations have come about that needs the continued support of the fellowship and from you. Lord, as long as I continue to willingly put you first, the rest becomes easier. So long as I continue to open my mouth about the things that are in my head, the fellowship is always there for me. Lord as long as I continue to do the thing I should do — I will continue to get better. And these things Lord, I turn over to you. Thank you Lord, Thank you Lord for the deliverance from darkness into the marvelous light

In Jesus Name, I pray
Amen

- 142 -

CPSIA information can be obtained
at www.ICGtesting.com
Printed in the USA
FFOW04n0824111117
43468808-42140FF

BOBBY THE BRAIN
WRESTLING'S BAD BOY TELLS ALL

Bobby Heenan
with Steve Anderson

TRIUMPH
BOOKS
CHICAGO

Library of Congress Cataloging-in-Publication Data
(for hardcover editiion)
Heenan, Bobby, 1944–
    Bobby the Brain : wrestling's bad boy tells all / Bobby Heenan
with Steve Anderson.
        p. cm.
    ISBN 1-57243-465-1 (hardcover)
    1. Heenan, Bobby, 1944– 2. Wrestlers—United States—
Biography. I. Anderson, Steve, 1965– II. Title.

    GV1196.H42 A3 2002
    796.812'092—dc21
    [B]   2002020635

This book is available in quantity at special discounts for your group
or organization. For further information, contact:
    Triumph Books
    601 South LaSalle Street
    Suite 500
    Chicago, Illinois, 60605
    (312) 939-3330
    Fax (312) 663-3557

Printed in the United States of America
ISBN 1-57243-668-9

Interior design by Amy Flammang-Carter
Cover design by Salvatore Concialdi
Cover photos courtesy of Mike Lano

FOR MILLIE

CONTENTS

FOREWORD

I always said that whenever there was a fight, Bobby Heenan was the one that got sued. Whenever there was a wrestling match that needed to be fixed, Bobby was the one to fix it. And whenever you were looking bad and needed to look good, Bobby could make you look good.

He was always the one in the middle of the shit, like the time he and I got in a fight one night with a fan in Atlanta. The fan ended up suing Bobby. Whenever someone would get hurt, it would be Bobby. He'd always step in the way and take the hit for us. Whenever things went awry, Bobby would fix it.

Bobby Heenan set the standard for professionalism behind the scenes and he was the consummate professional in front of the camera. There were a lot of guys who would step up to the plate, but you could always depend on Bobby. He was the one who set the example for what a professional was like.

The first time I met him, he was short and to the point. He put business before friendship. He made sure that he didn't let friendship mess up business, so he would always make sure that he could do business with you first. Then, if you did your job, he would offer you his friendship.

In the ring, he was great. The thing that always bothered me most was wondering, "Why is this guy managing?" His punches looked better than anybody else's. When I first met him, he looked young and strong and I just couldn't believe it. He was taking the falls. He was taking the abuse just to make other people look good. I just couldn't believe how much he contributed. But that was Bobby's nature.

He could have taken a different position in the business. He could have been the "Gorgeous George," or the "Pat Patterson, Intercontinental Champion," or he could have been the superstar, à la Jesse Ventura or Hulk Hogan, a blonde "Thunderlips" type of wrestler that was the top guy. Instead, Bobby worked with a bunch of other guys, making *them* look good.

In one given night, he would go out four or five times to the ring. He'd go out with Nick Bockwinkel and make him look good when he would screw up. He would make me look good when I was working with Bockwinkel. Then he would go out with Bobby Duncum and Ken Patera. I would go out there just once a night, do my damn job, get in my car, and drink my beer. He would go out there every night and make sure everybody looked good. It was the weirdest thing. He loved it. It was his life.

Bobby was the one who would make the matches with Bockwinkel. When it would get kind of boring in the ring, he would add stuff. Bockwinkel and I would be out of gas or blown up in the ring. We would do the old 1980 "Grab the Rear Chinlock Hold to Bore the Audience to Death" thing. Bobby would be out there working his ass off. We would be in a rest hold in the middle of the ring, getting our breath back, and Bobby would be pounding the apron, running up and down, and fighting with the fans. Just raising holy hell. He never rested out there. He always worked hard to keep everything going.

He was the one who helped me get Andre the Giant through Wrestlemania 3. Andre was very badly hurt and in a lot of pain. Bobby was working just as hard as Andre and I were to get the darn thing over with.

I don't know if Bobby is a "living legend." To me, a legend is mythical—a superhero—not real. It reminds me of something unattainable. Bobby was a legendary wrestler, *legendary*. He will go down in the books as someone who mastered the craft. Maybe he was a legendary craftsman.

Among the people that know the business, Bobby's name will always be on the tips of their tongues. The people who don't know the business don't know how hard Bobby Heenan tried to blend in. Bobby Heenan basically helped everyone. He was a master of his craft. And part of being the chameleon, the deception of being so good at what he did, was that he had to fit in normally amongst the wrestlers. Outside of the wrestling circle, he was like an oddball. But in the wrestling circles, he made sure that, in between the geeks, the freaks, the midgets, and the ladies, his spot didn't overshadow anybody.

He could have—he was so talented. He could have stolen your spotlight at any moment.

—Hulk Hogan

A NOTE FROM THE AUTHOR AND HIS FAMILY

I know there are probably going to be some wrestlers who are not going to like the things I'm going to say in this book. They'll claim that I'm talking too much about the business and smartening people up too much.

For the wrestlers that think I stabbed them in the back and talked out of turn about the business with the inside stories, I'm sorry they feel that way. But if they want to continue to go and lie, they can. They should understand that the "magic show" is over. The fans know how we do our tricks. Hell, some know them better than we do. To put it simply, there is no magic out there anymore. So, instead of lying to people, let's give them what they deserve. Let's tell them the truth about this business and the industry and entertain them in a whole new way.

I'd also like to thank my wife and daughter for everything. My wife, Cynthia, who has been with me through every phase of my life, is a very understanding woman. It's not easy being married to a heel, especially a heel manager. And then there's my daughter, who I have never had a problem with in my life. Although she did cut her hair all crazy one time. I guess she wanted to look like Hawk from the Road Warriors. She's married now and has a good husband. Everything has been great. They have stuck with me all these years through everything. Either they really love me or I made more money than I thought I did.

I've been shot at and stabbed. I've had people throw rocks, batteries, and cups of urine and beer at me. They even spit right in my face. That's because they hated me. And I was good enough at what I did to make them do that.

I have buried my mother and grandmother, raised my daughter, and fed my family, all with the money I made from the fans. So, it's time to screw them.

I want to thank you people. Thank you very much for hating me. I love you all.

God bless our memories, and God bless America.

And remember, a friend in need is a pest.

—Bobby "the Brain" Heenan

Where do I begin? The fact that I was a country "bumpkin" finally living in a big city gives my story a different perspective. When I first met Bobby, I was in awe. He was the first gentleman I knew who was able to carry on a conversation, plus he had a sense of humor to boot. Little did I know of the "man"; however, I was familiar with some of the people he spoke of. Bobby's never-ending stories kept me and anyone else around entertained from the minute we met him to the very end.

Nothing has changed.

Bobby and I became friends during his visits to Minneapolis. After months of dinners and parties, we became very close, and after four years, we developed a romantic relationship. He warned me that his life had not been the "normal eight to fiver" and would not likely change. Boy, was he right. There was never a dull moment nor a quiet moment. There were always people around whom he considered part of his family. I grew to enjoy this because I had come from a large family of mom, dad, brothers, cousins, aunts, and uncles.

The one normalcy, which made me love him even more, was the care he showed for his mother and grandmother. He had experienced a rough upbringing but was still able to provide for the two most important people in his life. To me, this was a man.

To show how our life started out together, our honeymoon came first, then we had the wedding and wedding night, which was spent with as many friends as possible. My mother and father, God rest their souls, didn't meet Bob until two days before our wedding. He was very endearing, and, of course, they were won over immediately. For our first night alone, we headed to the drive-in movies in his '55 Mustang convertible. I felt like I was Sandy in the movie *Grease*. Actually, we weren't alone, but with his best friend, Buster, and a case of beer.

Then came our daughter. Yes, we managed to get one in there. It was like Bob had received the best gift any one person could receive. He has taught her well. Jessica is all her father: humor, wit, caring, etc. What a twosome they became. Jess has an interest in sports to complement her dad's. What a handful. I've been on my toes ever since, but, damn, we made a great threesome (now a foursome since Jessica's marriage).

All Bobby has wanted to do is "laugh and make people laugh" and "love and be loved." He's done them all very well. We've had our ups and downs in life, but we could always depend on Bobby to keep us laughing . . . together. I've loved every minute.

—Cindi Heenan

People often ask me if I ever was hurt or upset when people called my dad "Weasel." Hell no. I probably started the chants. It was a tough life growing up with a father like mine—someone who was a world-renowned TV star and one everyone hated.

In elementary school, the boys used to be so mean to me. In my mind, I had to protect the business, as my father taught me. They used to make fun of me, not because they were really that mean, but because they were jealous and wanted in on the action, so to speak. The only thing the morons didn't know was that if they had been nice to me, they could have been a part of that cool world known as wrestling.

It wasn't easy growing up with a father who traveled all the time. He missed quite a few birthdays and Thanksgivings, and he was hardly ever there on Easter; he was usually overseas. But when he was there, it was magical. We're very similar, you see, and that made us the best of friends. Sure, we got in a few arguments over the years, but we are almost the same person. My poor mother.

He's the greatest father anyone could ever have. I have so much respect and admiration for him. He's taught me so much about life. I thought that when the time came for me to get married, he would never be able to let go, but that just shows you and me how much about my father there is to learn.

After my husband, John, asked me to marry him, I was scared that my father would feel pushed aside. I knew that my mother would understand, just like she always has. But I was my father's buddy, his "Didley," as he liked to call me. It was always the three of us and that was it. Now, a stranger was coming to take away his baby, but he really surprised me.

I know at first it was scary for him, but as the wedding grew near, he became more excited and wanted to be really involved with the planning process. He surprised both my mother and me. Now we are known as the "Fearsome Foursome." And my dad now has two buddies in both John and me.

He is the most awesome person I know, bigger than life. I wish that other people could know my father like I do, but you never will. But I hope in this book you can catch a glimpse into the man who has taught me so much about understanding and compassion—the man who helped mold me into the person I am today.

I know he has a million fans that adore him, claiming to be his biggest fan, even his number one fan, but I am truly my father's biggest fan. I always have been and forever will be, until the end of time. He's my rock. I probably don't tell him enough. I love him so very much. I want to thank him for being my dad.

—Jessica Heenan

Chapter 1

A TRIUMPHANT RETURN

"The Johnny Carson of the sports entertainment world."

Paul Heyman said that about me when I returned to the WWF at Wrestlemania X-Seven. He was right. Both Johnny and I are retired and out of work.

After I was released from World Championship Wrestling in November of 2000, I called Vince McMahon and told him I'd be available if there was an opening for me. He said that he'd talk to Kevin Dunn, his producer, and to call him back. Kevin Dunn called me back and told me, "Hang tight. We have a lot of respect for you and your work."

In February of 2001, the opportunity came up to do the Women of Wrestling pay-per-view. It was a lot of fun, despite the technical difficulties. It was something different, and I just wanted to get out of the house. I knew David McClane, the promoter and owner of the show, from Indianapolis and agreed to come in for it.

Meanwhile, I didn't hear anything from the WWF until the end of March, two weeks before Wrestlemania. Kevin Dunn called me again and said, "Would you come up and work one match, you and Gene Okerlund?"

That one match was the "Gimmick Battle Royal."

I went out there. My God, it was like night and day from the nightmare that was WCW. Everybody backstage was talking. Everybody backstage was friendly. I saw the people from production who I knew during my first run with WWF. Working with professionals again, going from WCW to the WWF, was like going from the Mud Hens to the Yankees.

Before I walked out to the arena to call the match with Gene, I was standing with the Iron Sheik. Right before he was supposed to walk out, he noticed that he didn't have a belt for his pants. He asked Butch of the Bushwhackers if he had one.

Butch said, "Yeah, but I have a 34-inch waist."

Sheik couldn't find a belt to keep his pants up. So he looked around and found some adhesive tape and taped his pants to his ass with the tape running through his belt loops.

I was standing there waiting to go out past the curtain. Paul Bearer was running the gorilla position. (The "gorilla position" is the guy who sits right by the entrance curtain to direct traffic, giving cues to the wrestlers about when to go out and handling other cues to those around ringside via headset.) He said, "Bobby, go." As I turned to leave, Sheik dropped his flag, the flagpole, and his turban. The curtain opened for me to go out, and this guy is bent over right in front of me with his pants falling down. The tape didn't take. "Will you get out of the way," I yelled. He can't move well because he has bad legs. So I stepped over him and walked out to the arena toward the announce position with Gene.

What a feeling. The fans remembered me, and the "Weasel" chants started. It was music to my ears. Even if it was for just one night, I was back in the WWF. I never should have left.

Sheik was the first one out. His pants were staying up. I remember saying, "By the time he gets here, it will be Wrestlemania 38."

When I sat down with Okerlund, I started calling him Tony (as in Schiavone). It wasn't a mistake. It was on purpose. But thinking about it, I should have known better than to confuse the two. Gene has talent and a job.

Afterward, I watched the rest of the show backstage. I attended a party back at the hotel. Vince McMahon and Jerry McDivot, his attorney, had a great conversation with me. Later on, I left the party for my room and went to bed. I haven't heard from them since.

Honestly, I don't know if I'll ever be back in the WWF. I don't think Shane McMahon, Vince's son, likes me. It has nothing to do with me so much as he thinks I walked out on his dad. Blackjack Lanza once told me that Shane asked him, "Why did Bobby walk out on my dad?"

Jack told him, "He didn't. Your dad said that if he can make a better deal someplace, then do it."

Gorilla Monsoon once told me, "If you're in this business for anything more than money, you're a fool."

Now, I may be "the Brain," but I'm no fool.

Chapter 2

THE EARLY YEARS

Where do I start my story? I was born Raymond Louis Heenan in Chicago on November 1, 1944. My dad left my mom when I was less than one year old, so I was raised by my mother and grandmother. Some people say I'm funny, but my mother, whom I always called Millie, is still the funniest person I've ever met in my life. She looked like a combination of Lucille Ball and Bette Davis.

One day, I stepped out of the bathroom after a shower, and the television was on. There was a show on similar to *You Asked for It*, and they were electrocuting an elephant for some reason. They put clamps around his legs and a guy flipped this switch. The elephant would stiffen up and there would be smoke everywhere. I guess they wanted the hide.

Amazed at the sight, I turned to my mother and asked, "Millie, why are they electrocuting an elephant?"

She came back with, "You ever try to hang one?"

In our neighborhood, we had a professional wrestler named Zack Melkof who lived down the street. Zack was a Chicago Park District officer. In the city, we had two kinds of police: the regular city police and the Chicago Park District—we used to call them "squirrel chasers." They were in charge of the parks, driving their motorcycles around and patrolling the area.

Zack used to go down to the beach and work out with rocks, picking up big ones and lifting them. He was a huge man to me in those days, but then again I was a 10-year-old kid. He had these cauliflower ears and a dark tan from staying at the beach all the time. He just looked like one rough, tough guy. My friends and I knew who he was because we saw him on television wrestling for Marigold in those days. He wasn't a star, just an underneath guy. I'd always tell him, "Good luck" before his matches. He'd snarl back, "Good luck don't help me much."

Zack asked my mother one day if he could take a bunch of neighborhood kids to the Marigold. She agreed, and me and a bunch of my buddies went with Zack. I sat in the front row of the bleachers, and I was instantly amazed. I remember a wrestler I saw named Johnny Case, who later on became a good friend of mine and a travel companion to Japan. When he wasn't wrestling, Johnny was the president of the Antioch, Illinois, school system. He was an educator and a very smart man. But in the ring, Johnny was a heel, the wrestling term for bad guy.

What amazed me that night was when Johnny told the crowd to be quiet, they made noise. And if he told them to say something, they were quiet. It was incredible to see how a man could control a crowd—how, when he flew through the air, the people would jump to their feet in excitement.

I was hooked right there.

This was something I simply had to do. Honestly, before that, I never knew I would do it. I actually wanted to be a baseball player. I was a big Cubs fan and lived only four miles from Wrigley Field.

After Marigold television went off the air, there wasn't much wrestling on that I can remember. At that time, we lived in an apartment hotel. My buddies and I would go into the lobby and wrestle in tag matches, taking bumps on the furniture, making our own show based on what we had seen.

In 1959, Vince McMahon Sr. started running his TV in Chicago, along with Fred Kohler, the local promoter. The show was out of Bridgeport, Connecticut, and ran for two hours from midnight on Saturday until 2:00 the following morning. My God, there was Johnny Valentine. There was Buddy Rogers. There was "Bearcat" Wright. There were the Kangaroos. There were the Graham Brothers. It was different from what I watched in 1954 from the Marigold. Again, it was on television and not live, but now I could see these guys up close.

I continued to be amazed. This is what I wanted to do. But, still, I didn't know how to do it.

When I turned 15, they sold the hotel that my mother was managing. My aunt, who was living with us, had cancer. We moved to Indianapolis to live with her until she had her operation and my mom could get back on her feet with a job. I was in the eighth grade for the third year, having been kept back twice. I guess my attendance was not so good. I used to prefer taking the bus downtown and sleeping in the tents in the sports department at the local Marshall Fields rather than going to school.

School was not for me. I just didn't understand why I had to know about the Boston Tea Party. I couldn't understand why I had to know about a guy named Magellan. I wanted to see wrestling.

My aunt died about a year after we moved to Indianapolis, but Millie, my grandmother, and I stayed there. It turned out to be the best place I lived, and I met the best people I could ever have grown up with. I used to hang around with a guy named Tom Mathis, a disk jockey with WIFE radio in Indianapolis. It was through him that I put on my first wrestling show. It was on a Saturday night at St. Rita's Boxing Gym in Indianapolis. I put a mask on and wrestled as the Avenger. I wasn't even in the business yet and hadn't been "smartened up" to what happened in the ring.

I was scheduled to wrestle Tom, who was known as one of the WIFE "good guys." I got in the ring and cut a promo on him. I had Scott Goodwin, an old buddy of mine, as my manager. We had a couple of girls with us and an atomizer, like Gorgeous George used to have. I wore a mask, tight wrestling pants, and boots made out of old hockey skates without the blades on them. I also had a jacket on that looked like someone had stolen a shower curtain from the local hotel.

We practiced in this big ring that Champ Chanee let us use. He was a policeman in Indianapolis and worked with youth boxing. We donated all the concessions and everything to the local boxing program. On that night, the place was crowded. Mind you, it only held 50 people, but it was fun because it was so packed.

The crowd loved Tom and hated me, with my entourage and atomizer. We worked two out of three falls and I put him over. Neither he nor I took my mask off because I had to put up the equipment there the following week and didn't want anyone to know that I was the Avenger.

Mathis worked from midnight until 6:00 in the morning on WIFE. On weekends he would do sock hops around Indianapolis. Sometimes, when he couldn't make it, Scott and I would take over for him. It was fun to work all these clubs with all these women.

Joe Dye, Jack and Mike Sugars, and Jack Nichols were these guys I knew who had formed a band—similar to what you'd see on *Happy Days*. Scott and I thought that it would be a good idea to manage these guys and get them into the dances around town. We'd look more important than just two guys playing records and, more importantly, we'd get more women.

They agreed to let us manage them. But the problem was that to work in the clubs, you had to join the union. If Scott and I paid $50 apiece, that would ensure that the band could get $150 a gig. But the most the band ever made was $50. The problem was that the band couldn't play anything and was so bad that we could only get into clubs where they paid $20 or $25.

So I thought I would use my wrestling knowledge and disguise them. I put masks on them and called them The Executioners, mostly because they murdered everything that they played. But they were so dumb. They'd walk into the club without their masks on and then sit in the dressing room with their masks on. I wanted them to do some choreography and move around a little bit. I had them try to play while getting on each other's shoulders. They messed that up.

Scott thought it would be a good idea for the two of us to be singers in the band. I told him, "We can't sing." We solved that problem by not turning our microphones on. We both combed our hair to look like the Righteous Brothers and wore suits with no lapels, ties, Beatle boots, and tight pants. And we played the tambourine. It really didn't matter what The Executioners played, they were so bad.

Every once in awhile, for protection from the audience, we'd get a couple of tough-looking guys in the crowd and let them play the tambourine. Just so we could get out of town. But we had a ball the whole time.

At that time in 1966, we had no money, so I dropped out of school, never finishing the eighth grade. I started working job to job to support my mother, my grandmother, and myself. I worked as an usher at a theater, a clerk at a hardware store and a department store, a milkman, and a car jockey at a Ford dealership, which is where I got the "call" for wrestling.

While I was at the dealership, I worked a second job at the Indianapolis Coliseum as a stagehand setting up the shows. The wrestling promoter there was Bulk Estes, and he booked cards with "Cowboy" Bob Ellis, Dick the Bruiser, Wilbur Snyder, the Shire Brothers, and Ray Stevens.

Ray was a man I really looked up to, and we became the best of friends. We wrestled each other, and I have had the chance to manage him. Ray could take a bump. He flew around the ring with his blond hair flowing. He was exciting.

I also met the original Sheik from Detroit, who became my first friend in the business. He really took care of me. He was an Arab from Beirut who didn't speak any English. He had this scary look and threw fire. He really terrified people, including me. He used to chase me down the aisle when I was selling Cokes and get the people all excited, thinking this madman was going to catch and hurt this poor kid.

After a couple of months, I worked my way around and got to know Russ Leonard, who put out a wrestling magazine called *Big Time Wrestling*. Every Tuesday night after work, I would take my mom to the hospital to see my aunt, hitchhike to the Armory, and sell Russ' programs out front from 6:00 to 7:00. Then I'd go around back and help the wrestlers with their bags and pick up a half a buck here and there. From there, I sold Cokes until 8:30, which was match time.

I would take my Coke tray and hide it behind the door, walk downstairs, put on a sweater that said "Championship Wrestling," and walk the wrestlers to the ring as a second for five dollars. During the match, I would run back, take my sweater off, and sell more Cokes. After the match was over, I would walk the guy back and bring the next guy out. That was my routine. At one point, I would have to go outside and wash the Sheik's car for an extra five bucks. I had a $52 a month mortgage at the age of 16, and I thought I was home free.

As time went on, I started setting the ring up in the Coliseum, carrying the jackets, and working as a second around the ring.

When I was 17, I would work some of the spot shows around Indianapolis. I did anything I could do to be around the business.

On January 10, 1965, I was working at the Ford dealership when I got a call from Dick the Bruiser. He told me to be at the local television station, Channel 4, on Tuesday afternoon for interviews. I had no idea what he wanted, but I was thrilled until he said, "I'll see you there, Bobby," and hung up the phone.

I thought to myself, "My name's not Bobby. It's Ray." I was sure he dialed up the wrong guy. I called him back and he assured me he had the right guy. "Be there at 1:00 on Tuesday, Bobby," he said. Bruiser called me Bobby because Buddy Rogers had a manager named Bobby Davis. They were in Chicago in the early sixties, and I started in 1965, so he just gave me that name.

I didn't know what the hell all of this meant. I went down there. Bruiser was there, along with this tag team called the Assassins. They were made up of a little guy named Joe Tomaso and a bigger guy named Guy Mitchell, and they wore masks. Dick decided to put me in as their manager.

So there I was. It was my first day with my first tag team. The problem was Joe wasn't there, but they still wanted to cut a promo with me and the Assassins. Dick decided to use a nearby mannequin, put a mask and a trench coat on it, and place it behind me and Guy. Guy did the interview because I didn't talk. I didn't know how to back then.

They told me not to say anything because I didn't know what to say ahead of time. It's my first day, and I'm standing there with one masked guy, two masks, and a mannequin—and I'm on my lunch hour. I'm thinking, "What in the hell am I getting into?"

After the interview, Dick told me, "At 6:00, be at the Holiday Inn on Highway 31. We're going to Louisville." In those days, there were no limos or first-class airline service. You met someplace, and everyone jumped in a car and rode to the town together. I went home and told my mother what I was going to do and how excited I was. I packed a bag, but I didn't know what to bring. I had my shower shoes, a soap dish, a towel, and a shirt. I wasn't sure if I needed any of that. I didn't know what to take.

I met Bruiser and Wilbur Snyder at the Holiday Inn. Guy and I got into the car and we started off for Louisville. Dick and Wilbur were sitting in the front seat and talking in this language I didn't understand. Later, I found out it was Carny. I didn't know about it then, so I really didn't listen. They're talking about this and that and I was counting cows thinking that I'm driving to Louisville, Kentucky, and I don't know for what. I don't know what I'm going to do. I know I'm going to manage, but I wasn't sure what I was supposed to do. I had been around and had seen what managers do, but I did not know what they wanted me to do.

As we arrived, Bruiser and Wilbur decided it was time to officially break me into the business. Bruiser threw this mask at me and said, "Put this on." As I slipped the mask over my head, he continued, "We don't hurt each other. We make it look like we do. And if you tell anybody what's going on, I'll break both your legs, your arms, and your back. And when you get better, Wilbur will break them."

I gulped, "OK, fine." What's funny is that I used to sneak down into the dressing rooms and listen to them talk. I knew it wasn't real from the beginning. I had been in a fight. A fight lasts 20 seconds, not an hour. I knew it was entertainment, but I played dumb.

I went into the dressing room with the mask on. These guys are walking by, and I'm introducing myself. I knew who they were, but they didn't know who I was. They were used to seeing me carrying jackets. Now, I'm in the dressing room with them, and I'm sitting there naked, wearing only a mask.

We went to the ring for a match with Moose Cholak and Wilbur Snyder. Moose was a big man, 6'5" and about 350 to 375 pounds. He wore a lumberjack shirt with the sleeves cut out, Levi's, and engineer boots. He was the most dangerous human being in the ring. He would hurt you during the instructions by just moving his hand and accidentally slapping you in the mouth. He was just so clumsy.

Vince McMahon Sr. gave him the "Moose" idea. Moose had a huge moose head with antlers made that he named Alexander. Inside the moose head was a football helmet and wooden horses for support on his shoulders. The first time Moose got in the ring with the moose head on in Baltimore, Maryland, he stepped over the top rope with this thing that weighed a couple of hundred pounds. He stood in the middle of the ring and folded his arms across his chest, trying to look real tough. He looked at his opponent, and, as he did that, he lost his balance. Here was this 375-pound man with a moose on his head, slowly going backward, waving his arms, and yelling, "Ohhhhhh!" He hit the mat and broke the antlers. After that, he quit wearing that moose head for a while, but he'd break it out every now and then for holidays. He made a great reindeer.

Thankfully, he didn't have the moose head with him in Louisville. Before the match, Bruiser gave me the finish. He told me to jump up on the apron with all four of us in the ring and then Moose would bring me in the ring and take the mask off me. When the time came, I jumped up on the apron. Now, I thought I was aware at that time of the kind of money that wrestlers were making. I was thinking in my mind, "I'll make $10,000 tonight. I have to be."

Moose pulled me into the ring, grabbed the top of the mask, and tried to rip it off. Well, no one ever taught me how to wear a mask, and I had it tied in about nine knots. I didn't know that you didn't have to tie the mask, you just tucked the strings up inside it so the other guy could get it off easily. There I was at 20 years of age, 150 pounds, and six feet tall. Moose had me by one arm and the mask, hanging me. I didn't know how to get the mask off. He finally reached in, broke the strings, and unmasked me.

I jumped out of the ring and ran into some hillbilly woman from Louisville. In case you didn't know, the toothbrush was invented in Kentucky. Anyplace else and they would have named it the "teethbrush." This toothless woman reached out and put her cheap cigar out on my neck. The cops grabbed her, and I ran back to the dressing room.

The next match was Johnny Valentine against the Bruiser. But Valentine wouldn't go to the ring. He had gotten into an earlier fight with the police and punched one of them and a fan. He went into the dressing room, shut the door, and put a chair in front of it with me trapped in there.

The cops were beating on the door, trying to get in. Tomaso, who knew Valentine, said, "What's the matter?" Johnny turned around, punched him, and knocked him down. I figured Johnny just punched a guy he knows, what is he going to do to me? I ran underneath a table.

"Wee" Willie Davis was the promoter in Louisville. He was about 6'10" and 400 pounds and famous for his appearance in the original *Mighty Joe Young* movie. Willie decided to take matters into his own hands. He grabbed one of the nightsticks, walked into the dressing room, and started whacking Valentine over the head. You could just hear his melon cracking. Finally, Johnny went down, the cops handcuffed him, and they took him out of there.

I got out from under the table, shaking and naked with just a towel. I dressed and got back in the car. I remember the drive home that night, not because it was my first match, but because of this horrible truck wreck. A man was lying on the highway outside the truck and he's on fire. You could hear him screaming as we pulled up, "Oh, God. God help me."

We pulled into Indianapolis at about 2:00 in the morning. Bruiser handed me five dollars for the night. I'm thinking to myself that I have to get up at 7:00 in the morning to go to work.

I've been to Louisville, Kentucky, managing some people I don't really manage. I was almost hung. I was burned by a cigar. I was almost beat to death by Johnny Valentine and a man with a nightstick. I saw this horrendous accident where a man was alive and on fire.

For five dollars.

And all I could think of was one thing.

This is for me. When can I go do this again?

After a couple of weeks, my boss at the car dealership found out what I was doing. He asked me, "How can you be in such a degrading profession?"

"Degrading profession? You're a car dealer," I said. "These people come through the doors. You take those poor bastards and drop them to their knees. All we're doing is entertaining people."

He told me he didn't want me to work there. I chased him around the desk, and he retaliated by firing me. I went home and told Bruiser that I didn't have a regular job anymore. Wrestling was what I wanted to do full time. I later found out that I didn't make a whole lot more than I made at the Ford dealership. Bruiser simply was not a good payoff guy. He would never give you 50 bucks, he'd give you 45. He'd never give you 100, he'd give you 90. I figured that every time you save 5 or 10 bucks on a payoff, you can make pretty good money.

I became "Pretty Boy" Bobby Heenan, a gimmick that I actually stole from Larry Hennig.

I started wrestling right away in addition to managing, because the promoters saw that I could take bumps. I never trained. I just knew how to work—like some people can play the piano. Some people can write. I can't do anything but wrestle. It came natural to me.

We would start working at midnight and finish at about 3:00 in the morning setting up the ring after ice shows or public skating. The other hobos they hired to help us would drift away. After they left, we would get in the ring and have tag matches. We just worked like they did on television. That was how I learned to work.

My "training" was with my friends. And I wasn't the only one to come out of that training as a professional wrestler. Some of them I brought with me to the ring. Jim Kunz wrestled as both Super Brucie, complete with a Superman T-shirt and cape, and Dr. S. T. Bernard, as in Saint Bernard. He even tagged with Bruiser in a match against me and Baron Von Raschke. Jim had bad legs and couldn't get around too well. He was funny, and he made the people laugh. He was 190 pounds with little bird legs. His trademark was this fist he made with his thumb between the fingers.

I'm just glad my friends got to play along with me.

Another man who helped me along was Tom Jones, who wrestled for Bill Watts in Tennessee and was a real nice man. He would work with me a little bit. He slammed me. I'd get him in a headlock and take him over. Still, no one ever taught me timing.

My focus was on managing, and, when I started, my thinking was that I had seen managers before and they were usually guys who were over-the-hill and hanging around to get a couple of paydays or extend their careers. The promoter would use him because of his name, and he could talk for a guy who couldn't talk.

I saw that these guys always managed the same way. They always carried a cane and hit a guy. I didn't want to use a cane, because if I used it, one hand was busy and I couldn't defend myself. Besides, I didn't want to hit anybody with a cane and have a lawsuit. I wanted my hands free. Plus, I took bumps. I couldn't take a bump with a cane because it's going to fly out of my hands and some fan is going to get it and give it back to me the hard way.

I thought to myself, "I'm going to manage like a wrestler and wrestle like a manager."

So when I stood on the floor and my man was getting hit, I was going to register it too. I was going to sell like my man is selling and react to every punch and kick along with him. I was going to show that I had an investment in this guy. If I was his manager, I sure as hell had to be concerned about him.

As a wrestler, I quickly realized that I would never be world champion because I didn't have the body. I wasn't going to the gym and working out all the time. I wasn't into it, and I didn't like it. I learned that you didn't have to be big or small. You just had to know how to work.

Promoters would use me both ways, because it was cheaper. They had a wrestler and a manager, and they only had one guy to pay to do two jobs.

The first guy I wrestled was an African American named Calvin "Prince" Pullins, who just happened to be the bouncer at Bruiser's bar called The Harem. He also worked at a local pawnshop. Prince was about 210 pounds and muscular, but not too big. At that time, I weighed in at about 180 pounds.

The ring at the Armory was real hard because it was actually a boxing ring. But on that night, they could have slammed me on ice. I was so high. I was so ready for my first match. But the one thing I forgot was to check on my endurance. After the bell rang, I immediately started begging away, but after about three times doing that, I was out of gas. I was so blown up from nerves.

I hadn't taken a bump yet and my tongue was hanging out like a cash register receipt. I couldn't get any air. I thought, "My God, I have to go eight minutes with him. I'll die. I'll never make it."

I'd go back to the corner and talk to Chris Markoff just to get my air back. He'd grab a hold of me and throw me back in. Prince would give me a headbutt, and I'd take a couple of bumps. I didn't know I even had air, but there was more coming out of me than I could breathe in.

The finish was that Prince had me in the corner beating me up and Markoff jumped up on the ring apron. The referee walked over to Markoff, and I pulled the proverbial "foreign object"—a bar of soap wrapped in tape—out of my trunks. I nailed Prince from behind, he went down, and I pinned him.

After the match, I remember thinking that I'd rather be a manager for five bucks than a wrestler for ten. This was hard. But it was fun because it was my hometown and I had all my friends there.

My wrestling and managing career went on from there. After the Assassins split up, I managed the Devil's Duo, Angelo Poffo, who is the father of Randy "Macho Man" Savage, and Chris Markoff, who was real backward and almost dyslexic in the ring. He'd say, "Watch the kick," after he'd kick you.

From there, Blackjack Lanza came into the Indianapolis area. He was a "babyface" (a good guy), calling himself "Cowboy" Jack Lanza. Wilbur decided it would be good to put Jack and me together by turning Jack into a heel.

I also managed "Handsome" Jimmy Valiant and Johnny Valiant. They were probably the worst tag team I managed in my life. They weren't very good. During the summers, we worked in Canada for a guy named the Bearman. He made Jimmy and I tag-team champions but didn't give us any belts. He didn't have enough money because it was a small-time promotion.

The Bearman would get one of his partners, appropriately named the Wolfman, to put up flyers telling where the matches were and who would be wrestling. But Wolfman put them over all the stop signs in town because he figured everyone would see them better. There were no stop signs in that town, just eight-sided wrestling posters.

The Bearman was also the owner of one of my most unique opponents. You guessed it—a bear.

Baron Von Raschke and I used to work in the winter against this bear, appropriately named Teddy. You're not going to believe it, but the bear could work. Teddy really didn't want to be there, because it was wintertime and he wanted to sleep. Some of the buildings we worked in had ice for hockey games. They put down homosote and wood over the floor, and Teddy would eventually feel it through his paws. So, he'd get in the ring and pee. I don't know about you, but there's nothing I love more than rolling around on the canvas in bear urine.

I'd get up behind Teddy, and I'd kick him right in the ass and say, "Guess who, Teddy," tag Raschke, and jump out of the ring. Raschke would accuse the bear of carrying a foreign object. He'd yell, "Referee, check the bear. He just went into his fur and got something." He'd tag me back in. I'd lock up with Teddy when he was standing and squeeze his foot twice. He would put his foot up and monkey flip me. Then I'd get up and go behind the bear and squeeze his shoulders twice and he'd reach up and flying mare me.

One night, I wanted to see how strong this bear was, so I grabbed him in a front facelock. He could turn his head any way he wanted to. He grabbed my hand and my leg, took me down, and started snorting up my leg and inner thigh. Now, I didn't know what he was going for, but I couldn't grab the muzzle to pull off of him because that was the finish and it was too early. The finish was supposed to be Baron and me taking the towel and wrapping it around the bear's neck to choke him. After that, Teddy would lie on his back. He sold! The bear sold for us! The trainer would then come in the ring and take the muzzle off. Teddy would stand up, and we would run away.

When a young kid would come in, he'd have to wrestle Teddy for a couple of matches. We would all see that the kid was nervous. We'd reassure him and say, "Let the bear just play with you."

After the kid would leave the dressing room, one guy would be designated to go to McDonald's and get packets of honey. We'd put the honey on our hands and slap the kid on his ass on the way out.

Naturally, as soon as he got in the ring, the bear started licking the honey and terrified him. What a sight. A big bear lying on top of this new wrestler, licking his ass with the guy screaming bloody murder.

Raschke and I often joked about wrestling Teddy. One day, we were in between shows where we were wrestling him. We drove past a circus caravan. Raschke saw two giraffes sticking out from a truck, looked at me, and said, "Well, I guess it's going to be a tag tonight."

I worked in the Indiana territory from 1965 to 1969, doing a lot of fair dates in Indianapolis and Chicago. At the Armory in Indianapolis, Bruiser and Wilbur Snyder became the promoters. They would tape six matches on a Tuesday night starting at 8:30. There were 75 guys in the back and 20 fans in the audience. After two hours of taping, the arena emptied because people had gone home. Bruiser and Wilbur would make the wrestlers dress up in their street clothes and sit in the stands. The building had only one bleacher and camera, so it looked like there were 100 people in a packed arena. Half the guys would doze off, so Bruiser would tape the audio from a Bears game to make it sound like 50,000 people were cheering with only a few guys in the audience, some of them sleeping.

I worked at a promotion in Pittsburgh that had television and wanted the crowd to look bigger as well. But they could get only about 20 people to come to television, so they had a backdrop curtain with the faces drawn on it, which made it look like 50 people were there. That was a lot for them.

But no matter how many people would attend, the promoters would always have their own "count." They would tell you that the house was $10,000 when it was actually $8,000, just to make you feel better. But they paid you based on $6,000.

During that time, I was the first manager used for the National Wrestling Alliance in St. Louis. We used to do TV on Monday nights from the Chase Park Plaza Hotel in St. Louis. The promoter was Sam Muchnick, who I can safely say never liked heat ("heat" is how wrestlers refer to the reaction of the crowd). He would have only one interview every three weeks, and it was always the babyface cutting the promo.

It wasn't studio TV, but a dining room with a ring in the middle and tables and chairs all around. The men came in suits, and the women wore furs. The hotel served dinner during the matches, which were all clean finishes with no disqualifications. There were heels and babyfaces, and there was some heat. People would yell and scream, but no one threw anything or jumped out of their chairs and tried to fight anybody.

The matches never spilled out onto the floor. You didn't bang a guy's head into a bowl of soup. No one powerbombed a guy through the table. I've never seen anything like it in my life.

It was the damnedest thing you ever saw.

Chapter 3

THE "BRAIN" IS BORN

When I arrived in the American Wrestling Association (AWA) in Minnesota in 1969, there was already a "Pretty Boy" named Larry Hennig, who teamed with Harley Race. At first, I used "Gorgeous" Bobby Heenan, but I didn't like it. Everybody was a "gorgeous" something. I wanted to be different. I started managing Blackjack Lanza and Dr. X, who was the Destroyer on the West Coast. AWA promoter Verne Gagne didn't want to use him with that name because he thought everyone knew the Destroyer was Dick Beyer. Blackjack and I did a short program with him, and we wound up unmasking Dr. X. Much to Verne's shock, it didn't matter who he was. None of the Minnesota fans knew Dick Beyer.

I was in Japan with the Destroyer in 1983. Destroyer will not take his mask off for anything, even to this day. He's retired now and does a radio show in Buffalo wearing his mask. I spent a lot of time with him in Japan, and he was a huge favorite over there. He lived there for about 10 years, spoke and wrote Japanese, and ran an office where he sold his memorabilia. He even appeared on a *Laugh-in*-style television show, but he always wore that mask.

I rode with him to Yokohama instead of taking the bus back to the hotel with the other wrestlers. It was the weirdest experience of my life. I was in a car driving 80 miles an hour through the streets of Tokyo, sitting on the driver's side of the car with no wheel and a masked man driving on the passenger side. Dick wore that mask everywhere. He wore it on the airplanes and trains. But one day, he was sunning on the roof of a hotel with the mask off. As he was walking downstairs, one of the waiters came walking by.

"Oh shit," he said.

I said, "Dick, what's he going to say? He doesn't know who you are."

Just like the fans in the AWA.

He was a great masked man and always protected it. And he still does. That mask has been seen by so many people, he could sell advertising on it.

I stayed in the AWA for two years but decided to return to Indiana in 1971. Three years later, I left Indianapolis for good when I was screwed on a payoff. We had a show at Market Square Arena. The building had just opened with Glen Campbell, and the second show was wrestling with Dick the Bruiser versus the Sheik on top of the card. I worked as a babyface manager for Dick, and naturally I turned on him at the end of the match.

We sold out Market Square Arena with 18,000 people. Bruiser gave the Sheik $2,000. He gave me $600, saying, "If you can make more someplace else, you can go do it."

On that day and others, I remember what Bruiser said when he started me. "What I did was give you a break."

I shot back, "No you didn't. You did it so I'd run errands for you. I just lucked out and became able to make you and me a living."

I gave my notice and finished up to go back to the AWA. Again, I didn't want to be "Gorgeous" anymore, and I couldn't use "Pretty Boy" because of Larry Hennig. So, Wally Karbo and Ray Stevens came up with my new name. Wally told me, "Well, you're smart. You're 'the Brain.'"

Ray said, "Yeah, you're the 'Brain.' You're 'Bobby the Brain.'"

Wally Karbo came across on television as bumbling and not very bright, but that was because he was always nervous. Verne would constantly be yelling at him. Sometimes for good reasons.

Another guy in the AWA was Ivan Putski. His gimmick was supposed to be that he only spoke Polish. Wally was Polish too, and everybody knew it, so he was supposed to act as Ivan's translator. During one of Putski's interviews with Marty O'Neill, Verne wanted Wally to go out there. He even told him what to say.

As the interview was going on, Marty said, "Could I get Wally Karbo out here?"

Wally walked onto the set.

"Wally, you're of Polish descent, aren't you?" Marty asked.

"Yes," said Wally.

"Well, I'm trying to find out about Mr. Putski here. I'm trying to find out how much he weighs. Could you ask him?"

Wally turned to Putski and, instead of asking the question in Polish, yelled, "How much ah-you weigh?"

I was in the production room with Verne as he was slapping his bald head hard in frustration. I told him, "You didn't think he was going to do it right, did you?"

He may have gotten that wrong, but Wally was the best liar in the world. I used to tell him, "You have to hire a guy to call your dog, because not even he believes you."

After my father-in-law was killed in an accident, my mother-in-law gave me his car, a Mazda station wagon. Wally told me one day, "You know, pal, I need a car for the lake."

"I got just the car for you," I told him.

"How much you want?" asked Wally.

"How about $1,000?" I said.

He agreed to that, but a week later Wally gave me a check for $900. I told him, "I said $1,000, Wally."

"You said $900."

I wasn't going to argue with him because if I did get that extra $100, he'd get the money back from my paycheck somehow.

I looked at the check he gave me. It was a payroll check from the Minneapolis Boxing and Wrestling Club. Verne bought Wally my car, and I had to pay taxes on it.

Wally wasn't a dishonest man, except when it came to paying us and lying about it. But it was more fun to catch him in a lie. In spite of that, Wally would always help a guy out. If a guy lost money at a poker game, Wally would give him $200 and bail him out. A guy called him once and asked him for help. Wally met him and loaned the guy a couple of hundred bucks. The guy asked him if he wanted to buy a television for $100.

Wally figured the guy was on the skids and he would help him out. The cops ended up arresting that guy and Wally for possessing stolen merchandise. At Wally's first appearance at the St. Paul Civic Center after the story was in all the papers, the fans went nuts when he came out, chanting, "Wally, Wally, Wally."

He was more over (popular) than at any point in his career.

I had an idea. I told him, "Do you know how to get rid of Verne? It's easy."

"How?" he asked.

"You go to Kmart and buy five TVs. When Verne's out of town, take them over to his house and put them in his barn," I said. "Then, you tell the cops that you can turn them on to 'Mr. Big.'"

He thought about it for a while. Then he said, "I don't know anybody with a truck."

As you can see, just having basic conversations with him was tough. I had to call him one day over my payoff.

"Wally, I haven't been paid in a month."

He said, "Oh pal, I'm on the phone with Eddie Graham in Miami. He's got an outdoor show tonight and it's raining like hell." Then he hung up.

Now, Miami had nothing to do with the AWA. It had nothing to do with my call. I just paid hard-earned money to call him and got a weather forecast to a place I wasn't going to.

The AWA had a private plane, and I needed to find out when the plane was leaving from Flying Cloud Airport in Eden Prairie, Minnesota. I asked Wally, "What time does the plane leave?" He said, "Ask the pilot when you get there." He'd give you answers like that.

Wally would tell you to go have an interview, but he didn't want you to mention any specific match or opponent. I don't know why, but he'd say, "Go have an interview, but don't say nothing."

Even though he was our boss, Wally liked to party with us. Denver was a great place to work because we'd party all night after the show, but we would be real hungover when it was time to get on the plane. I saw him at the airport in the morning in bad shape with just one sock on.

When we landed in Minneapolis, I noticed as he was walking in front of me that he had two socks on.

I called out to him, "Wally, where did you find your other sock?"

He said, "Oh pal, they was both on the same foot."

Wally had this girl drive us from Dawson, Manitoba, 300 miles north of Winnipeg, back home to Minneapolis. Ray and I were sitting in the back. We didn't know where we were going. Obviously, we were lost. Ray and I didn't care much because we had some beer and a bottle of wine with us. We had to stop to find out where we were. Wally walked into a nearby hotel to ask for directions.

Ray and I were standing outside the car when a police officer pulled up and asked us what we were doing. I told him that we were hitchhiking.

"Whose car is that?" he asked.

"The guy who went to the hotel."

"Whose wine and beer is this?"

I said, "It's his."

The cop walked into the hotel. A few minutes later, Wally came out, glaring at me. He got into the car, slammed the door, and screamed, "That cop fined me $200 for having an open bottle in the car and picking up hitchhikers!"

I was in Winnipeg one night when I was coming out of the door and some fan spit at me. I don't mind a guy taking a shot at me, but I don't like to be spit at in the face. He held it for a while too, because it was like a cup of water. Two guys held him for me, and I saw that he had only a couple of teeth left. I figured I would take them all. I hit him in the mouth and knocked them out.

Wally called me the next day, "Oh, there's going to be trouble, pal. Did you hit a guy last night?"

I said, "Yeah."

He asked, "Where were the cops?"

I told him the truth. "They were holding him."

George "Scrapiron" Gadaski was a referee and a wrestler in the AWA. He was a good guy and always in shape. He wasn't a pushover either—he was tough. George also put up the ring before every show. He made every town. He'd be the first one there to put the ring up at noon, wrestle or referee, and drive all night all by himself. The ring was always set up on time. You could always count on George. Verne and Wally would always complain to him about how much money it cost to maintain the ring. George would always give the excuse, "These are big guys."

The ring was put up with four posts, a shell around it, and plywood boards cut in sections. The wood broke sometimes. Wally complained about the budget and how much it cost for the wood for the ring.

"Well, you put the ring up, Wally," George would say.

"Well, goddamn it, you put it up," Wally would fire back and drop the subject for the time being. They'd argue like that all the time.

George died from a brain tumor years later. Verne and Wally went to George's funeral. After the service, everyone went back to George's house for cake and coffee. But Verne was standing outside for the longest time, and no one knew why.

He was staring at this barn George had built. The wood looked familiar. Then it hit Verne. George had built himself this huge barn out of Verne's wood that he had constantly requested for the ring.

He called Wally outside and showed him that George had stolen his wood.

"No, Verne," Wally said. "George is dead."

That was Wally.

When they moved the AWA offices out from the Dykeman Hotel to the Shelard, that killed Wally. For 50 years, he roamed downtown. He knew every store owner, bank teller, bartender, waiter, hooker, street person, and paper man. They moved him out to the country in a big building. It wasn't fun for him anymore. Wally's life was that hotel.

I didn't have a place to stay once. Wally offered up the Dykeman: "I'll take care of you. I'll get a good room for you, pal."

I got in the room and pulled back the curtain. The view in this "good room" was a wall.

"Thanks, Wally," I said to myself. He's been gone for years, and I still say that to myself.

When I came back to the AWA on July 10, 1974, I managed Nick Bockwinkel and Ray Stevens, who was my idol in the business.

Ray Stevens was married to a woman wrestler who was about 10 years older than he was. She was tough, but Ray claimed she wasn't all that tough. He would say, "I used to have her on her knees twice a week, begging."

"Did you hit her?" I would ask.

"No, she was telling me to come out from under the bed and fight like a man."

Ray was very talented, but Nick was conscientious about his profession. He cared about keeping in shape and about his appearance. He always wanted to do the right thing for the business, always protecting it. He was 100 percent for the business. Ray Stevens was the opposite of Nick. He would protect the business too, but Ray would stay out all night. While Nick was having his Ovaltine and cookies at 10:00 while reading *National Geographic*, Ray and I were going out at around 11:00.

Nick and I were in a plane coming from Houston to Minneapolis after working for Paul Boesch (a promoter in Texas). I saw this guy with a Hawaiian shirt and uncombed hair like Kramer on *Seinfeld*. I was sitting in the last row, and Nick was sitting across from me. I always preferred sitting in the last row because I know for a fact that a plane doesn't back into a mountain.

After the plane took off, the guy walked by me, reached for the emergency door, and tried to open it. I pulled my seat belt off, grabbed the guy, and threw him over my seat. I put my foot on his throat and pulled his hair up. I yelled, "Can I have some help here?"

Nick just sat there, calmly stirring his coffee. The guy isn't resisting me or fighting me. He was a tall guy, but not a big guy. Nick looked up and said, "Sir Robert, why are you beating up the passengers?"

He called me "Sir Robert" because I was knighted by Lord James Blears, a promoter from Hawaii, on the shithouse floor of the St. Paul Civic Center with Nick's belt. I was on my knees and everything.

"Nick," I yelled, "I'm not beating up the passengers. The asshole is trying to leave."

Nick just couldn't understand why I was fighting this nut. Like there was nothing else to do but take on the guy in 14F.

I found out later that the guy had just been released from a mental home and was trying to find the bathroom. We landed in Memphis, and they took him off the plane. The pilot came back and thanked me. I said, "Don't thank me. How about a couple of free, round-trip tickets?" I wound up with two little bottles of vodka.

Nick knows a lot of big words. He's the only guy I know that if you ask him what time it is, he tells you how to build a watch. He used big words around Ray Stevens and me. Ray and I had the same education. One day, Nick was talking about a paradox. I didn't know what he meant, and it must have shown on my face. So Nick asked me, "Do you know what a paradox is?"

I said, "Yeah, it's where you put two boats."

"No, it's two doctors," Stevens said.

I said, "No, it's two long dogs."

The next day, Nick asked us, "Have you guys been reading about the egg deficits they're having in Guam?"

Ray said, "Hey, we're still working on paradox. Let us get through that."

Baron Von Raschke always told Nick Bockwinkel, "You're living proof that a man can be educated beyond his means." How true that was and is today.

Nick was fun to rib. His AWA championship belt was made by the inmates at the Denver Prison. When he saw it, Nick said, "Isn't it awful big?"

I said, "Nick, you could be wearing a license plate."

The belt had Velcro in the back. It was hard for Nick to put it on himself, so I would hold the belt in front of him, wrap it around his waist, and attach the Velcro. Once I had a cigar in my mouth and he was wearing white trunks. I took the cigar out of my mouth, touched the end of his private area with the ash, and put the belt on. He walked to the ring with this little black dot and said, "Why are they laughing, Sir Robert?"

"You got me, Nick," I said.

I always hated one-hour "broadways"—time-limit draws—with Nick. Sitting on a chair for an hour and watching Nick is a long time. Nick was wrestling this kid from Bolivia, and he wasn't having a very good night. He was putting holds on this guy and hurting himself.

I said to myself, "I can't take any more of this," and I left the ring.

I walked to the back and Joe Blanchard, the promoter, said, "What are you doing back here? You're supposed to be out there with Nick."

"I can't, Joe. He's ruining my career. It's just one of those nights where everything doesn't work."

I made a suggestion. I said, "Joe, you go out there." He walked out to the ring and came back quickly.

"What do you think?" I asked.

"Stay here," he said.

While Wally and Ray came up with "the Brain," the "Weasel" nickname came from the Crusher. He used to sing songs about them and about chasing me around the ringpost. "Pop goes the weasel," he'd sing, but the man couldn't carry a tune. He always said that weasels were no-good, sneaky guys that did bad things. So, Crusher decided that the name fit.

The Crusher was an old guy from Milwaukee. Hell, he was an old guy when he was 20. He was a hard worker from the factories and always thought that every promoter was out to screw him. What he didn't realize was that he had 20 good years in a territory where he lived. He would take off in April or May and come back in October. He would get in an argument with Verne, quit, and take the whole summer off. Then he'd come back in the fall, get in a major program, and draw big money.

Verne always thought Crusher was selfish, wanted too much, and wasn't as over as he thought he was. Crusher felt the same way about Verne—that Verne thought he was more over than he really was and he would steal from Crusher.

Back in those days, the babyfaces hung around together and the heels stayed with each other as well. That's the way it was in those "kayfabe" days. ("Kayfabe" is wrestling slang that refers to protecting the business. To "kayfabe" basically means that the wrestler keeps the inner workings of the business to himself and doesn't share them with the fans. Sort of like a magician doesn't reveal his tricks.) If Verne caught you riding around with the "other side," you'd get yelled at but not fired because he kept a pretty small crew.

We were in Bismarck, North Dakota, with Crusher, Jim Brunzell, Larry Hennig, and a few other guys. The only time the heels and the babyfaces saw each other was in the hall. We started talking with each other in this hallway, some were even playing cribbage, when all these people walked out. They saw us all together. Our first thought was that they would think we all hang together and we needed to protect the business.

For some reason, we all started fighting each other.

There we were, 30 guys in the hall hitting each other with working punches. I hit Crusher with a cribbage board, and he took a bump. That's right. The only bump that man ever took was in Bismarck, North Dakota, in the hall of the Budgetel.

We turned around and there was no one there. They were on the elevator and could not have cared less. I had a big knot on my head from a cribbage board. Another guy hurt his knee. We thought we were keeping them from being smart. I think it was the other way around.

The AWA was a different place to be. Coming from Indianapolis, this was the big leagues. Verne Gagne had a lot of talent that worked those winter towns. He didn't run Miami or Tampa. He had Winnipeg, Denver, Milwaukee, Green Bay, Chicago, Minneapolis, St. Paul, and Omaha. It was a great place to work because you didn't have to work every day. You worked maybe four days a week. Maybe five. Sometimes three. The two best territories in those days were the AWA and the WWF (World Wrestling Federation).

In spite of that, I left the AWA in January of 1979 to go with Blackjack Lanza down to Atlanta. He asked me to go with him, and I agreed. Verne didn't want me to leave and didn't know how to explain my absence. That was around the time that Woody Hayes slapped the kid on the sidelines of a nationally televised college football game. I told Verne to tell the fans that I slapped Stanley Blackburn (the AWA "president"). On television, they announced that I was "suspended" for one year.

Atlanta was National Wrestling Alliance (NWA) country. They did things differently. When they wanted to switch the NWA world title, the promoters in the alliance would vote on who should be the next champion. The new champion had to put a deposit of around $25,000 on the belt, so if the champ ran off with the belt, they kept the money so they could buy another one. When it was time to give the belt back, the champion would get the money back with interest.

If you didn't want to do the finish that night, too bad. The champ had to. With the world champion, there were usually only three outcomes: go to a one-hour time limit, get disqualified, or win. If the champion was defeated without approval of the board, he would forfeit the deposit.

The NWA board controlled everything. They would give specifics on dates and places when the champion would win and lose the belt. Even the president of the alliance made 3 percent every night the champion worked.

In Atlanta, I had a version of the Bobby Heenan Family with "Killer" Karl Kox, Masked Superstar, and a guy named Dr. Judo, whom I managed only once. His real name was Bill Howard, and he was known for "doing jobs" (losing).

We were sitting in a restaurant and a woman walked up to me. "Are you Bobby Heenan?"

"Yes," I said.

She looked at Kox. "Are you Killer Karl Kox?"

"Yes."

She looked at Bill Howard. "I don't know you."

Bill laid on his back. "Now do I look familiar?"

Even when he walked into the building with his Dr. Judo mask on, fans would chant, "Howard's a coward." They knew who he was.

Killer Karl Kox was a great friend and a tough, tough man. He is originally from Baltimore and now retired in Dallas. And he had a rather unorthodox style.

One night, Karl was wrestling Dick Murdoch in Louisiana for "Cowboy" Bill Watts. Before the match, he was sitting in the dressing room and he was rubbing a Hershey chocolate bar so it would get real soft. Before he walked out to the ring, he took the candy and put it down the back of his trunks.

During the match, he told Murdoch to give him an "ass bump." Murdoch picked him up and dropped Kox's rear end on his knee. Kox worked his way around the ring, wobbling and selling it in a comical sort of way. He reached down the back of his tights as all the people were laughing, not knowing what he'd do next. Out of his trunks, he pulled out this big, brown hand.

The fans went wild. Kox started bringing his hand to his nose about a half-inch every four seconds, sniffing it. The people were holding their noses because of this Hershey bar mess. He smelled it one more time, turned his head away, and turned back to his "soiled" hand.

He licked his fingers.

People started running and screaming, holding their hands over their mouths. Kox went back to the dressing room pleased with his heat. Watts fired him.

I wrestled a tag match with Kox in Rome, Georgia. In the middle of the match, I looked over to our corner and he was gone. I was by myself. Apparently, he had to go to the bathroom. He came back with three feet of toilet paper hanging from his trunks. He walked back toward the ring but went around the ring to the concession stand to get a hot dog.

I was taking bumps, but no one was watching me. They were all watching Kox lie down on the hot dog stand to eat his snack. He finished with his hot dog and Coke and walked back to the ring, still with the toilet paper hanging out of his trunks. I tagged him. He stepped in and they beat him immediately. Damnedest thing you ever saw.

Macon, Georgia, had its own champion. Ralph Reed, the promoter, made Kox the Macon champion. Kox came back from a match to the dressing room, took his belt, and threw it in a garbage can. The next day, the promoter asked him if he had his belt. Kox lied to Ralph and told him that the ring attendant never brought it back. Reed had another one made. The first night he had it, he threw that belt away. This went on for a long time.

Kox confided in me, "They don't understand. I don't *want* to be the champion of Macon."

Even though Kox had two good eyes, he owned a glass eye. When we would go to restaurants, he would drop it in his soup and call the waitress over with one eye shut. He would fumble around with his spoon in his soup as she stood there, wondering what he wanted. Eventually, he would find that eye and scoop it up with the spoon. He took it off the spoon, shook it off, and palmed it so it looked like he was putting it back in his eye socket. He would "pop" it back in and smile at her. She would run away screaming.

Kox would also sit in the locker room with the young Japanese wrestlers. As he fumbled through his bag, he would shout, "Goddamn it, someone stole my eye. I can't find my eye." He threw everything out of the bag. Actually, he had taken that eyeball and put it between his "cheeks." As he bent over to look around, the Japanese boys would see this eye staring back at them.

One of the scariest moments down there was when I was dangling in a cage over the ring while Kox was wrestling Bob Armstrong in Atlanta. I don't like heights. I can take a slam off the top rope, but the wrestler better be there to slam me when I reach the top, because I can't stay there. All 230 pounds of me were in the cage. I looked down, and the only things holding me up were two guys holding the rope. If one of the guys decided to scratch his ass, I was a dead man.

If that wasn't bad enough, I had to throw powder to Kox, but I had on black pants and a black shirt. I pulled out the powder, and it got all over me. It was ridiculous. I was ready to take a leak and leave.

While I was in Atlanta, I worked with the great announcer Gordon Solie. He was excellent. He did his homework and knew all the body parts. He coined the phrase, "It's going to be a 'Pier 6 brawl.'" Didn't they get in fights on Pier 5? Why doesn't everyone go to Pier 5? Nothing happened there.

He respected the business and respected the boys. I went to his memorial service in 2000 with my wife, Cindi, and Jimmy Hart. We weren't sent there by WCW or anything. I went there because I lived in Tampa where Gordon was cremated, and I had great respect for him. Vince McMahon sent a video that they showed on a screen in front of the church. It had Jim Ross, Jerry Brisco, and Pat Patterson talking about working with him. And Gordon never even worked for the WWF.

Even Wade Boggs was there. A month before Gordon died, Boggs asked Jack and Jerry Brisco if he could meet Gordon. Wade told me later, "I sat and talked to Gordon for a half hour and felt I knew the man my whole life." He did the eulogy with Brian Blair. But not one representative from WCW was there. Tony Schiavone (who was their TV announcer and producer at the time) said, "We didn't know where it was."

Tony Schiavone, of all people, should have been there. Because he was supposed to be some kind of half-assed producer.

One time Gordon got involved in an angle and was fired. Nick Bockwinkel and I flew from Hawaii to Atlanta. Nick had the AWA championship at that time and was working in an NWA town. We were there to do a big show at the Omni. The promoter wanted to use us in a couple of weeks to do television down there. We had to clear it with Verne, and he OK'd it.

At that time, Nick's finishing move was the "figure four," but he hurt himself putting it on people, just like he did with the "Oriental sleeper." He just couldn't put them on his opponents. I used to tell him from ringside, "It's time for the 'Oriental piece-of-shit' that you use."

Nick was wrestling Steve Regal, Wilbur Snyder's son-in-law, and beat him with the figure four. Nick wouldn't break it, and I jumped in the ring and yelled at him to keep it going. Gordon came in the ring, yelling, "Stop it, please." Nick put the figure four on Gordon. Mr. Wrestling II, a popular wrestler at the time, ran into the ring and we all split.

Eddie Graham heard about it and fired Gordon because his deal with Atlanta was that Graham could use Gordon, but Gordon couldn't be touched by anybody. No one should ever touch an announcer. You don't see football players beat up John Madden or Pat Summerall.

I guess Nick and Gordon just wanted to show how dangerous the hold was. But Eddie brought Gordon back after a couple of weeks.

There wasn't a whole lot of money down in Atlanta. Ole Anderson was the booker. He didn't talk to people nicely, and it wasn't fun being around him. Nobody liked him. I worked there from January to November without a day off. I was ready to go back to the AWA.

Chapter 4

BACK TO THE AWA

I went back to the AWA around Thanksgiving of 1979. I did an angle with Lord Alfred Hayes where his man, Super Destroyer Mark II, who would go on to be Sergeant Slaughter, turned on him and introduced me as his new manager. We ended the story line a few months later when Alfred lost a "Loser Leaves Town" match to me. I never found out why Alfred left. He was a dear friend of mine. He went to Montreal, and the poor man wound up managing Billy Robinson. He almost went nuts because Robinson was such an obnoxious Englishman.

He always worked stiff (actually hurting his opponents instead of pulling his punches). I told him one day, "Billy, everything you do in the ring is beautiful. And it hurts."

Nick and I also reunited, and he was named the AWA world champion again after Verne defeated him and retired in 1981. I told Verne once, "If you beat Nick one more time, you get to keep him."

Nick would go on to lose the title to Otto Wanz in August of the next year. What a piece of shit Wanz was.

That whole situation was a scam. Nick didn't tell me the finish that night. He gave me another finish. I walked out to the ring with him, and Wally Karbo was sitting ringside. It was weird because Wally never sat out there.

Otto was stumbling around the ring like he usually did, and they went to the finish where Nick banged his head into the turnbuckle and fell back with Otto with both their shoulders on the mat. Otto raised his shoulder and beat Nick. I jumped into the ring and ran over to Larry Lisowski, the referee. Keep in mind that I'm still working. Wally ran behind me and grabbed me, yelling, "Don't hit him. Don't hit him."

I said, "Why would I hit him?"

"Because Nick lost," Karbo said.

I was working. I told him, "I don't care if Nick lost or Nick won."

I got in the ring as Nick was pulling himself up from the second rope, and he asked, "What happened?"

I said, "You lost the belt, Nick."

"I must have hit my head."

I walked back to the dressing room with him. He was still acting groggy. "Nick, quit working," I told him.

"That was a rib on you," he said.

"I knew you were working," I said, "because you grabbed the second rope and you knew where it was. What are you ribbing me for?"

I found out later that Verne told Nick not to tell anyone the finish, not even me. The reason they switched the belt to Otto is because whoever was the champion in Otto's little "Disneyworld" he lived in got the return match in Austria. The last champion (Verne) that the now former champion (Nick) defeated got to be the new champion's (Otto) manager.

Verne and his wife got a trip to Austria. I didn't go.

Another time I saw something like that was when Dick Murdoch was double-crossed in St. Louis in a match against the Bruiser. They told Bruiser that he was going to beat Murdoch. They told Murdoch that he was going to lose the first fall but take the second fall, and in the third fall, they would go to the time limit.

Dick Murdoch lost the first fall, and that was it. It was only a one-fall match. Murdoch never knew.

I was really insulted when Wanz beat Nick. They told me a different finish where Nick would go over on Wanz. Nick told me a different finish, and I'm still not over it. I should be, I guess.

Otto was such an idiot. He was in Japan with us, and we all went to this German bar in Tokyo. They'd bring you these big bones with meat on them and piles of potato pancakes. Otto would eat so much that he couldn't fit it on the table. He'd put the potato pancakes on a chair next to him. When he was stuffing his face with this food all around him, I would take three or four toilet paper sheets and put them in the sweatband of his hat. After two weeks, his hat would be sitting on top of his head like he was Lou Costello. He thought he was gaining weight in his head.

Not being told the finish of a match was a major indignity, but it was not the only indignity I would suffer in my career. We were sitting in the dressing room one night, and I was getting ready to go on vacation for a week. I jokingly said, "I'll probably come back to find out you guys have a weasel suit you got me wrestling in."

A light must have gone off in Verne's head as he was listening to me.

I continued, "I could throw Greg [his son] in, load my tail, and hit him."

"Load your tail?" Verne asked.

"I'm just kidding," I said.

I came back from vacation and Wally told me, "You're not going to believe this, pal. I've got my brother making you a weasel suit." A comment in a dressing room had come true. His brother measured me for a weasel suit that had a tail, feet, and a zipper.

I had "hotpants" matches with the Crusher in the late sixties. I was managing Blackjack Lanza at the time, and the stipulation was that if Crusher beat Jack, he'd get to put me in hotpants. So, Crusher obviously would beat Jack, knock me out cold, and slide the hotpants on. I would wake up and find these orange pants on me. I'd try to get them off of me, and I'd trip and fall.

The first match with the weasel suit was in St. Paul. Greg asked me what the finish was. I told him that he was going to beat me and put me in the suit. Their first idea was for Greg to pin me quickly.

"Why would I get in the suit then?" I asked. "'The Brain' would tell you to stick it up your ass."

The promoters asked me, "How are you going to get in it?"

I reassured them, "Just let him beat me."

Greg beat me that night, and of course I refused to put the suit on. Referee Marty Miller gave me to the count of 10 to put the suit on. I walked away, Greg ran out, nailed me, and rolled me back in the ring. He picked me up in the ring and put me in his sleeper hold.

I would wake up real groggy and then start to stare at my hands. Only I had paws. Then I saw I had a tail. So I would start chasing my tail and take bumps in the ring. Wally's brother made the bottoms of the feet real slick, so I was slipping all over the ring. I finally got the suit off, threw it in the air, and walked underneath it. It would land on me, and I would start fighting it all over again.

I wasn't the only one trying to rip that suit off. One night in Peoria, I was lying out cold in the ring, and some mark came by and ripped my tail off.

Greg was a good "weasel suit" opponent, but he never became the AWA world champion like his father did. Verne never made Greg the champion because he wanted only one world champion in the Gagne family. Verne could have had that kid in wrestling school and hired Dan Gable and others to teach Greg to shoot. ("Shoot" is wrestling slang for actually punching and kicking, as opposed to the loose pro wrestling style.) Not with Verne. Greg was tag-team champion and international television champion, but that was it.

Greg and Jim Brunzell were members of the "High Flyers" and held the AWA world tag-team title. They always got along, but Brunzell always felt that he would never be treated as well as Greg was. That wasn't going to happen because Greg was Verne's son. Period. Jim felt like the second banana. Jim wanted to wrestle as a single and face Nick for the heavyweight title. He went to Charlotte for a while, but he wasn't as over as he was in the AWA. Remember, if a promoter wants you over, you'll get over. Brunzell trained at Verne's school and paid Verne a percentage of money for so many years for the training. As far as I know, Brunzell was one of the only wrestlers to live up to that agreement.

Verne got his money from other sources as well. He used to sell this product called Gerispeed, a vitamin supplement. It sold pretty well. He was wrestling in Detroit around the late fifties or early sixties. Before a match he was going to have with Verne, Bruiser found this old, dirty bum outside the building. He offered the guy 20 bucks to wait outside the door. When it came time for Dick's interview, he found the guy, who had since fallen asleep or passed out. Bruiser slung the guy over his shoulder, brought him to the set, and told everyone that this guy had been on Gerispeed for five years and look how much he improved his health.

Another weasel suit opponent back then was Buck "Rock and Roll" Zumhofe. I watched him one night with his jumpsuit and the big radio he carried around and thought to myself, "I could make money with this kid." I really didn't know Zumhofe, but I thought I could have some fun with him.

We had an angle in the early eighties where I was wrestling Kenny Jay on television and Buck came out with his radio. I turned to him, and Kenny rolled me up for the pin. I acted mad and was ready to fight Zumhofe. He put the radio down, but the dummy didn't have the back on it, and all the batteries rolled out. The music that was supposed to be irritating me suddenly stopped.

So I just kicked him in the head.

Although we didn't wrestle in "Weasel Suit" matches, I worked against Brad Rheingans, who was a former Olympic wrestler. Wrestling Brad was like wrestling a cab. He wouldn't bend. He couldn't move. It was the worst. It was like working with a refrigerator.

I wrestled Brad in his third match in Ladysmith, Wisconsin. They wanted me to do the job for him. Of course. I'd do anything I could just to get the match over with. You couldn't bend him or anything. He was so strong and he had that mentality of shooting. There were 100 people in the arena that night. He beat me and started leaving the ring.

I shouted, "Hey, asshole!"

"What?" he asked. He couldn't hear me.

"You, asshole!"

He got in the ring.

"Take your straps down," I demanded.

"What?"

"I said take your straps down, asshole."

He took his straps down. I took mine down, too. I said, "Put 'em up. Put 'em up, asshole."

He put up his fists.

I looked at the crowd and shouted, "The guy does anything I tell him," and I left.

I would really mess with Rheingans in the ring. Usually, when you are wrestling a guy and you want to hit him and have him hit you back, you'd say, "One, two." I'd get Brad in the ropes and say,

"One," and hit him. He'd try to hit me back. I'd say, "I said one." And he'd stop in midpunch.

I would have him in a headlock and call a high spot. Usually I'd say, "Shoot me in, hit me with a tackle, jump over me, get it again."

So I told Brad, "One tackle. Don't get it again." I'd shoot him in; he'd hit me with a tackle. He'd come off the other ropes.

"I said not to get it," I'd say. He'd stop.

But wrestling that "cab" sure beat Mad Dog Vachon pounding on me. He was violent.

I was wrestling him one night in Hamburg behind Zumhofe's house near a railroad track. The Dog dragged me to the track and laid my neck across it.

He said, "Stay here."

I asked, "How long?"

"Until the fucking train comes," he growled.

You would have to let Dog beat on you and let him know you could take it to get his respect. He didn't like guys like Jesse Ventura and Billy Graham. He always said, "They're pussies. They can't take it."

When Mad Dog chopped, he didn't just chop. He had small hands (or paws) like little shovels that would rip into your flesh. When Mad Dog won the AWA belt in Texas, the promoters were going to have him drop it to Billy Graham. Graham gave it back, saying, "Brother, I don't need this. A guy could get hurt out there."

Violence also defined Frank Goodish, who wrestled as "Bruiser" Brody. But Frank was always out to screw promoters because he was another guy convinced that they wanted to screw him. We had a show at the Showboat in Las Vegas. Someone had gotten sick before the show started. A custodian cleaned it up with a mop, put the mop in a bucket, and left it out in the hall.

Goodish found it as he was walking out to the ring. He stood in the ring with this wet mop full of vomit and started throwing it around at the people. Who is going to come back to a show with that?

He missed shots. He went to Chicago once and, because no one picked him up at the hotel, he turned around and went home. In Indianapolis, I gave him the finish for his match with Jim Brunzell. He was supposed to go 20 minutes and get disqualified. He didn't wrestle one minute. He walked out with a cartload of chairs, knocked the ringside seats over, and went out into the stands.

The referee asked, "What should I do?" I told him to count him out.

He wrestled Nick once for Paul Boesch in Houston, Texas, and he actually behaved himself. He didn't know Nick, and he liked Boesch because he paid a lot of money. Boesch was the best payoff guy in the business and a very fair guy. He would always pay me in cash with a big envelope—compared to the ones I got in St. Louis, which I could slide under a door.

Frank was not about to blow Houston, because he was from Texas and he wanted to work around there. He would never stay in a territory. He'd go in and out. When he'd come in and stick it to a promoter, he never realized that there were guys underneath working that territory who depended on that once-a-month, big show for money. He didn't understand that if he went in and screwed it up for that promoter, he was screwing all the little guys at the bottom too. That's why I never had any respect for Frank Goodish.

It was enjoyable working for Verne, and I didn't have any problem with him. He was fair with me, and the only conflict I had was when I left for the WWF. It's funny. I called Vince McMahon Sr. before I went to Japan in 1983. I'd call him every six months about coming in, but he wouldn't use me. He had Lou Albano, Grand Wizard, and Fred Blassie. The last time I talked to him, he said, "Something big is going to happen, and I can't use you now.

Taking advice from Chris Markoff during my very first match.
Photo courtesy of Bobby Heenan's personal collection.

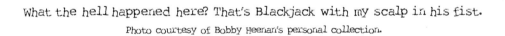

What the hell happened here? That's Blackjack with my scalp in his fist.
Photo courtesy of Bobby Heenan's personal collection.

A post-match examination
of my messed-up face.
Photo courtesy of Bobby Heenan's
personal collection.

Recovering from a bloody beating.
Photo by Michael Lano (wrealano@aol.com).

That's me on the floor there, writhing in pain.
Photo by Michael Lano (wrealano@aol.com), reprinted courtesy of Bobby Heenan's personal collection.

Posing with heavyweight champion Nick Bockwinkel.

Photo courtesy of Bobby Heenan's personal collection.

Tasting the turnbuckle courtesy of Greg Gagne.

Photo by Michael Lano (wrealano@aol.com).

That's me being bloodied by Pat Patterson.
Photo by Michael Lano (wrealano@aol.com).

Chomping on a cigar, hanging out with Blackjack Lanza.
Photo courtesy of Bobby Heenan's personal collection.

A younger me posing with Blackjack.

Photo courtesy of Bobby Heenan's personal collection.

There'd really be trouble. But you'll hear about it." He wouldn't tell me what was up. When I went to Japan, he died of cancer, but he had already sold his promotion to his son, Vince McMahon Jr.

Verne didn't want me to leave, but I wanted to because Vince McMahon made me an offer I couldn't refuse. It was almost double my pay. I was going to do the TV from Madison Square Garden on the MSG channel. It was a chance to do more things. I was 44 and ready to make a change. I didn't want to work past 50.

I could see with Vince McMahon's imagination and his television product that he was better than P. T. Barnum. Even the boys in the AWA watched his tapes. It was exciting. It was different. I had an opportunity to go with Hulk Hogan, Gene Okerlund, and David Schultz. Vince made me feel like a star. Verne was a wrestler. Bruiser and Wilbur Snyder were wrestlers. Everyone has their own feelings about Vince, but he was always fair to me. He always made me feel like I was worth something. Some promoters would talk down to their workers, but not Vince.

Verne was so mad when Vince was taking over. He claimed that he was going to run Brooklyn against Vince. I told him there was no place to run there. He needed to upgrade his product. I said, "There are four gas stations on four corners. No promoter owns anything. No one owns a town. He has the right to go there. Vince has the right to come here." He didn't like to hear that, but it was the truth.

I never quite found out if this was true, but the Iron Sheik told me that when he went to New York and beat Bob Backlund for the WWF title, the next show was supposed to be Sheik and Backlund in a return match. That's what Backlund thought. It was actually Sheik versus Hulk Hogan at the next show where Hogan was going to get the belt.

Arnold Skaaland went to the ring with Backlund that night, and, during the match, Iron Sheik got Backlund in a "camel clutch." Skaaland threw the towel in, but Backlund didn't know anything about it. Skaaland was told by the WWF to do it. I don't know if that was a way to protect Backlund so he didn't have to give up, but Backlund was upset about it. On top of that, he didn't get the return match. Hogan did.

Sheik told me that after he won the belt, Vince was going to go national and have his television all over the place. Verne called Sheik and said, "You come to Minneapolis with the belt, and I'll put you over Nick Bockwinkel. You'll be the AWA champion and the WWF champion. We'll unify it to the AWA championship. Plus, I'll give you $100,000."

Sheik thought about it. He told me, "Verne Gagne started me, but he never made any money for me. Vince McMahon Sr. has always taken care of me and gave me the belt. I've made good money with him."

He turned Verne down and told Vince Sr. about the phone call. That's why you will always see the Iron Sheik used by the McMahon family. They appreciated his loyalty. Again, I don't know if it's true or not, but I suspect it is.

Hulk Hogan's departure from the AWA started when he came back from Japan in 1983. He didn't want to work for Verne because of some discrepancy over T-shirt money. The AWA sold all our T-shirts, but we never got a dime for anything. No one did that I know of, except for maybe his son, Greg. Verne even made up a battle royal shirt once with all our faces on it.

The AWA was scared that Hogan was going to try something during his last match with Nick Bockwinkel for the AWA title in St. Paul toward the end of 1983. They even gave Nick two finishes. I just laughed, saying, "This isn't going to happen. This is business."

Hogan never showed up for that match. He had signed with the WWF. David Schultz, another wrestler, didn't show up either, and Verne fired him. David got a little mad about that, to say the least.

I was out back having a cigarette outside the television studio. Everybody was on lunch break when Schultz walked by me, saying, "Hi, Bobby." He was wearing a baseball cap, pants tucked into his cowboy boots, rodeo gloves, and a lumberjack coat. This guy looked ready to fight.

The only people left in the studio were Billy Graham, Blackjack Lanza, and Verne and Greg Gagne. Schultz walked into the studio, went right up to Verne, and said, "Don't you tell anybody I was fired because I quit. I sent you a telegram last night."

"Get the hell out of here before I have you thrown out," Verne yelled.

"You ain't gonna do nothin' to me, you old, bald-headed man," Schultz shouted.

Verne looked at him and realized that he was in a television station. He didn't want to lose his show over a brawl. He walked out to get some assistance.

Greg shouted at Schultz, "I'll go with you." Graham and Lanza held him back, which was a good idea or Verne would have been planning a funeral for his son.

Schultz finally left, but he was wound up tighter than a cheap watch and ready to go. And that wasn't the end of the departures.

Gene Okerlund left soon after that. The AWA had its number one babyface gone, a top heel, and a top announcer. Their main guys remaining were Bockwinkel, Greg Gagne, and Verne.

I was next.

When I was ready to leave the AWA, I called Hogan and told him I wanted to go to New York. They had already asked me three or four times. He said, "Call me back in five minutes."

I called him back. He said, "I just talked to Vince. When you get home, call him."

I called Vince on a Friday night from Denver. I couldn't take it anymore and wanted to make a change. The AWA was going down, and Vince was really on a run. I saw what the wrestlers were making from the WWF. I wanted to make that run. I had a good money offer and was treated with respect.

51

I wanted to be a part of it.

After I accepted the offer from Vince, I called Verne at home. His wife told me that he was over visiting Greg and his grandson. I called Greg's house and asked him if Verne was there. Greg said, "No, why?"

"Well, I need to talk to him about something."

"Is it anything important?" he asked.

I figured Verne was there, so I cut to the chase, "I was made an offer by the WWF."

"Oh, those bastards. They're after it again," he grumbled.

"I'm going to take it," I said. "It's a substantial offer."

Strangely, Greg said, "Go ahead."

I asked him later why he said that. Greg said, "Because usually the guy won't go. Nine out of ten times, we win." Smart mentality.

I guess Greg "found" Verne, because he called me back quickly. "What is it, Bobby?" he asked.

"There's something I want to talk to you about. The WWF called and they made me an offer."

"Oh, those bastards. They're after it again," he said, mimicking Greg.

"I'm going to accept the offer."

"You're what?"

"I'm going to accept the offer."

"Tell it to me face-to-face," Verne said.

"Are you going to be in the office this afternoon around 1:00?" I asked.

"Yes."

I hung up the phone and told my wife Cindi, "I'm going in to give my notice."

I really didn't know what they would do to me. Verne lost Hogan, Okerlund, and Schultz. He was going to lose me, which meant that Nick wouldn't have anybody. He lost Nick's main opponent and his manager. It would be a big dent. But Vince's ratings were going up. He was getting more popular every week.

Before I went to the office, I made a blade to protect myself. They didn't know it then, but they will now if they read this. I greeted Mary Ellen, who was Verne's sister-in-law and the secretary. She was a very nice lady.

I walked into Verne's office and kept my hands in my pockets the whole time. Verne shut the door, turned around, and said to Greg, "Let's get him and throw him out the window." We were up 20 floors.

I sat down on the couch and said, "Go ahead. You'll make my wife a very wealthy woman."

They both sat down, one on each side of me. "We're just kidding," Verne said. "Tell me what's going on. What happened?"

"Vince called me and made me an offer," I said. "It's twice what you're paying me to do Madison Square Garden television and manage."

WWF managers in those days worked only TV, and they'd go home and get paid for every town their man was at. I would have less travel and could be home with my daughter, who was five at the time.

Verne made me an offer. "I don't know where I'll get it," he said. "But I'll get it to you."

I knew he meant well, but he's still business. I think he liked me, but I told him, "I have to look out for myself now. You have a big home on Lake Minnetonka. You have all this land and money. I want that. Now is my chance to advance myself and have it."

"I'll finish out my dates," I told Verne. "But I won't work with Brad Rheingans."

The reason I wouldn't work with Brad is because he was new. Verne had just started him and had donated a lot of money to the Olympic committee. Brad's an Olympian from Minnesota.

Verne is from Minnesota. Verne probably told him that he would give him the belt someday. Brad didn't know me. I didn't know him.

I didn't want him out there breaking my leg or neck accidentally on purpose.

He's the only man I didn't trust, but not because I felt he was dishonest. He was so green and young and might have hurt me not knowing what he was doing.

I finished off my dates. On my last night, I thanked Verne for everything. I was done with the AWA.

These days, when I see Verne, he thanks me for finishing up dates. He told me, "You're the only guy who gave me proper notice." I consider him a friend to this day. But if I thought they were going to hurt me or touch me on the day I gave my notice, I was going to take that blade and cut the top of my own head off. Let the courts sort it out.

I think Vince McMahon thought he could come in and buy everybody out and they'd all get scared and run. He thought that someone would give him a fight, either Verne, Fritz Von Erich, Eddie Graham, Bill Watts, or someone else. But their mentality was gone. They all had to have money, because they never gave it to the boys. They didn't have the ability to create like Vince. They couldn't keep up with him. They were still stuck in the sixties, and Vince was going into the new century.

The mentality of a promoter in those days was to spend the least amount of money to draw the most. Vince already had the money from his father and investments he had made.

I didn't get much heat for jumping to the WWF. I did get a call from Harley Race, who was a promoter at that time in Kansas City for the NWA. He said, "Bobby, I hear you're going to New York. We've been friends for 30 years. You can't do this to us."

"Harley," I said, "I've got to look out for myself and my family."

He agreed and wished me the best of luck. In the end, the wrestlers didn't care what a guy did because they knew that if the opportunity came to them, they would do it too. You had to do it for yourself. In pro wrestling, there is no insurance, no benefits, and no retirement. Besides, when I got to the WWF, I was seeing guys I worked with before, like John Studd, Sergeant Slaughter, and Pat Patterson.

It wasn't any different.

Chapter 5

JOINING THE WWF

Joining the WWF was not the first time I met Vince McMahon Jr. We met at an exhibition for Muhammad Ali in Chicago in 1976. Ali was preparing for his match in Japan with Antonio Inoki. I walked in with Al DeRusha and Nick Bockwinkel. We introduced ourselves. Vince just looked up and nodded. A very cold reception.

Vince always wore these wild-colored outfits. I told Linda, his wife, that if they put a light in the closet, that wouldn't happen. She just shrugged and said, "He likes colors."

Every year, Vince had a tailor come down from Rhode Island to make his suits. The tailor matched the lining, shirt, tie, and everything. Vince kept his suits in this big cedar closet at his home. He would wear the suits in the winter, but when spring came, he would give them all away. Every season, a new wardrobe.

I guess if I ever see a bum lying in the alley wearing an orange suit, I'll know where he got it from.

I never had a conversation with Vince until that day I called him from Denver to come in to the WWF. When you first meet Vince, the honeymoon starts, but it's over real quick. You could always talk to Vince. He always had time to listen to me and gave me some good advice. He said, "Remember this. Two people can solve any problem, unless one's an asshole."

At the Garden that night, I met Vince for the first time since the Inoki-Ali fight, but I made the mistake of having a cigar. Vince barked, "Put that out." He hated smoking.

We were doing *Saturday Night's Main Event* in Milwaukee in 1989 when Randy Savage turned on Hulk Hogan to set up Wrestlemania 5. Jesse Ventura was in the back smoking a cigar. Vince noticed right away and said, "Who the hell is smoking here? Put that out." That was Vince's only pet peeve. The only time I saw him get mad was when someone smoked. Jesse put his cigar out in the announcer's dressing room.

Later on, I saw the cigar in an ashtray. I picked it up but wasn't sure what I was going to do with it. Later, I was in Vince's dressing room talking to him. Vince had his tuxedo on, and I noticed his other clothes hanging on a rack. After Vince left, I took Jesse's cigar and put it in the breast pocket of Vince's suit coat under his hankie. I never found out what happened, but I'm sure Jesse got blamed for it.

Vince always wanted to be a worker. He was 14 or 15 when he started hanging out with Dr. Jerry Graham. Jerry had a Cadillac and would drive down Broadway in New York with the top down. There was Vince wearing a red, ruffled shirt and bleached blond hair. When his old man found out about it, he went nuts.

My first appearance in the WWF was in Madison Square Garden in New York. I walked to the ring, got on the microphone, and said I was looking for new talent. It was funny. I walked into the Garden that night and everybody knew me. This was before the business went national, but those fans bought the wrestling magazines. Some promoters, like Verne Gagne, never understood the value of those magazines. I told him that if fans are going to pay three bucks for a lousy seat to see some wrestlers, they'd pay 50 cents for a magazine with every wrestler in it.

I was originally supposed to manage Jesse Ventura in the WWF. Vince asked me if I'd mind, and I agreed because we always got along. When I got to New York, Vince told me that Jesse had some circulation problems in his legs and he couldn't be there. He asked me if I wanted to work with John Studd. Again, I agreed. I just wanted to be there. I would have managed Donald Duck. In fact, I think I have.

The following Sunday, the WWF had a show at the Met Center in Bloomington, Minnesota. I wore a mask to the building that night and came in the back way. I put a rock in my shoe so I could change my walk, which I think is distinctive because I'm bow-legged. I even changed luggage. No one knew who I was. I walked past fans who followed the AWA and into the dressing room where I saw Roddy Piper. I shoved him. He turned around like he was going to hit me. I took the mask off to reveal who I was.

Studd got in the ring and said he had a new manager. I walked out, and the "Weasel" chants started up like I was never gone.

John was a real nice, quiet man. He loved his family and always wanted to be home. He always wanted to do the right thing. I would get annoyed with people on the plane bugging me when I was trying to sleep. He would say, "Be nice," and would sign the autograph. He was a real decent man, and the business was far below him. I don't remember him ever even saying "damn it" or swearing at all. He was a lot like the Howard Sprague character in *Mayberry RFD*.

John and I were in Pittsburgh working a show. Sometimes you'd get a ring announcer who wasn't with the company—some old guy who didn't like wrestling and didn't want to be there but loved the 50 bucks and the night out from "Maude."

The announcer got in the ring and grabbed the microphone that hung from the ceiling. He announced Studd but didn't announce me. He walked out of the ring, and I grabbed the microphone—I was ready to announce myself. The guy controlling the microphone obviously didn't want me to have it, so he pulled it up as I was introducing myself. We started this tug of war. I grabbed the microphone with both hands and pulled hard. The wire broke, and the microphone hit me on the face, bloodied my nose, and knocked me on my ass.

Studd looked at me and asked, "What happened?"

"You know, I don't care if they ever know who I am," I said. "I want to get out of here. I just beat the hell out of myself with a microphone."

I was glad to be working with old friends like Studd, Gene Okerlund, and Hulk Hogan. One night in New York City, Gene was out on the town with Hogan, if you know what I mean. Gene always liked to suck up to him. Hulkster would pay the bill and let him come back to the hotel in his stretch limo.

Gene arrived at the hotel and immediately staggered upstairs to go to bed. About 4:00 in the morning, Gene, with nothing on, got out of bed to relieve himself. He walked to the bathroom door, opened it up, and shut it behind him. He immediately realized that he wasn't in the bathroom. He was in the hall of the 12th floor, naked as the day he was born—except with a mustache.

At first, Gene did not know what to do. He walked over to the window, took the drapes down, and wrapped them around him. The elevator took him to the lobby with Gene covered in the window dressing. He told the desk clerk who he was and that he had stepped outside of his room instead of going into the bathroom.

The desk clerk laughed and said, "Don't worry about that, Mr. Okerlund. Mickey Mantle stays here and he usually brings a 'friend' up to his room. When she steals his watch, he chases her out of the room. The door shuts behind him and he comes down here the same way too."

Later, I told Okerlund, "Gene, you're a hall of famer."

Hogan, on the other hand, is a legitimate "hall of famer." I remember that night in 1979 when I was wrestling in Marietta, Georgia. You have to understand that the buildings weren't like the way they are now, where you have 20,000-seat arenas with rails around the ring, police protection, and pyro. The Cobb County Civic Center held about 2,500 people and, on that night, there were 1,500 there.

I was wrestling a tag match. It was the first time I met my partner for that night. He was 6'7", weighed 310 pounds, and had this enormous amount of hair on his body. On that night, he shaved all the hair off except for a big heart of hair on the middle of his chest.

After the match, we jumped down to go back to the dressing room and he was walking ahead of me. Some fan jumped out, and my partner stopped in his tracks. He didn't know what to do because he was so green. He hadn't wrestled that much, let alone faced off with a fan. He was nervous. I said, "Let me ahead of you." So I went to get ahead of him and I start walking. The mark jumps out in front of me. I grabbed the guy and threw him to the ground, and the Marietta police hauled him away.

My partner that night, Sterling Golden, went on to do something more in wrestling. He got rid of the boots and trunks and got new ring wear—this time yellow.

I always kept my distance from Hogan because of our ongoing feud from the eighties in the AWA. Even when he turned heel in WCW, I didn't root for him because I wanted to protect the business. The hottest angle I was involved in was Hogan versus Andre the Giant. I fought him in the AWA and the WWF for all those years. Why, all of a sudden, would I turn after one week if I didn't really like the guy? It didn't make sense. I talked about how I liked what he was doing, but I didn't like him.

Hogan was the one who got me into the WWF, and I was the one who got him into the AWA. When I left Georgia in 1979 and returned to Minneapolis, I told Verne about this guy. I said, "He's huge, has a hell of a body, and people look at him in awe. He's a little green, but he can get better."

Back then, I could tell that Hogan didn't care about wrestling. He cared about entertaining and making money.

Hogan went from Atlanta to his first run in the WWF. Vince McMahon Sr. always gave guys Irish names like Bugsy McGraw and Blackjack Mulligan. He gave him the name Hulk Hogan. He was doing well in New York. One night, Sylvester Stallone was at one of his matches and saw him. He sent word back to the dressing room that he wanted Hogan to play Thunderlips in *Rocky III*.

When I came back from a tour of Japan, Verne brought in Hogan. He was hot from the beginning. They tried to make him a heel and gave him a manager named Johnny Valiant, who wasn't a very good one. Hogan was beating two to three guys a night in handicap matches, but the people just loved him. Hulk Hogan and the Crusher were the biggest things to ever hit the AWA.

Hogan was the logical one to go after Nick for the belt. I was managing Nick at the time. Perhaps to get Hogan over as a heel, they should have put him with me and made Nick a babyface. But I don't know if I could have done that, even with my heat.

The AWA was doing great business before Hogan, but after he showed up, they were selling out. We worked in St. Paul, doing $150,000 to $200,000. But with Hogan versus Bockwinkel, they had to rent the building next door and put in closed-circuit television. They did over $300,000.

He was phenomenal. I've never seen a character or wrestler like that. Andre was a phenomenon, but I wasn't with him every day when he was starting out as a babyface. I wasn't in a territory with him. I was with Hogan in Atlanta, Minneapolis, and New York and saw him become a superstar—a phenomenon like nothing before.

I've heard the question, "Why didn't they give Hogan the AWA title?" many times. They were going to in St. Paul. It was Hogan's last match before he went over to work for Antonio Inoki in Japan and make some big money. Verne came into the locker room and told Hogan, "You're going to beat Nick, and we're going to give you the belt. I want you to call Inoki and tell him I'm doing your booking since I own the champion."

Verne thought Hogan was dumb enough to fall for it. But Hogan was smart and he learned that he couldn't just get the belt; Verne would book him, his program with Inoki would be changed, and he would make less money.

Hogan turned down the offer. Verne said, "OK, then get disqualified," thinking Hogan would change his mind because Verne was taking the belt away.

He didn't. That was the whole deal. He didn't want to be controlled by Verne, and he would have been. He wanted to be free to go to Japan in the winter and make $100,000 a day. The Japanese treated him like a king. What it all came down to is that he didn't need the AWA as much as the AWA needed him. And that was the beginning of the end for Hulk Hogan in the AWA.

I've been watching pro wrestling for 46 years, and I have never seen people react to anybody the way they did to Hulk Hogan. I've never seen anything like the control he had over them—the way they dressed like him. The way people cut their hair like him. People made themselves bald to look like him. The amount of merchandise this man sold was unreal. I saw people cry at ringside when Hulk was in trouble. I've seen kids look at him like an idol, somebody they thought they'd never get to see. I've never seen an athlete like that in my life. Sure, it's acting, but still he's an athlete. A lot of people say he's not a good athlete, but he's a very good one. He puts a lot of asses in a lot of seats, and that's how I judge how good of a guy he is.

Vince decided to use Tiny Lister, who starred with Hogan in his first movie, *No Holds Barred*, as Zeus. He was a big guy with this goofy eye. But Vince was going to make him into a wrestler, and Hogan had to work with him. The guy had never been in the ring in his life and had no idea what it was about. Vince pulled off a pay-per-view with Hogan walking Zeus through everything. He took a guy who was big, green, and couldn't see, and got him through a whole program, doing interviews, and ending up with a pay-per-view match that made money. Despite what other people think, I say Hogan was a fairly good hand in the ring.

Hulk Hogan's fame did create a lot of jealousy among other wrestlers. Hogan and Jesse Ventura never liked each other. Jesse was terribly jealous of Hogan, who always drew more money than him. Hogan knew Jesse didn't like him, and he would do things to piss Jesse off all the time.

Ventura was never a threat to Hogan. Jesse had a great ability to talk, but once that bell rang and the boa came off, he couldn't take bumps. He wouldn't even have been a good job guy. In the AWA, the promoters teamed him with Adrian Adonis, and Adrian wondered why he always got pinned instead of Jesse. (It was because Adrian could do it better.) Jesse had a good talk and he dressed as odd as anyone, so he made himself amusing to people. Jesse could draw you money, but nothing like Hogan.

I don't know why Jesse left the WWF in 1990. It was probably something about Hogan because that's why he left WCW. Jesse thought Hogan got him fired, and Hogan was glad Jesse was gone. Jesse wouldn't put him over on TV. He would just sit there, rock in his chair, and not say anything about Hogan. Sometimes he would sound unprepared, but Jesse was very smart, and he could make it sound that way. If he didn't want to put someone over, like Hogan, he just acted like he didn't know much about him. It didn't help the product, and it wasn't what they were paying him for.

They should have just put the two in a room and let them go at it. But Hogan would have come out on top.

I remember when guys would get their booking sheets to see where they would be wrestling. At the height of its popularity in the eighties, the WWF was running three shows a night. The guys would be in Seattle one night, in Tampa the next night, the next night in Boston, and then in San Diego. They would crisscross the country. Guys didn't care about that. They looked to see if they were on the same card as Hogan. Or should I say cards?

Hogan, Paul Orndorff, and I were working a program. Business was on fire back then in the mid-eighties. We were at Nassau, Long Island, on a Saturday night. It was sold out with 20,000 people. The main event was Hogan versus Orndorff, and they put us on third. A lot of promoters always put the main event on last. Vince always put the main event on third or fourth so he could have an intermission and announce a return match with a stipulation on the next card and sell tickets to that event.

When we got done there, we ran out of the building. The WWF took us in a limo to MacArthur Airport and put the three of us on a private Learjet. The three of us got on the jet—Hogan in yellow, Orndorff in red, and me in my sequined suit. We looked like Liberace's backup group.

We arrived at O'Hare in Chicago, which is an hour behind New York, at 10:30 for another sold-out show. The police from Rosemont picked us up and drove us to the Rosemont Horizon. We drove down the ramp and quickly got out of the car. Blackjack Lanza, one of the agents, told us, "Keep going straight on. Intermission is over." The three of us walked to the ring and did the same thing we had done two hours before, a thousand miles away.

Business was good because of Hogan and Vince. From that came Wrestlemania. From Wrestlemania came a lot of memories, both good and bad.

There was a big party after Wrestlemania 1 at the Rainbow Room. Liberace, one of the celebrities who appeared on the show, was sitting by a chair with his hand on a rail. I was on the other side of the rail with my wife, talking to people. I leaned back and accidentally sat on Liberace's hand.

"Oh, excuse me," I said.

Liberace looked at Cindi and said, "Nice tush."

I never found out if he was talking to her or me.

I was in the hospital the morning of Wrestlemania 2 in Tampa, Florida. I had a myogram done where they shot dye in my spine. In 1983, I broke my neck in Japan after this kid named Onita came off the top rope with a legdrop and dropped his leg on my face. I never had pain in my hand, just from my wrist up to my neck. It bothered me for years, but we didn't have any insurance. No one would take care of you, so I didn't have enough money to have an operation. I couldn't take the time off. I had a wife and a kid to feed.

Someone from the WWF told me that if I didn't make Wrestlemania, I was fired. I checked out of the hospital that morning after having a myogram the day before. The nurse asked, "Where are you going?"

I said, "I'm going to Los Angeles to wrestle. See you later."

I caught a plane to L.A., and we did Wrestlemania. I took a red-eye back, returned to the hospital, checked in at 5:00 in the morning, and went back to bed. That's the way they browbeat you. You had to work or you were fired. Talking to me like that, it was a disgrace.

I managed King Kong Bundy in the main event against Hulk Hogan at that Wrestlemania. He was fun. He wore a black tunic to the ring, and he was lily white with a bald head. I used to call him Shamu, because he was white and black and about the size of the whale. We were sitting in first class on a plane to San Francisco. Bundy was asleep. The stewardess asked me, "Anything I can get you?"

I said, "Yes, I'll have a scotch and water."

She looked at Bundy. "Would your friend like anything?"

"Yes, bring him a pail of fish."

Bundy heard what I said. He leaned over on me and slept the whole way to San Francisco practically on top of me. He got me back.

I also managed Hulk Hogan's opponent in the main event of Wrestlemania 3, Andre the Giant.

The morning of Wrestlemania, I had breakfast with Andre before we went over to the Pontiac Stadium. Andre had his usual—an omelette and six bottles of wine. When we arrived at the building, we met up with Vince McMahon and adjourned to the steam room of the Detroit Lions training center to go over the finish for the evening and discuss what would go on in the ring.

Vince was telling us that we were going to the ring on these forklifts, heels (us) first and then the babyface (Hogan). They would raise the forklifts as high as they could, maybe seven or eight feet in the air. They would have these five-by-five platforms, ring ropes, and everything. Vince told us that the forklift was so big that it could only back up to leave because there was no room for it to turn around.

Andre had a question for Vince: "How big are the aisles?"

"Well, they're pretty big," Vince responded. "Why?"

"I'm going to push over Hogan's forklift."

Vince was shocked. "While he's on it?"

Andre said, "I don't know."

"Andre," Vince said, "you can't do that. There's a guy driving it."

"I don't care."

After the meeting, Vince pulled me aside. "If he starts to push the forklift over, watch him."

I said, "Vince, me and 93,000 people will watch him. And that's all we'll be able to do."

Everything worked out. Andre didn't tip anybody or anything over. When I was up on that forklift with Andre and we started going out, I knew he wasn't going to do anything. He couldn't get back from the ring to get Hogan anyway because his knee was bothering him.

We went out and saw 93,000 people, a world indoor attendance record. That didn't click in my head right away. What clicked in my head was, "I wonder how many people are watching this on pay-per-view." I'm riding on this forklift in front of all these people and I thought, "My god, this is history." Records can be broken, like the ones set by Babe Ruth and Roger Maris. This record will hold. To be part of it was a phenomenal experience.

At Wrestlemania 4 at Trump Plaza, Donald Trump bought the show. He came backstage to meet the boys with about five bodyguards and Ivana, his wife at the time. He was a real nice guy and shook hands with everyone back there.

Rick Rude and I went out for our match with Jake Roberts. During the bout, Jake put Rude over the security rail backward right in front of Ivana. He told Rude to move. Jake grabbed his snake out of the bag and charged him. Rude ducked, and the snake went right into Ivana's face. She flew backward in her chair with her chalice of wine on the floor and her legs up. I thought, "Oh God, if Vince hears about this, we're in trouble."

I looked over at Trump. He winked at me. He was glad she got knocked on her ass. Ivana stood up, dusted herself off, and told her bodyguard, "You should have shot the fucking snake."

I also wrestled at Wrestlemania 4 in a match with the Islanders against the British Bulldogs and Koko B. Ware. In those days, the Bulldogs would bring an actual bulldog, named Matilda, to the ring. Sometimes, they would sic her on their opponents. But Matilda wouldn't go for the wrestler, she would only go for his shoe. During the match, I was supposed to go to Matilda so she would chase me out of the ring and down the aisle. Then, I was supposed to fall down, and she was supposed to bite me on the arm, which was protected by a dog suit.

I was practicing in the dressing room with her. Nothing. I couldn't get her to do anything. The only thing she would do is fart. Dynamite Kid, one of the Bulldogs, fed her hot dogs all day. This big bulldog would not bite me. She just sat there and farted.

I'm in the ring with a dog suit on that was made for a guy who wore a medium suit. It felt like it was made up of carpet, and I couldn't breathe in that bastard. The end of the match came, and I took off out of the ring. Mind you, I was already blown up. I hadn't wrestled in two years, and it was a long way from the ring to the dressing room. I saw Matilda coming behind me with Davey Boy Smith. But she wasn't running fast. Davey was trying to force her to run.

I couldn't go any more. I fell down in the aisle. I told Davey to let her jump me right there. Matilda got on top of me and started sniffing the dog suit. Obviously, she smelled another dog on it, because she began to hump me. She wouldn't bite me, just hump me. I thought, "Oh my God, it has come to this now. All the way from the Assassins to being a dog chew."

I got up, walked back to the dressing room, and told the boys backstage, "Don't worry about the payoff. I already got screwed."

At Wrestlemania 6, I'll never forget a woman who was sitting in the front row with her husband. I managed the Barbarian that evening, and he used to wear a leather and fur vest with chains. It looked like he found it on the road. After the match, this woman and her husband came backstage, and she approached me to see if she could have his vest.

I went back and asked the Barbarian and he said, "No."

I told her that he wasn't there.

The woman turned out to be Mary Tyler Moore. What the hell was she going to do with leather, fur, and chains?

Wrestlemania 6 also featured my ring return against Terry Taylor, who was then known as the Red Rooster. For the record, it wasn't my idea to give him that gimmick, and I didn't want to manage him anyway. Vince asked me if I would. Sometimes you say yes just for the TV exposure. Besides, it was stupid enough, and I thought I could have some fun with it.

That Wrestlemania match was a popcorn match. It was right before the main event, and that's when people go out to get their popcorn. It was timed, and we had some spots set up to go six to seven minutes. Vince walked up to us before the match. "All we need is 30 seconds."

I told Terry, "I'll give you a turnbuckle charge, you move, I'll hit the post, and bounce back, and you pin me."

"But we've got five minutes of spots to do."

I told him, "After the match, when we get to the back, you can do them."

They wanted him to work less for the same money. He really was a "Red Rooster."

My last Wrestlemania was the ninth one. Everyone was dressed up like they were from the Roman empire. I was supposed to come out on a camel wearing a toga. Now anybody could come out on a camel properly, but I decided to come out backward just to be "the Brain" and be different. Randy Savage even pulled my robe up to reveal my bright blue shorts. Wearing that muumuu was kind of scary. I kind of liked it.

Chapter 6

FROM MANAGER TO BROADCAST JOURNALIST

Just like a pretty girl doesn't like other pretty girls, Andre the Giant didn't like big wrestlers. I remember when Manute Bol—a basketball player from Nigeria who was taller than Andre—would come to the Capital Centre in Washington. Andre would never go out and meet him because of something Vince McMahon Sr. told him. Vince said not to let anyone see Andre with someone who is bigger than he is. Andre had to be the biggest man in the world.

John Studd wanted to be the biggest guy in the business, but he couldn't because of Andre.

When Andre would work with Studd, he would really bump him around. Studd couldn't take bumps because of his size. He would get in the ring with Andre and get pulverized, even losing some hair and getting some teeth loosened. Andre wanted Studd to stay on him and beat him down, and John simply didn't want to make him mad.

On television, Studd would say he was the real giant, and I think Andre believed some of his interviews.

I wasn't aware that the WWF was going to turn Andre heel in 1987. He walked up to me one day and said, "We're going to have some fun, boss." I was confused because I wasn't managing him at the time.

A few days later, Vince approached me and said, "Andre would like you to be his manager."

That was quite an honor. No one had ever managed him before, and he never wanted to be associated with anybody else. Andre always talked for himself. I think he just felt I was over and he could trust me.

It was Andre's idea to pass the torch to Hulk Hogan and to have the match at Wrestlemania 3. The finish was clear. Hogan would make a comeback, slam Andre, and pin him. But you have to know that once you got your hands between Andre's legs and lifted him up, if he wanted to go forward, you couldn't stop him. He could hold you down and tell that referee, "Count!" That referee would count. I would have even run in the ring and counted.

I don't think Hogan ever wanted to work with Andre because I don't think he trusted Andre. Trust is very important in the ring. And when Andre wanted something, he took it. Baron Von Raschke once explained to me why Andre had bad teeth and even worse breath: "Do you know what that's from? Eating handfuls of villagers."

Andre was a natural heel because he grew to hate people. Fans would walk up to him and ask questions like, "How tall are you?" "How much do you weigh?" and "Are you Andre the Giant?"

No, he was Willie Shoemaker. Who do you think he was?

He turned babyface at Wrestlemania 6 when he lost the tag-team title he held with Haku. After the match, he was supposed to attack me and slap me around. I saw that big paw coming down, but I moved to the left. I thought he was going right to left, but he missed me. His hand moved back to the left, and I was moving my face to the right, and he connected. He was paint-brushing the hell out of me, and I couldn't tell him to stop. It was like driving a golf ball in a bathroom. I didn't know where he was coming from.

But turning back to a babyface didn't change how he felt about the people.

While I would have memberships to all the airline clubs so I could go into the lounges and not be bothered, Andre wanted to sit in the hall. But everybody would bother him, and in turn he would swear at them. I'd ask Andre to come into the lounge with me, but he refused. Again, it was something Vince McMahon Sr. told him years ago. Everyone must see him, and he must be out in public. Andre became bigger than life, and he hated it.

Andre did have an escape. He had a favorite French restaurant in Connecticut. The food was just like his mom used to cook. He could sit there in quiet and nobody bothered him. They served liver, tongues, lips, and lungs. I used to call the place "The Autopsy Grill."

They had an old guy at the "Grill" named Charlie who played the piano. I told him once, "One of these days, you're going to be on the menu here."

Before his WWF career, Andre would travel the country, wrestling in many territories. At that time there were at least 30 in the United States and Canada. Everyone who worked with Andre referred to him as "Boss." Why "Boss"? Think of the old question of where a bear sleeps. Anywhere he wants to. Replace "bear" with "Boss," and that summed up Andre.

He even held the *Live with Regis and Kathy Lee* show hostage. Regis wanted to go to commercial, and Andre kept threatening Regis, yelling, "No."

Andre hated to wrestle in the AWA. Verne Gagne always booked him to wrestle twice: a match on the card and the battle royal.

Andre thought he was a special attraction and should wrestle only once.

He would have said something about it, but he was usually booked higher up on the card with an opponent that would draw. Even though he hated doing it, Andre worked twice for the good of the promotion. But when he would work the singles match, he'd wrestle only a couple of minutes. And although he won most of the battle royals, there were times when he would just throw himself out of the ring if he was in a bad mood. However, not before backing up six wrestlers in the turnbuckle with his rear end and executing a unique, lethal, and very common "finishing move" for him: passing gas that sounded more like thunder.

Nonwrestlers were not immune to Andre's "finisher." He would do it in elevators with a bunch of old women in there. He'd scowl at them and yell, "Quit it."

Andre's mood would depend on the town. We were in Rapid City, South Dakota, with the AWA, and he clearly didn't want to be there. He got in the ring, obviously tanked, looked at everybody, and again eliminated himself from the battle royal.

A few days later, I was serving as the agent backstage when Verne Gagne walked up to me and said, "I hear Andre is finishing his matches too early."

I said, "Well, that's Andre."

He said, "You keep him in there."

I said, "Verne, if I had a Thompson submachine gun, I couldn't keep him in there. When the man 'goes home,' he 'goes home.' Goodnight, Mr. Gagne."

I bumped into Andre once at O'Hare Airport. I hadn't seen him in about 10 years. This big paw grabbed me by the shoulder. I turned around, and there he was with his plaid suit and big hair.

"Boss, how have you been?" I asked.

"You have drink with me," Andre demanded.

"I can't. I've got to catch a plane to Omaha. I've only got 10 minutes."

He wouldn't let go. "No, you have drink with me."

"No, I have to go, please."

"Well, good to see you."

Andre left, and I walked about 10 more steps when a couple of businessmen—Bob Newhart types—asked me, "Who was that?"

I said, "I don't know, but I was on my way to my plane and he grabbed me and asked me to go into the bathroom with him."

They both screamed, "Oh my God," and ran in the opposite direction of where Andre was going.

Andre used to like to have a few eye-openers in the morning. Well, in the afternoon and at night too. We were sitting in a bar on 47th Street in New York. Andre sat there and played cards while consuming 86 beers.

One day, he had maybe seven or eight double or triple vodkas at the airport waiting to board a 7:00 A.M. flight. After finishing his "usual," he got on the plane. Immediately, he started pulling up the armrest in first class to give himself more room.

The flight attendant walked up and asked him, "Sir, can I get you anything?"

"Yes. Screwdriver," Andre said.

He finally pulled the armrest up and sat down. The flight attendant came back and handed him a screwdriver—an actual screwdriver, a Stanley screwdriver.

Andre looked at the screwdriver, then at her and said, "What would you have brought me if I had said 'Bloody Mary'?"

I approached the flight attendant and took her into the galley. "This is something that might get you by in life," I said to her, imparting some words of wisdom. "A guy gets on the plane and it's 7:00 in the morning. He's got a plaid suit on. He's 7'4" and 550 pounds. He's got hair like the MGM lion. And he's drunk.

"Don't bring him tools!"

We went to the Marriott in Kansas City. At midnight, they had "last call." The bartender came up to me and asked, "Is Andre here with you this time?"

"No," I said.

"Oh, thank God," the bartender said. "Last time he was here, I gave him last call and he didn't want to leave. I told him that I could only stay as long as he was drinking."

Andre ordered 40 vodka tonics and sat and drank them until 4:00 in the morning.

I met Rob Reiner at the Comedy Awards in Los Angeles after Andre died. He was the producer of *The Princess Bride*, a movie that Andre appeared in.

I introduced myself to him. He said, "Boy, Andre was quite a guy."

I said, "He certainly was."

"Do you know what his bill was at the Hyatt in London the month we shot the movie with him?"

"No."

"Forty thousand dollars. And there wasn't one movie on the bill. He never left the bar."

Women loved Andre. One night, he "got romantic" with a petite young lady in his hotel room. The problem was he didn't bother to close the curtain on his first-floor hotel room. Sheik Adnan al-Kaissie and some other Arab gentlemen walked by and witnessed the whole event. There was Andre the Giant with his big mane of hair and this small young lady. I asked Adnan what it looked like.

He said, "It looked like a lion raping a rabbit."

Andre had his share of women. Flight attendants would approach us on the planes. "We have to ask you guys something about him. Could we?"

"I know what you're going to ask us," I'd say. "You're going to ask how 'big' he is."

"You don't know, do you?"

I held my hands apart wide.

"See, I told you," one stewardess would say to the other.

One night, we were in a bar in Atlanta owned by Tim Woods, who wrestled as Mr. Wrestling. Andre saw this woman who was quite well endowed on top. He walked over to her and said, "Let me see them."

The girl took her bra off under her shirt, gave it to him, and said, "If you go across the street and put it on the horse, I'll show you."

Across the street was a bar called The Crystal Club. On the roof of the bar was a wooden horse. Andre, at 3:00 in the morning, forced the cook out to the roof of the bar with a ladder. Andre climbed to the top of the horse and put the bra on it while the poor cook was holding the ladder.

He climbed down the ladder and returned to the bar. The girl was long gone by then, but the horse across the street never looked better.

WWF referee Tim White once said that Andre had no shame. He used to drive Andre's van to the arenas. I'd ride with him, and Arnold Skaaland would play cards with him. We were in Glens Falls, New York, for a television taping. WWF television was always set up with every inch of the backstage area used. Andre couldn't find a place to play cards so he moved his table to the other side of the curtain, which was the hallway where people would be coming in later.

There he was, playing cribbage with Tito Santana. Around 7:00, people started to walk down the hall and Andre was sitting there playing cards—naked. And he actually finished the game.

Andre never wore a coat. It could be the dead of winter. He would be wearing shoes with no socks, pants, and a shirt that was open. Sometimes he wore a sports coat, sometimes not—he would if he decided to take it off the car that night or it wasn't covering the pool.

When he wasn't sitting around in the nude, Andre had a tendency to leave his shirt open in public. Once we were eating at a Chinese restaurant when the waitress ran up and yelled, "Button shirt. Button shirt."

Andre ignored her.

"Button shirt!"

Andre said to her, "If I can't show you my chest, then I will show you my ass."

And he mooned the whole restaurant.

Andre was sitting in a country and western bar with his shirt wide open. A little bouncer walked by and said, "Hey, you have to button your shirt."

Andre said nothing and kept drinking.

"I told you to button your shirt."

Nothing.

The manager walked up to him and said, "Sir, you have to button your shirt."

The manager called the police. "Barney" showed up, all by himself. "Sir, you have to button your shirt."

Andre said nothing. The cop actually called for backup.

Several officers were now in the bar. The sergeant approached him and said, "You have to button your shirt."

Andre said nothing.

"OK, stand up," the sergeant said, obviously ready to take Andre into custody.

Andre stood up and never stopped. The cop watched him get out of that chair and kept watching and watching and watching, realizing how big Andre was.

The sergeant turned to the other cops, "You know, it is hot in here."

A Japanese wrestler named Kochika tried to break Andre's leg once just to see how tough he was. What a mentality this man had. He was 6'3" and about 260 pounds facing a guy the size of Andre.

I asked Andre, "What did you do to him, Boss?"

"Do you know how to put on a full nelson?" he asked.

Picture a full nelson. One wrestler stands behind another wrestler. The first wrestler (in back) puts his hands in front of the second wrestler and then brings them up behind the neck of the second wrestler so that the first wrestler's arms are wrapped around the arms of the second wrestler.

I said to Andre, "Yes."

"Then I stood in front of him."

I was trying to picture Andre having this man in a full nelson and then stepping in front of him with his hip.

"What did you do then?" I asked.

"I fell forward."

"What happened to him, Boss?"

Andre put his hand over his mouth, laughed, and yelled, "Coma!"

Japanese fans are funny. In America, if you run into the stands and attack the fans, you get sued. In Japan, you can chase them and throw chairs at them. Tiger Jeet Singh used to take his saber sword and slap people with it. Stan Hansen used to take his bull-whip with the cowbell and whip people with it. The fans would run like hell, and when you stopped chasing them, they'd sit back down like nothing happened.

I managed Andre once in Japan. He was supposed to wrestle on the roof of a supermarket five stories up. They asked Andre not to chase the people because they thought the people might run off the roof.

Andre said, "For $10,000, I won't chase them."

The promoter came back and gave him 10 grand.

After Wrestlemania 3, I "sold" Andre to Ted DiBiase. The WWF wanted somebody to work with Andre as a tag-team partner. I couldn't manage DiBiase because he had Virgil. It never made sense to me. I sold Andre, the only man who could win me a championship, but I kept "the King" Harley Race. Go figure.

A few years later, I wanted to get out of managing altogether because of my neck. It was a great career, and I had done nearly everything except manage a woman or wrestle a woman. (That wasn't by choice. It just never came up. Bruiser didn't use them. Verne Gagne didn't use them either when I was in the AWA.)

I was managing "Mr. Perfect" Curt Hennig at the time I retired, and I "sold" him to "Coach" John Tolos. John was one of those old-timers hanging around and looking for a payday.

I became a "broadcast journalist," a term that Vince McMahon came up with. When I was doing color commentary while being a manager, it was very hard. I could never get the other guy over because I had to talk more about my man. I couldn't get the other heels over. If I managed Rick Rude, I couldn't talk about how good Ted DiBiase was because I had to put all my attention to my wrestler or I didn't consider myself a good manager.

"DiBiase is good," I'd say. "He's got millions and millions of dollars in Swiss banks. But look at the body on Rick Rude. I know money buys everything, but Rude is at his peak right now."

If I said nobody could beat DiBiase, that means my man couldn't beat him. Being just a commentator was easier. I could be middle-of-the-road and still be the heel. It was an easy transition and no problem at all. It was something I wanted to do.

In all reality, wrestling doesn't need a play-by-play guy. Most play-by-play guys came from radio, where you'd have to describe everything because no one was seeing it. You don't need to do what Tony Schiavone does. It was best when it was me and Mike Tenay and we would talk about the angle they were working, what would happen the next time the two wrestlers met, and what they were capable of doing.

You don't need to call out moves, like clotheslines and Irish whips. (Actually, I think I knew an Irish whip. Her name was Madeline, and she was from Connecticut.)

Jim Ross was always very prepared. The times I worked with him, he always had everything down, including football, baseball, and amateur wrestling stats. He's a very educated and well-prepared announcer. He's not well liked by a lot of guys because he was put into positions where he had to deal with contracts and other people's money that didn't belong to him.

Randy Savage was great to work with too. He was very professional. If I had a territory, I would have Randy, his brother Lanny Poffo, and their father Angelo working for me. Because they'll always be there on time. They'll always care about the business and do what is right. They know what they should do and shouldn't do. They're businessmen.

Lanny's heart was in the business because he is from a wrestling family, but he was in the shadow of Randy. That's the way things work sometimes. Jack Brisco was more valuable than Jerry. Dory Funk Jr. was nothing like Terry. Lanny needed a gimmick, and he needed a manager. And even though he managed guys like Curt Hennig and the Beverly Brothers, none of the guys wanted him around for the most part. They didn't look at him as a manager but as an underneath guy. Associating with him made them seem "underneath." (An underneath guy is someone who isn't in the main event—an undercard or midcard wrestler.)

Vince was tremendous to work with on television. At the beginning, I was scared because I didn't like working with the boss. But Vince wasn't the kind of guy that ever yelled at you. If you screwed up, he would calmly tell you how you should do it.

I was doing an interview once where I was making fun of Bruno Sammartino and how old he was. Vince walked by and bumped the camera. "Uh oh," he'd say. "Retake." Most bosses in this business would yell, "Cut, goddamn it, you can't say that."

Not Vince. He pulled me aside and quietly said, "Bruno really doesn't like it when you talk about his age and things like that."

He was smooth. He never yelled. I went out there and did it the way he wanted it. I'm the kind of guy who could never play for Vince Lombardi. If you yell at me, I'll go home. If you compliment me and give me a pat on the back, I'll work harder. I'm not the kind of guy who is motivated by yelling.

Verne was a yeller. That's why he didn't have any hair; he would knock it off his head with his hand. He'd never say, "Jesus." He'd say, "Jeez." He'd never say, "Christ." He'd say, "Cripes." He would get so mad.

About a year after I retired, Vince approached me with an idea. He told me that Ric Flair was coming in and was going to eventually take the WWF title. He wanted me to manage Flair. From the first time he told me about it, I didn't want to do it. I was still hurting. I lost my heart for it. I used to like to take bumps at the end of matches and be brought in and thrown into the turnbuckles. I didn't love to work and it wasn't fun anymore. And my deal was that I wasn't going to manage anymore. But I knew that if I didn't do it, they would dump me over it.

Flair told me that Hogan wanted to work and go on the road for six months with me.

Flair came in with the WCW title belt, and we showed it on WWF television, but the attorneys got involved, so we had to stop. I agreed to manage him, but I only lasted 10 days. I just couldn't work anymore. It hurt so bad, I couldn't sleep at night. I never took pills or medication. I had beer, scotch, and wine to help.

Flair would say, "You don't have to do anything, just stand there."

I said, "I can't. I'm going to reach a point where I have to move. When my man is hit, I've got to sell it."

The travel schedule was grueling as well. You worked ten days on, four days off, ten on, three off, four on, three off, ten on. That's the way it went all the time. But if you finish up in Seattle, one day is used up for travel. When you get home, you have laundry and bills, and you're counting the time. "I've got 28 more hours here," you'd say. You'd go to bed and the next day you'd get up and have to rush everything in one day. "I have one day left," you'd say.

I had to carry wrestling shoes, trunks, three sequined jackets—which weighed a ton—and pants and a shirt for *Prime Time,* a show I cohosted with Gorilla Monsoon. I carried my manager shoes, which were Reeboks, but everyone called them my "Weasel Wedgies." Not to mention clothes to wear on the street. I had a lot of luggage to carry and I had to carry it on, because I needed it to arrive where I was going. Carrying all those bags, renting cars, and rushing to planes was really hard. On my off days, I had to go to Baltimore and do *Prime Time Wrestling.* Then there might be a personal appearance. Sometimes I didn't get a day off.

Jim Neidhart worked 80 days in a row. I asked him, "How many frequent-flier miles do you have?"

He said, "How the hell do I know? I'm never home to answer the mail."

The travel reminded me of one year I worked with the AWA. Once a month, I would go finish up in Toronto on Sunday and fly to Chicago and then 10 hours to Honolulu. I was off Monday night, and Tuesday I could go to the beach all day. On Wednesday night, I would work. Afterward, I would take planes from Honolulu to Los Angeles to Denver to Minneapolis to Winnipeg. I'd work Winnipeg Thursday night and get up at 6:00 the next morning to do TV interviews until 10:00. I'd fly from there to Denver to work and then to Minneapolis the next day to tape the TV show and then rush to the airport to catch a 5:00 flight to Chicago. From there, we would rent a car and drive 70 miles to Rockford. We'd stay in Chicago that night, but the next morning, we would drive 250 miles to Green Bay. I would then drive to Milwaukee to catch a plane back to Indianapolis.

I managed Flair for a short period of time. I just didn't want to be on the road. This business is funny. When you want to do something, they won't let you do it. But when you don't want to do it, they *make* you do it.

Curt Hennig replaced me as Flair's "Executive Consultant." I was an influence on him and he even wore a suit with "Mr. Perfect" embroidered on the back. Vince McMahon called it his "Bobby Heenan Starter Kit."

A few months later, in November of 1992, the Ultimate Warrior left the WWF. The WWF wanted to turn Curt babyface and team him with Randy Savage at Survivor Series against Flair and Razor Ramon, also known as Scott Hall. I told McMahon to have him turn on me on *Prime Time Wrestling*, which had become a roundtable show with me, Curt, McMahon, and other WWF wrestlers. I would say something bad to Curt, he'd grab me, and I'd start begging. He could dump some water on me, and I'd turn chickenshit.

I suggested to McMahon that Flair go out first at the 1992 Royal Rumble and win it. He had him come out second and changed it to make it his own idea. Vince liked to do that. When Sean Waltman joined the WWF in 1993, I came up with his gimmick name of the 1-2-3 Kid. He was going to wrestle Scott Hall, and I suggested that Hall put him over. Scott didn't care, so he did. We were in the car going back to Connecticut with Vince, Pat Patterson, and James J. Dillon. Vince asked, "What should we call him?"

"We should call him the Lightning Kid."

"Can't do that," Vince said. "There's already something with that name."

"Why not call him the 1-2-3 Kid?" I suggested. "He just got a 1-2-3."

He actually liked that idea and used it.

Flair was a natural from the beginning coming into the WWF. When he first started with Verne, he was the size of Dusty Rhodes and had brown hair. My first encounter with him, from what I was told, was when he was a fan and I punched him in the mouth one night outside of the Minneapolis Auditorium. I don't remember that, but he told me the story much later.

Flair got his break down in Charlotte, North Carolina, after a plane crash that almost ended his career. Just looking at him, you knew that they had to put the world title on him. Nobody had hair like him. Well, Hogan did, but he had only half of it. Sort of like a convertible with the top down.

Flair always wore the nice clothes and the Rolex watches. He wouldn't mind ripping those clothes apart during interviews. Thousands of dollars it must have cost him, but I'm sure the Crockets (promoters in the mid-Atlantic area and in the NWA) compensated him for that.

Flair had the colorful attire and the "Whoo." You could just see that he was the next "Gorgeous George." The torch went to him. Flair came on the scene and he was never nervous. He always admired me and Ray Stevens, and I appreciate him for that. He always spoke highly of us, and I can only talk about Ric like that. He was a tremendous performer. He never laid on his ass. He never took a night off, and he went out there and took slams off the top rope for anyone just to get them over in a match.

Chapter 7

TOUGH DECISIONS

During my final years with the WWF, there were investigations about steroid use and molestation of young boys who served as ring attendants.

There was no doubt in my mind that wrestlers used steroids. Hulk Hogan admitted it. Other people have. Other people haven't. In my experience, I've never seen a guy shoot himself up. They didn't do it in the dressing room around me because I didn't do it. I never saw it. Besides, this is a cutthroat business and there would be some guy who would run to the promoter and say, "I saw so-and-so with a turkey baster up his ass. What do we do?" Vince McMahon was acquitted and cleared of any involvement. Honestly, I simply don't know if steroids were in the WWF locker rooms or not.

There was a big stink made about it. That trial cost Vince millions of dollars and the jury found him not guilty. It came down to Vince having a lot of money and a great lawyer. Justice prevailed. I had to go before the grand jury about steroid use in the WWF. I told them the truth—I never saw steroids. I saw a lot of guys with paper bags, but that was it.

I know that George Zahorian, the doctor who was convicted in another trial, would show up in Hershey wearing a long, white coat and carrying two big doctor bags. There would be a line outside his door. I went to him once to get some water pills to lose some weight I was retaining. He offered to give them to me for five bucks a pill. Then he told me I'd have to urinate all the time. I couldn't do a broadcast for three hours when I had to pee every 30 seconds. Besides, I could have gotten a prescription for the pills from my own doctor.

As for the molestation, these were young guys who wanted to get into the business like I did. Many were troubled souls from broken homes. When I saw them, I could tell they had problems. I put up the ring too when I was a kid. I carried the jackets as well. But I was never propositioned by a man or forced into a sexual relationship to get ahead in the business or keep my job.

At least Crusher didn't kiss like he was gay.

No one ever propositioned me. I knew Mel Phillips, a WWF ring announcer, was a little odd because of the stories I've heard about a foot fetish, but that's all hearsay. I don't know the personal lives of the rest of the WWF staff and whether they were gay or not.

I didn't pay attention to those guys. I don't look at guys. When I get into the dressing room, I try to rib them—hide their shoes or do something important.

There are single guys who fool around. There are married guys who go back to their rooms alone. There are guys who want to "smoke" a little. There are guys who want to drink a little. And there are guys who don't do anything.

I was at Video One, Vince's television studio. When Vince would audition announcers, he would always want someone else to do an interview with them. They would send me in with the person who was auditioning to do two different kinds of interviews, one with a babyface and one with a heel. The prospective announcer would introduce me and I would walk onto the set. When I'd play the heel, I'd say, "Where did you come from? How did you get this job? Do you know somebody with power?" Some would come back with stupid comments.

One day, I'm in the studio and I see this person auditioning. (He later sued the WWF claiming that a WWF employee sexually harassed him.) I overheard Vince say, "Who the hell is that?"

"That's the guy that's auditioning for the announcing job," said one of the production people.

"Huh," Vince grunted. That was never a good sign.

The new announcer came to a production meeting and he was introduced to everyone. I never saw anyone approach him. Vince simply didn't like his style. I heard the stories about him getting propositioned, but I don't think he was around long enough. Vince didn't even know who the guy was. As Monsoon would say, "Don't commit his name to memory. He won't be here that long." And he wasn't. It just didn't work out.

Vince told us that when everything was going good, people wanted to knock you and bring you down. We thought that's what was going on. Nothing ever came of it. Vince is still in business and he still has his people.

My WWF contract was up in 1993, and Vince McMahon gave me an offer for a new contract. A week later, he told me that he couldn't honor that offer and wanted me to take a 50 percent pay cut. I didn't want to do that. I was tired of going to New York, tired of crowds, and tired of people. It was just hard to get around. I decided it was time to go.

At the production meeting before my last show, Vince asked me how I wanted to leave. I told him to have Gorilla Monsoon just throw me out after going through my bags and finding stolen towels, light bulbs, ashtrays, and phonebooks. Everything from a hotel. That's what "the Brain" would do.

Pat Patterson asked me, "Why don't you have a bra and panties in there too?"

"Well, Pat, I think when we travel, you and I pack differently," I told him.

Vince agreed to it. So Gorilla came to ringside where I was doing commentary. He threw me and my bag out of the building. I gave my farewell and walked around the back. Gorilla was waiting for me in his car, and we drove to the LaGuardia Holiday Inn.

We quietly stood in the elevator, which took us to the floor where our rooms were. I turned to him and said, "Well, nine years together. Good luck, partner." I shook his hand. He went his way. I went mine.

I got into my room. There was a big basket of fruit in there, all bananas. I called Gorilla. "I have some bananas here. Do you want them?" He came down the hall, and I gave him his favorite fruit. We must have hugged and cried for an hour.

Gorilla Monsoon's real name was Robert Marella. Before he wrestled, he was a singer in Toronto called Gino Marella.

Doing *Prime Time* in a studio and voice-over work for *Wrestling Challenge* was repetitious since we were seeing the same match four to five times a week. But working with Gorilla Monsoon was a joy—the highlight of my career. He was the most honest, gentle, intelligent man I ever met.

He had a tremendous mind. He was educated and smart. And he knew about the human body, including all the muscles and parts.

He would yell, "He kicked him in the gluteus maximus."

I'd say, "Yeah, he kicked him in the butt."

He loved to gamble, playing blackjack and cards. He always carried about $25,000 in cash. I would ask him, "What would you do with all that money?"

He'd say, "What if I want to buy something?"

"What? A house?" I said. "If you're driving through Green Bay, maybe you should buy the football team and a bratwurst."

He was very family oriented and when Joey, his boy and a referee for the WWF, was killed in a car accident, that took his heart out of him. When I left and there was no more *Prime Time*, his desire to work diminished.

Prime Time Wrestling, the show we cohosted on the USA Network, was the number one show on that channel. We didn't have the number of homes with cable that they do today, but we were getting sixes and sevens in the Nielsens. We didn't just do wraparounds of the matches; we sat there for three hours and watched them. Gorilla wanted to do it that way. If something happened in a match, we could talk about it. And we never once used a script.

The best *Prime Time* we ever did was on Halloween one year. We sat out on the set with Monsoon wearing a big ape suit with his sports coat over it. He was wearing his Rolex and his ring that said "Gino" on it. We did the whole show with him wearing the mask.

Toward the end of the show, we took one of the cameramen who was the same size as Monsoon and put him in the gorilla suit with the jacket. Monsoon was standing offstage when the cameras started rolling. I was wrapping the show up when Monsoon ran onto the set with luggage, saying, "I'm sorry I'm late."

"Who the hell have I been with for two hours?" I cried. And we went off the air.

In addition to his television duties, Monsoon would sit backstage in the aptly named "Gorilla position," directing traffic during tapings. On television, the finishes of the matches were carefully timed out. If it was a six-minute match, Gorilla would say to Mel Phillips, the ring announcer, through his headset, "Give it to 'em, Mel" after four minutes. Mel would put a pencil in his mouth. When the referee or the wrestlers saw the pencil in his mouth, they knew they had two minutes to finish the match.

The appropriate time came and Gorilla said, "Give it to 'em, Mel." Mel put the pencil in his mouth. But the wrestlers wouldn't "go home." "Home" signifies the dressing room and "going home" means that you end the match. Monsoon kept yelling into the headset, "Give it to 'em, Mel." By this time, Mel had four pencils in his mouth and no one was looking at him.

The 6'8", 400-pound "ape" calmly put his headset down and walked into the arena, past all the people who don't know the inner workings of the business. He got to the edge of the ring and bellowed loudly enough for everyone to hear:

"Go home!"

We stayed in touch after I left. I would visit him and we would talk on the phone every week. Gorilla is one of my best friends in life. He is dearly missed by me and my family. I love that man.

One of the few times I didn't work with Monsoon was when McMahon wanted to do a half-hour program called *The Bobby Heenan Show*. It was basically a half hour within the block that *Prime Time* had. I would have guests on the show, including Heather Hunter, who was a porn star.

McMahon had Jim Troy go to the USA Network to make the deal, but the guy never went and did it. McMahon had a contract with USA for two hours of wrestling. The USA claimed that they weren't getting two hours of wrestling, but 90 minutes of wrestling and a half hour of *The Bobby Heenan Show*. They were never talked to about it and never gave their OK. That was different programming in their eyes. We ended up doing only four episodes.

The Bobby Heenan Show was fun, but it was hard to do at first. There was no audience and no band. I was making fun of these people on the show, but there was no timing and no one laughing. It was like looking in the mirror and telling yourself jokes. It just wasn't funny.

The Rosatti sisters served as my "Oink-ettes" for the show. They were really sisters and longtime wrestling fans from around

Poughkeepsie, New York. Vince liked them for some reason and always gave them front-row seats. They weren't "rats" (unattractive wrestling groupies) and didn't do anything with the boys.

One night they were sitting in the front row of Madison Square Garden wearing pig snouts. I had Howard Finkel give me the microphone. In front of 20,000 people, I said, "Be quiet for a minute. This is very important."

I pointed to the Rosattis and their pig snouts. "Look at these three. Look at their faces. Can you imagine that?

"They're actually wearing lipstick."

Vince eventually changed the format of *Prime Time* because he likes change. I also think that the original *Prime Time* was doing so well, there was a jealousy factor with some people. I've learned that, in this business, there are some that will cut their nose off to spite their face.

Vince and I cohosted the new *Prime Time*, this time with a "live audience" that was actually WWF office employees. After work, they'd have to come over and sit in the audience. And they couldn't go home until we were done. We taped three shows, and Vince was the kind of guy that if he started live TV at 8:00, he started at 8:00. But if he started taping at 8:00, he started at 10:30 because he didn't have to go on the air live. He ran everything during the show, taking phone calls and being bugged by people with problems and questions he had to answer.

We'd usually be done by midnight. Regular wrestling fans would have gone home. The employees were not even allowed to go to the bathroom during the taping, because you would have empty spots in the audience. We weren't the Academy Awards where we had people to fill spots. It was a long day for all of us.

On the show, Vince would still wear colorful outfits, but these were wild-looking sweat suits—merchandise he was advertising for the World Bodybuilding Federation. I would tease him, "Obviously, some cheap motel is missing a shower curtain."

Sean Mooney, another WWF announcer, eventually took over for Vince on *Prime Time*. After Sean left the WWF and was passing his resume around in the television industry, he never included his job in the WWF. He didn't even mention Titan Sports. There was absolutely no mention of wrestling. He was a handsome guy and looked good on TV, but maybe he was too good-looking. Maybe he would have looked too good in one of those sweat suits. Vince would not have liked that.

I left the WWF in December without a job. I really wanted to get into acting, doing commercials and endorsements. But no one wanted to touch me because of wrestling. I soon realized that to be an actor, you have to live in Los Angeles and be out there for all the calls. I didn't want to fly from Tampa.

I got a call from Eric Bischoff at WCW, and he made me an offer to work one day a week for the same money Vince had offered me. At that time, my daughter Jessica was going to the University of Alabama. I lived in Tampa and would work in Atlanta, which was only 200 miles from her. Once a week, I could go up and see her for lunch. That's why I took the job with WCW.

Chapter 8

WCW

In WCW, I began what would be the worst six years of my life. It was more unprofessional than any place I've ever worked.

I knew going in that it wasn't going to be the same as the WWF. I already knew guys who were there who had told me that it was run like a circus. I went there for the money and to be closer to home. The first week, I was in the booth to do voice-overs for the television shows with Tony Schiavone. I watched a guy throw a drop-kick, and it missed by about four to five inches. Tony didn't say anything.

I'd try to cover it by saying, "You know, Tony, a lot of people don't have that resiliency, when they see a drop-kick, to get out of the way and move back."

"Cut," Tony said to the production crew. He looked at me and said, "Don't cover it up. Don't bring any attention to it."

Inevitably, that missed drop-kick would show up in highlights after the match.

After a year there, I wanted to go back to the WWF. Around that time, I was calling a match with Brian Pillman against Eddie Guerrero at a Clash of Champions in January of 1995. I told everybody from the outset never to touch me. That was just a given. To this day, I have a bad neck. After my surgery in 1995, the doctor told me that he didn't know if my neck was stronger or weaker than it ever was.

When I did TV, I never watched the ring to call the action. I watched the monitor. You have to call what you see. I saw Pillman outside of the ring and I started talking to Tony Schiavone. I couldn't see Brian at all. Pillman came up behind me and pulled my coat down over my shoulders. I didn't know if it was a fan or what.

I stood up and said, "What the fuck are you doing?"

I threw my headset off and started walking up the aisle. I stopped myself and thought, "No, I'm going to finish it."

Eric Bischoff didn't like what Pillman had done. I said, "Hey, you hired the guy. What's he coming over touching me for?"

Pillman apologized too. I said, "That's OK. You scared me. I didn't know who it was."

They have since erased those tapes. There is no record of it anyplace unless someone taped the live broadcast. I honestly thought I was going to get fired for that.

I didn't like the idea that they didn't tell us what was going on. You never felt wanted there. You always felt like the foster kid from a domestic dispute who had to stay somewhere for a month. I made friends there who were professional and nice, but other than that, most of them were lucky to be working and have a job. They didn't have the training, mentality, or desire to do anything right. They were all very lucky to be with such a hillbilly company.

Begging off Pat Patterson. Although here in San Francisco Pat was one of the "good guys," everywhere else he went he was a heel.
Photo courtesy of Bobby Heenan's personal collection.

Me and the newly unmasked Super Destroyer Mark II–the future Sergeant Slaughter–who I managed at the time.

Photo by Michael Lano (wrealano@aol.com), reprinted courtesy of Bobby Heenan's personal collection.

With Ray Stevens (left) and Nick Bockwinkel (right).

Photo courtesy of Bobby Heenan's personal collection.

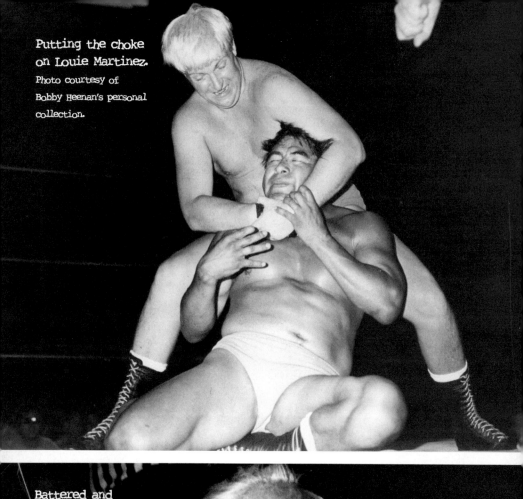

Putting the choke on Louie Martinez.
Photo courtesy of Bobby Heenan's personal collection.

Battered and bloodied once again.
Photo courtesy of Bobby Heenan's personal collection.

Moving in again on Louie Martinez.

Photo courtesy of Bobby Heenan's personal collection.

A much younger me with Angelo Poffo (left) and Chris Markoff (right).
Photo courtesy of Bobby Heenan's personal collection.

Cutting a promo with Angelo Poffo (left) and Chris Markoff (right).
Photo courtesy of Bobby Heenan's personal collection.

Being restrained by
the police while
going for the blade.
Photo courtesy of
Bobby Heenan's
personal collection.

With AWA World tag team champions Blackjack Lanza (left) and
Bobby Duncum (right).

Photo by London Publishing, used with permission.

With "Cowboy" Bob Orton.

Photo courtesy of Bobby Heenan's personal collection.

After production meetings in the WWF, Vince McMahon would say, "Let's go have some fun." After WCW production meetings, we'd say, "Let's go see if there's any free food left." But you'd go there and it would all be gone.

People from production would walk by you and they would never say hello or talk to you. There was this makeup girl who was promoted to executive producer because she was "taking it" from one of the other producers. She looked like Mount Rushmore and smelled like Grey Poupon. She couldn't put her own face on. She was going to make *me* look good?

There was another girl that worked there whom we called Wendy Turnbuckle. She was just a slob. She was clumsy and always spilling water. She'd grab a rag to clean it up, and she'd pull our headsets off.

One day, I saw her at the airport. Apparently, Wendy was a diabetic. She was lying on the floor of the terminal and gave herself a shot in her ass through her jeans. Of course, there was a croissant from Burger King lying next to her. Picture a big pig lying on the floor with a needle sticking out of her ass.

I leaned over to the guy sitting next to me and said, "Usually, when they use those dart guns, they'll take the tusks right off of her."

Everybody hated their jobs. It was the funniest place. For example, if someone was in charge of tapes and someone was in charge of pens, the person in charge of tapes would say, "Don't touch that tape. I'm in charge of it. I have to move that." The person in charge of pens would say, "Would you like to use my pen?" The tape person would say, "I don't want to get involved in that." They would do only what they had to do. No one would ever help anybody.

The production department wouldn't show replays with a guy coming off the top rope into a table. They'd show a guy locking up at the start of the match. They missed the good stuff. WCW always wanted to start a match in progress or show someone coming out of a limo. You don't see the Super Bowl start with a guy running the ball. You have to have an opening and the announcers have to talk about what you're going to see—set the stage for it. People who turn on wrestling and see a guy coming out of the car and walking into the building, they think they've missed something. They don't know where they're at in the show.

Keep in mind that the only reason to be in business is to draw money. You do that by increasing ratings and selling more advertising time so you get more people in the seats in the arena.

When the "Cat" Ernest Miller did his James Brown impersonation with the cape and the shoes, it was cute and people liked it. Someone got the idea to have the real James Brown come to the Cow Palace in San Francisco.

They signed James Brown for $10,000 for one night. At the beginning of the angle, Miller brought out a James Brown impersonator. "Cat" claimed it was James Brown. A couple of minutes later, the real James Brown came through the curtain. He got in the ring and did a little dance. Miller acted astonished.

Now, if someone is a promoter, booker, or writer and knew what they were doing in this business, the average moron would tell you that you announce that you're going to have James Brown at the show. You get him to come in a day early or have him do some sound bites for the local radio stations.

Eric's idea was, if the people missed it, they would buy the next pay-per-view. But what he didn't know was that the secret to selling anything was to advertise. He gave away 10 grand for nothing.

WCW even put the belt on actor David Arquette, which was a bad idea. But there was one nice thing about that whole situation: the money that Arquette made wrestling in WCW went to the families of the late Brian Pillman and Owen Hart. He didn't even know them. Everyone made fun of him, but they would have made fun of me if I had the lead role in *Gone with the Wind*. I don't belong in that part. He didn't belong as champion.

But that was WCW's philosophy. Double-cross everyone. Fool everyone. These ideas would make *Good Morning America* and the *Today* show. They laughed at poor Arquette and you never saw him on those phone commercials again.

Goldberg was the hottest thing that WCW ever had. People were standing outside the building chanting his name. Mark McGwire came to Atlanta because they both like to work out. Goldberg went to Fulton County Stadium and McGwire ripped off Goldberg's shirt and rubbed his bat on it. That year, he hit 70 home runs. Vince McMahon would have had people take McGwire to the Louisville Slugger company picking out the wood. He would have shown Goldberg working out in the same shirt before the visit.

WCW didn't send anyone to the stadium because it wasn't their idea. They never wanted to take responsibility for those kinds of things.

No one would make a decision on anything. And the decisions they did make were bad. They made Kevin Nash the booker, along with Terry Taylor and some other guys, and Nash went out and beat Goldberg, the hottest thing WCW had.

Nash shouldn't have beaten a man that was over like Goldberg was. The time to beat Goldberg was when it was time to pass the torch. Andre did that for Hogan. He let Hogan beat him. Plus, WCW needed to go all the way with Goldberg and build him up. But they didn't have that capacity.

Nash always loved showing two guys fighting in the back. But the camera would cut back to us and we would never comment on it. He had to do it like a television segment, as if we didn't know what was happening. When he would do something in the back, he would always clear out the hallway. He should have had people walking by to make it look normal. They always had fights in abandoned parts of the building. Why would they be in that part of the building? No one else was there.

When Goldberg's winning streak ended, that was the beginning of the end—that and the match between Hogan and Nash where Hogan pushed Nash down with one finger and pinned him. All that with 40,000 people in WCW's own backyard of Atlanta, the home of the company. After that show, Mike Tenay (another announcer) and I told Tony that the handwriting was on the wall.

He shot back with, "You bunch of paranoid sons of bitches!"

How are the Braves doing, Tony?

When I worked with Mike Tenay, we used to call his wife, Karen, "Fingers." Any saltshaker on a restaurant table went home with her. Mike never took a bump for a living, but he did when Jeff Jarrett hit him with a guitar. Most of the guitars were gimmicked. That one wasn't, and it hurt. I always wondered how many times Jarrett could hit someone with a guitar. He went through more of them than Johnny Cash.

Tenay was the perfect guy to make fun of with all the knowledge he had. Lee Marshall was hard to work with because he wouldn't come back on me like Monsoon did. What he didn't understand was that I'm six feet, 230 pounds, and a sneaky coward, and I used to wrestle. Monsoon used to wrestle and he was bigger than me. So, I was playing the coward and I had to back down from him. Marshall was just a dumpy-looking announcer. I couldn't be afraid of him and couldn't act that way. Just like I couldn't act afraid of Tony.

But Tenay was perfect. He would put me in my place with a whole bunch of words that had me confused. I would try to figure out what he would say about me, but I wouldn't fight him. Marshall was the kind of guy you'd want to hit. Guys like Gordon Solie you had respect for and wouldn't touch. Gene Okerlund, too. I never liked guys grabbing Gene during interviews.

Some would say that grabbing someone as if you were really going to assault them takes away your credibility, but that's ridiculous. If you're a masked guy who just ate a chair and teamed up with the Wolfman against two midgets and a woman in a cage, where is the credibility in the first place?

Mike is a real smart guy. Everything I needed to know I'd ask Mike because he eavesdrops on the wrestling world. He always did his homework but was dissatisfied in WCW. He would ask questions, and people would just scratch their heads. It was fun working with Mike, and I respect him and "Fingers" a lot. Wait a minute. Where's my wallet?

Eric Bischoff hired Steve McMichael to be a color commentator because Bischoff was a mark for McMichael. ("Mark" is normally a derogatory term that refers to a wrestling fan who believes that the sport is real; in this case, however, it just means that Bischoff had a blind devotion to McMichael and ignored any of his shortcomings.) McMichael was not a good wrestling announcer. And it's not because he was not a good announcer. For example, I couldn't do hockey for a couple of reasons. First, I can't say the names. They look like eye charts. Second, it's very hard to do hockey because it goes back and forth very quickly. McMichael was a good athlete and a good football player, but he just didn't know what to say or when to say it when it came to wrestling.

McMichael would say, "That guy is going to kill him," when you would never say that. I also think he found professional wrestling hard to get excited about and treat as real when he came from the Chicago Bears and the Super Bowl.

McMichael eventually became a wrestler. He debuted at the Great American Bash in 1996 when he teamed with Kevin Greene against Arn Anderson and Ric Flair, whom I managed that night. It was a match where McMichael turned on Greene and joined Anderson and Flair.

I don't care how good a shape you're in, whether you were a wrestler or a basketball player. You still can tell when a guy is out of wind. McMichael may have been able to play football all those years, but wrestling is different. A wrestler can blow up just from being nervous.

I was outside the ring, and I saw him on all fours sucking air. Just when I saw his stomach go in, I gave him a stiff boot in the gut and knocked the wind out of him. Back in the dressing room, he said, "Weasel, you got me."

"You can't tell anybody that," I said. "You played 10 years in the NFL. You have a Super Bowl ring. You're going to tell everyone that I kicked you and knocked the wind out of you?"

He never told a soul. I told everybody.

Up until the time I arrived in WCW, I never heard a wrestler say, "Let's go out there and put on a bad show," to screw the people. In WCW, I heard a couple of guys say that they had a bad match and they hoped they killed the town so they didn't have to come back. Whether there were a million people in those stands or 50, just entertain them. The fact that there were only 50 people in the stands was not their fault. It was the promotion's fault because they're not good enough on television to get people interested to come out and watch.

There were so many factions in WCW. Kevin Sullivan was the booker one week. Then it was Kevin Nash. Then Terry Taylor, who would never tell anybody the truth. Jimmy Hart would help. Arn Anderson would try to do his best. Mike Graham would try as well. But no one was told anything. One group wouldn't talk to another group. One group kept secrets from another group.

At Vince's production meetings, we would go over every part of what's going on. Anything to add? Anything to subtract? It would go on for two to three hours. I'd go into WCW production meetings, and they would read us a paper and that was it. I could read. Sometimes we would go out there for television, and we wouldn't get a format sheet until the second or third match.

WCW would also try to do these ridiculous "worked-shoots." One day in the hall, Diamond Dallas Page got in a fight with Buff Bagwell. They both wanted everyone to believe that it was real. But they were working, fighting in the hall in front of the boys. Dave Finlay, one of the other wrestlers, and I were sitting there laughing our asses off because they were using worked punches.

The ideas were interesting too. When Paul the "Giant" White, now known as the "Big Show," fell off of Cobo Hall at Halloween Havoc 1995, he came back for his title match with Hulk Hogan after falling off a 17-story building. They were going to put a fish in his trunks and say he fell into the Detroit River. I told people that they expected him to fall off the roof, so they put air bags on the ground to cushion his fall. What else are you going to say? A guy fell off the building and came back for his championship match?

No one at WCW knew how to promote the big man. He didn't know how to be a giant because he started taking bumps right away. Andre would never do that. The Giant was just a big guy who was an average wrestler. He was not a true "Giant."

The Nitro Girls were good. I didn't like them in the beginning because I didn't like Kimberly Page, who is married to Diamond Dallas Page. She had a bad attitude. She would say hi to you only if she wanted to. Before she was a Nitro Girl, she was just Dallas Page's armpiece. When she became the Nitro Girls' choreographer, she wouldn't talk to anyone. I didn't care. One less person I had to bother with.

The Nitro Girls could dance, and they looked good. But they started making them into wrestlers. They couldn't work, and no one wanted to see them work. It's like Elizabeth and all the other female managers. You can't have a woman manager. There's no payoff. If a manager gets involved in a six-man, the payoff is the cage match. You can't throw a woman in a cage and get blood all over her. And a man can't beat up a woman, unless it's Sherri Martel, who could kill anyone. No one wanted to see a man slam Liz or punch her. But they would want to see them do it to me.

The WWF is a wrestling company that needs television to survive. WCW was a wrestling company that just happened to be on TV because it was owned by a television company. We were the only thing making them money. We had better ratings than the Atlanta Braves, but WCW was always the whore sister of the Time Warner family—the kind that goes out every night, turns tricks, and makes money. The family lives in a big home, drives new cars, and dresses nice. But they don't want to tell anybody where they're getting the money.

We were making more money than any division of that company, but no one wanted to give us any credit for it because it was wrestling.

WCW was like the City of the Living Dead. No one spoke and there was no camaraderie. The underneath guys didn't like the Mexicans. The middle guys like Chris Benoit, Dean Malenko, and Eddie Guerrero were never going to get a break because Bischoff liked to use Kevin Nash and other big guys.

Most of the people in WCW couldn't find their ass with both hands.

I suggested an idea once on an angle with Cactus Jack and Maxx Payne. Eric told me, "We do all that. You just stick to announcing. You're just an announcer."

I said, "Fine." I never gave them another idea. It hit me. I would go in and get my check every two weeks. I had first-class airfare, expenses, guaranteed salary, medical, and I only worked a couple of days a week. I didn't care about anything. All I cared about was doing my job right and getting my money. I didn't care if a guy came out dressed like a goose. I just wanted to get out of there. It wasn't fun anymore. When it's not fun, it's hard to work and it comes across.

WCW was run by people who were not in the business. Sam Muchnick was never in the business. Neither was Dennis Hilgaard. Neither was Wally Karbo. But they knew how to promote. These guys in WCW, it wasn't their money, it was Ted Turner's money. They didn't have any idea how much money they were making or losing, nor did they care.

Sure, *Nitro* was number one for 83 weeks, but that was because of Vince McMahon. He was running those vignettes on Hogan being old and Savage being old. It made people aware of where Hogan and everybody were, so the fans started watching WCW.

During that time, the announcers were criticizing the WWF product on the air. I never knocked Vince one time. Eric Bischoff asked me once, "Are you still working for him?"

I said, "No, Eric, I'm not working for him. The reason I don't knock him is that I spent 10 years there. How stupid would I look to rip on the WWF? I'm hired by this company to put over this product. Sears people don't talk about JCPenney."

One night Vince had a prerecorded *Raw* show against a live *Nitro*. The WWF switched their title that night to Mankind. Eric announced the finish and what was going to happen on *Raw*. His mentality was that people would know the finish and not want to watch it. Everybody watched it. Vince did a seven that night in the ratings. We did a two.

Bischoff was even challenging Vince to matches in the ring. If that match ever happened, Vince would have killed him. Eric Bischoff is like every other guy that got into wrestling that didn't have the wrestling mentality or wasn't from the business. This guy was a kickboxer. I always called him "Kung Fu Charlie." He won different colored belts from some strip mall doing Tae Kwon Do with a bunch of 11-year-old kids barely touching each other.

Bischoff never did anything but kickbox. He'd threaten people. He was going to kick this guy's ass and this and that. I never had a problem with Eric. He gave me three contracts and two raises. But he just wasn't a friendly guy. He even admitted it when I asked him to go have a few beers with me.

To put it simply, Eric Bischoff wanted to be Vince McMahon. Vince is Neiman Marcus. Bischoff is Wal-Mart. He just couldn't be Vince. He didn't have it. Maybe he does for other things, but not for the wrestling. He told me one day, "I'm going to put the stake in Vince McMahon's heart, pull it out, and do it again."

That stake is located in someone else's body. And it's in a different area.

Bischoff would say to me, "You never took a company to the top for 83 weeks like I did."

I've been to the top in a lot of companies for 36 years, not for a year and a half. That's success if you can do it for more than that. Vince has done it. Bischoff hasn't.

They wouldn't tell us the finishes of the matches of the angles that were supposed to air. Bischoff justified that by saying, "We want you to react like it was a shoot."

I told him, "If it was a shoot, you know what we'd do? We wouldn't say anything. Because we've never seen one in the ring. Maybe it would be better to tell us so we can enhance the product."

We didn't even know that Hulk Hogan was turning at the Bash at the Beach in Daytona during the summer of 1996. They kept him in a car the whole time. We didn't even know he was in it. I knew he was there because I saw Brutus Beefcake, who is a long-time friend of Hogan's, hanging around.

They were so touchy at Turner. I used to make midget jokes when I worked for the WWF. Once I said, "Don't ever touch a midget. You never know where they've been. I saw the Haiti Kid doing sit-ups the other day under a '57 Chevy."

Nitro had a Mexican midget battle royal. Eric approached me and said, "Don't do anything insulting."

"First of all, Eric," I said, "you're talking not to Ray Heenan but to the character of Bobby Heenan. There are 12 midgets out there with masks on. What is Bobby Heenan going to say?"

"You can't. Midgets will write in."

"They can't reach the mail slot," I responded.

"Bobby," he said, "be careful."

What was I supposed to do? They all got in the ring and the only thing I could come up with was, "It looks like the ride at a daycare center."

I told Bischoff once that I could save him a fortune with the Lucha Libres.

"How?" he asked.

"You're bringing 12 guys in from Mexico City," I said. "Why don't you bring in two and keep 10 masks? They are all built the same and do the same moves. No one will know the difference."

Vince Russo took over for Bischoff in October of 1999. He said from the outset that he was going to hire actors. Anybody could do wrestling, he thought. He wanted to do everything in the business that worked and do it the opposite to see if it would still work. That mentality shows how well WCW was doing before the WWF bought them.

Russo was the editor of the WWF magazine. Everyone talks about how he and Ed Ferrara were writers there for WWF television. Truthfully, if they would give 20 ideas to McMahon, he would choose one of them and then turn around and do his own thing. Those weren't their ideas. Those were McMahon's.

Russo had no presence on television. He wore jeans and New York City T-shirts. He didn't look like an executive or the head of a company. Of course, neither did Eric. He started in WCW wearing suits, but then he became the boss.

Both Russo and Ferrara snowed WCW into putting all their faith into them. They were getting $500,000 a year apiece.

Russo didn't like me. He wanted a more youthful look, like an MTV look. So he replaced me with Mark Madden, a loudmouth slob from Pittsburgh who liked hockey. He shouldn't have been in that job.

I was with the company for six years. I missed two days of work—one for my mother-in-law's funeral, one because I had strep throat.

I called Tony Schiavone the day I was sick and he said, "That's OK." But Terry Taylor went nuts. He couldn't wait to hire Madden because they were both huge Internet fans. They called Madden and flew him from Pittsburgh to do *Nitro*.

Tony double-crossed me too. He would always say, "Knowledge is power," but he'd never tell you what was going on. He is a very insecure man.

Tony always had to have the higher chair in the middle. He told the stagehands that he had to have the middle chair higher. He would sit down, and I would reach for the lever so he'd sink. He got mad at that.

Tony was a real minor leaguer. For no reason other than to look like the WWF, management decided to change the look of *Nitro* and move us down to ringside, where, by the way, it's hotter with the lights on you. Tony decided to change his look and wear a leather jacket to the set. I think he maybe should have checked the calendar, as it was July. He was soaking wet the whole night, and Tony Schiavone doesn't keep well in warm weather.

Tony has not spoken to me since I left WCW. He never said good-bye to me. He knew it was coming, but he never told me that they weren't going to renew me. If knowledge is power, he wanted that power. In the time I worked for him, he never had me over to his house once even though we lived close to each other. I had him over to my house twice.

After I was released from WCW, I was out on New Year's Eve with the Tenays in Atlanta. My wife went to use the restroom downstairs. Cindi came back to tell me that Tony and his wife were at the bar. I walked downstairs and sat across the bar from Tony and just stared at him. Tony saw me and then would try to avoid looking at me. Finally, he left.

The next day, he told Tenay that he and his wife had to go home. They couldn't even eat because they were so upset. He couldn't figure out why I would stare at him and not acknowledge him. I told Mike what to tell him: "It's obvious I can't trust you. It's obvious you don't like me. There's nothing to say. So, if I can't trust you, I'm going to watch you."

I ruined his New Year's.

One week after I got sick with strep, Tony told me, "You're not going to be doing *Nitro*. They are going to try out different guys to see how they'll work down the road."

I said, "OK, what do you want me to do? Do you want me to do the pay-per-views?"

I figured I would ask Vince Russo. I approached him and asked him if he needed me for the pay-per-views. Tony ran up and stood right in front of me, probably winking at Russo. Russo said, "I'll get back to you on that."

He never did.

About the same time, WCW was fighting a lawsuit over racial discrimination filed by a bunch of wrestlers who felt the company wasn't using enough minorities. Suddenly, they made Booker T their world champion. They had Stevie Ray do the announcing. The Cat became the commissioner. If the allegations came up in court, WCW could defend themselves by saying that they had a black world champion, a black commentator, and a black commissioner.

They took me off *Thunder* and had me doing *Worldwide*, which was taped in Atlanta for syndication. It was just a horrible show with no production values. I was doing that once a week for 40 minutes. That was fine with me. I had lost my desire anyway. I didn't want to go to Sturgis, South Dakota, and all those goddamn places.

The pay-per-views in Sturgis were dangerous. All the bikers arrived at noon, and the pay-per-view didn't start until 7:00. They drank all day in the hot sun. There was no flooring, just gravel, which gave them something to throw.

I did the commentary with Tony Schiavone and Dusty Rhodes. When I walked out to the announcer's table, the people cheered me and I waved to them.

Dusty nudged me and said, "I thought you were a heel."

"Not when they have rocks and we're stationary. We wave to them."

All my desire was gone. I don't know if it affected my performance because I didn't know if it was bad or good. No one ever told me. We all have good and bad days. There were some matches that nobody cared about. There were some things you just could not hype. It's like a guy bringing you an 80-year-old hooker. She doesn't look good, so why does it matter?

In November of 2000, with my contract up in December but with an option for another year, my telephone rang. They didn't even have the class to bring me in. Craig Leathers, who hired the beautiful "Grey Poupon" lady, called me.

He said, "Bobby, I have some bad news."

I thought, "Oh no, they're going to re-up me."

"They decided not to pick up the option for the next year."

"How come?" I asked him.

"You make too much money for what you do."

I said, "Give me more to do."

"There isn't anything to do."

"You took me off *Nitro*, *Thunder*, and pay-per-views," I shot back. "You're paying three people to do what I did and still paying me my money."

Then Craig had the balls to ask me if I would work until the end of the year.

"Craig, you just fired me. You want me to work until the end of the year? I'll tell you what. I've never taken a vacation in the six years I've been here. I have three coming. I'll take the first three weeks of December off and come back for the last week. I sure hope I'm not rusty."

Needless to say, I didn't come back.

They wanted me to sign a paper to get paid until the end of the year, but it said that I wouldn't knock WCW in any way or make fun of them. They sent me the paper. I sent it to my attorney. They sent me another paper that said that if I didn't sign that paper and send it back, they'd consider it signed. They wanted to make up their own rules. That's how the company was run.

My time in WCW was over. I wasn't worried. I had saved my money. And I always told Cindi, "Two can eat as cheap as one if you don't eat."

Chapter 9

WORKING THE TERRITORIES

I've worked with a lot of veterans—guys I looked up to as a young fan. The older guys in the business would have big cauliflower ears from roughing them up during the matches. Other guys just wanted to look tough, so they took hot towels and covered their ears to heat them up. Then they would pinch their ears with pliers just to make them look like cauliflower.

One night, I was driving my 1967 Falcon with Gene Kiniski. Before I knew what hit me, Gene reached over, bent my ear down, and smacked me on the side of my head. I screamed, "Gene, what are you doing?"

He said, "You gotta look the part, kid. I did that for [Wilbur] Snyder."

Another veteran who nailed me when I wasn't looking was Haystacks Calhoun. But he was a real jerk. Calhoun was 6'2" and about 600 pounds; he wore overalls and a big beard and wrestled barefoot. He worked a battle royal with me one night. He wasn't even in the territory at the time. He was one of those guys who went from one territory to the next to see if he could get work. These guys didn't really care about the town. They just wanted to pay their way to the next town.

Calhoun had a tendency to come up from behind and hit someone with a knuckle in the back of the neck or head or just do something shitty to his opponent. He wasn't tough at all. He was just a slob. Sure enough, one night he hit me with his knuckle in the back of my head. I had had enough of this guy. I went out of the ring and walked over to the timekeeper's table, keeping one eye on Calhoun standing in the corner. I picked up the timekeeper's hammer that he used to ring the bell, walked back to the ring, and smashed Calhoun's 10 little toes.

I threw the hammer in the ring and walked away while he was jumping around the ring like a Lucha Libre, screaming in pain.

Jerk.

I wrestled a six-man tag once in St. Louis where I teamed with Blackjack Lanza and Waldo Von Erich against the legendary Lou Thesz, Pat O'Connor, and Whipper Watson. I witnessed first-hand how *not* to wrestle Thesz and the consequences of it.

Thesz was in the ring with Waldo when Waldo grabbed Lou by the top of his head to take him over. Lou had thinning hair on top, and he wasn't going anyplace. He moved out of the head-lock and slapped the piss out of Waldo.

Waldo tagged in Lanza. Jack knew what to do. He got Lou in a headlock, pulled him by the hair on the side of the head, and Lou went over. He just didn't want anyone to touch the hair he had left on top.

"Cowboy" Bob Ellis solved his thinning hair problem by wearing a wig during his matches. He'd get a lot of juice, which meant he bled a lot. He'd lie on his back and cut himself underneath the rug. You never saw it.

One day, Baron Von Raschke, Ellis, and I were standing in line at the airport. Baron had a wig too, but he never wore it. He would just fold it in his pocket and goof around with it, turning his head while the wig stayed in the same direction. I asked Raschke for his wig, and I threw it on the floor in front of Ellis.

I tapped him on the shoulder, "Is that yours, sir?"

He frantically grabbed the top of his head.

Poor Bob. I never dropped an elbow on anybody because my arms weren't that big and I didn't think it would hurt anybody. I dropped an arm on Ellis once and knocked all his teeth out. The problem was I did it backward, and he sat up. All his teeth were gone.

"Oh my God," I told Bob after the match. "I'll pay you. I'll get you a new set."

Bob said, "Don't worry about it. When I was in the army, I stole 12 pairs of dentures."

Chief Wahoo McDaniel was a tough man. He went to the University of Oklahoma and was a football player drafted by the Dallas Cowboys, but he also played for the Denver Broncos, the New York Jets, and the Miami Dolphins. When he made a tackle in New York, the public-address announcer would say, "The tackle was made by who?"

The crowd at Shea Stadium would chant, "Wahoo, Wahoo, Wahoo." He was over that much as a linebacker.

I told him once on television, "Gee, Wahoo, you played for Denver, New York, and Miami. If you were any good, at least one would have kept you. The last big trade they made for you was from the Jets to Miami. Miami got Wahoo McDaniel, and the Jets got two Sno-Kone salesmen and a parking lot attendant."

McDaniel started wrestling in the WWF but got in a fight with Vince McMahon Sr. over money. He turned over a table full of tickets and cash and walked out. They never used him again. He was one of the few legitimate Indians in wrestling, and what an attraction he was. When he put his headdress on, Wahoo looked like the south end of a northbound peacock. But he could throw a chop like no one else.

Wahoo was a rugged guy with a reputation for toughness and stories to back it up. He once ran from his dorm to downtown Tulsa on a bet. Another guy bet him that he couldn't drink a quart of motor oil. Wahoo took the bet and did it. He told me that the only effect from it was that every time he would sweat he smelled like a truck.

Wahoo McDaniel had lost a "Loser Leaves Town" match with "Superstar" Bill Eadie in Columbus, Georgia. The following week, Wahoo came back with a mask as "Mr. Columbus." But he wasn't smart enough to change his ring style. He still chopped because he didn't know how to throw a punch. He had never done that.

That night, we wrestled a battle royal. Wahoo was trapped in the corner by a couple of guys. I went down the ring apron, took the laces from the back of his mask, and tied it to the top rope. Wahoo chopped everyone away, but he couldn't move because his head was caught on the turnbuckle. He was running up and down the ropes, yelling for the referee to untie him.

There was nothing like a good rib, and that wasn't the only one. If you don't pull ribs or have a few drinks, and if you take this business too seriously, you'll go nuts. You get off a plane and you have to wait 45 minutes for a car. It's longer to wait in line than to fly sometimes. Travel is just a pain in the ass.

I used to get to O'Hare at 6:00 in the morning from Seattle and had to change planes to get to Tampa. There's nothing to do in the morning. I would take black shoe polish and put it on the earpieces of phones. I'd watch people talking on the phone and look around. Later, I'd see them walk through the airports with their suits, luggage, and black ears.

I'd pull a lot of ribs on Pepper Gomez. He was short, and when we would get in the car to go on long trips, I'd put telephone books in the front seat so he could sit up and look out the window. He'd get embarrassed and mad.

When I wrestled Pepper, I never called "high spots" in the ring, I'd call "low spots." When we would work, he would usually shoot me into the ropes and I'd give him one tackle, he would drop down, I would jump over him, and he would get it again. Then, I threw him into the ropes and he would tackle me. I would drop down, and as he came back to jump over me, I'd raise my body up about an inch and he'd catch his toe and trip.

I'd whisper, "Can't you get those little legs up higher?"

We were wrestling at a fairground in Portland, Indiana. The ring was on a track with a slight incline. I hit Pepper, he hit me, and I took a bump out of the ring on the low side of the ring. I ran around to the high side and rolled in. He chased me around to the same spot, but his nose was on the apron.

"Very funny, amigo," he'd say.

A week later, Renee Goulet and I were wrestling Dr. Big Bill Miller and Pepper at the Richmond, Indiana, ballpark on July 4. It rained up until two minutes before the show. The sun came out, and all I could think of was, "Oh, God. We are going to get muddy and dirty."

During the match, I spotted this huge mud puddle behind the chairs. I told Pepper, "Take me out behind the chairs and nail me. I'll take a bump in the puddle."

Pepper said, "OK, amigo, but don't get me dirty."

Now, what could he have been thinking?

He took me out by the puddle and nailed me. I took a bump on my back, turned on my stomach, and grabbed Pepper's ankles. I pushed them together as he shouted, "No, amigo, no," and fell facedown in the mud. His first instinct was to dig himself out, so I jumped on his back. He dug himself deeper in the mud with me on top of him.

Pepper got up and he couldn't even see. Goulet picked him up and slammed him in the mud again.

We went back to the ring, and Bill Miller, who was 6'6" and 350 pounds, yelled out, "Don't get me dirty."

I sized him up and yelled back, "There's not a chance."

We ended up getting counted out. The four of us went to the back and showered for an hour. I had mud and gravel where I didn't know I had places.

Red Bastein liked to have some fun in the ring as well. In Portland, "Playboy" Buddy Rose, a guy who was about 5'11" and 310 pounds—he looked like the Pillsbury Doughboy, a big, roly-poly guy—was wrestling Roddy Piper with Bastein as the referee. Bastein was checking Rose, his fingertips and around his trunks and shoes, looking for something illegal. As he reached around Rose's trunks, he took his plug of tobacco out of his mouth and dropped it down the ass of Buddy Rose's white trunks, similar to what "Killer" Karl Kox did with the Hershey Bar in Louisiana. Rose didn't know what hit him.

The bell rang. Rose told Piper to give him an "ass bump." Rose sold it, and you could see this big spot getting bigger and bigger. Rose knew there was something in there, and he knew he didn't have an accident.

So he reached into his trunks, took the tobacco out of his trunks, and threw it on the mat. The people in the crowd were going nuts.

That was a common theme of ribs. Andre the Giant used to shit in the tubs in Japan because he couldn't get in the bathrooms. They were more like phone booths.

When Jerry Lawler first came to the WWF, there was some payback to be had. We had a show in Sacramento, and I know at least three guys who shit in his crown, including the Undertaker and Steve Keirn. All those guys worked for him at one time in Lawler's promotion in Memphis, and they weren't treated well.

I would have my fun on the interview set as well. I was being interviewed by Marty O'Neill. I walked out to the set with a picture in my pocket of two lesbians together.

"You know what I'm going to use on Crusher tonight?" I'd ask him.

"What?"

I'd take out the picture and show him, "Look at that."

Marty said, "I'd say he's in trouble, because I've never seen anything like this."

When Wally Karbo would try to force Nick into a match, I would write down on a piece of paper the amount it would cost to get Nick in the ring. Wally would look at it and sigh, "Oh, pal."

The note would always say, "Fuck you, Wally."

Mr. Fuji, a longtime wrestler and manager, was a great ribber on the planes. Guys would be out all night partying, and they'd want to sleep on the plane. Fuji would say to them, "Take this, brother," and offer them a Halcyon. They'd be so out of it, he could perform surgery on them. Not Fuji. He would just paint their nails and shave their eyebrows off.

One of the Nasty Boys came home one night to his hotel room after partying. His wife was trying to call him and couldn't get ahold of him. The next day he was sleeping it off on the plane, and Fuji painted a black nose and whiskers on him. He got off the plane, went home, and his wife asked where he was.

"I was in my room all night. I didn't do anything."

Keep in mind that he was saying this standing in front of her looking like a pussycat.

That wasn't the only way to get a guy in trouble with his wife. I heard of other "ribbers" putting lipstick on and kissing the other guys' shirt collars or underwear so their wives would see it when they did the wash.

I had my share of fun on planes, and not just fighting the passengers. I discovered how to lock and unlock bathrooms from the outside. Where it says "occupied" or "vacant," there's a little nub in there to unlock it in case someone is in there getting sick. But that meant you could lock it too.

On one trip, Pedro Morales was sitting in the front row of the plane while I was sitting in the back right next to the bathroom. The plane took off and I could see him looking back at the bathroom sign. I knew he had to go. The seat belt sign turned off, and I saw Pedro get up. Before he could see what I was doing, I shut the bathroom door, popped the sign over to "occupied," and sat back down.

Morales walked up to the bathroom and saw the "occupied" sign. "Oh shit," he said, and started knocking on the door.

"Amigo."

No one answered.

"Amigo, I've got to piss."

He finally made his way back to his seat, but he kept looking back. I got up and opened the door, and he saw me. He jumped up as I shut the door and locked it. He ran back to the bathroom door and saw it said "occupied." I noticed that he was wearing a pair of gabardine pants, which was funny because he always had trouble pronouncing that word.

"What the hell is going on?" he shouted at the door. "I'm going to piss my gabardinos."

At the World Bodybuilding Federation event, the WWF had David Hebner, who has a twin brother named Earl that also works for the Federation, serve as an agent. Linda McMahon walked up to me and said, "I'm so embarrassed. I can't tell David and Earl apart. Which one is he?"

Of course I said, "It's Earl."

A half hour later, David walked up to me and said, "I'm nervous as hell. Linda McMahon keeps calling me Earl. I don't have the guts to tell her I'm David."

I didn't say anything. I found Linda and told her, "Linda, I made a mistake. That's David."

I went back to David and said, "Keep answering to Earl."

That went on for the whole day.

A very popular rib was called a "Mabel." A new guy would come into the territory, and we would find him the most attractive "arena rat," or wrestling groupie, which was hard to do if you've ever seen them. We'd introduce him to her, and he'd make friends with her. She was our "Queen Rat." So they would make a date to go to her place that night.

She'd mix him a drink and tell him to go in the next room and make himself comfortable. The front door would open and she'd shout, "Oh no! What are you doing home?"

She'd run into the next room and shout, "It's my husband. Run out the window!"

The guy would be crawling out the window when the "husband" would run in with a gun filled with blanks and "shoot" her. The wrestler is out the window, running down the street with his pants tucked under his arms or just a pair of argyles on. The "husband" was one of the boys with a blank pistol.

He'd show up for work the next day, and we would tell him what happened. Some guys would get mad. Others would laugh.

Wrestlers would always figure out a way to turn the tables. There were two guys in Canada who wrestled as the Kelly Twins. They were identical twins, and it was impossible to tell them apart. One would meet a girl and take her up to their room while the other was hiding in the bathroom. When he was done "being romantic," he would go into the bathroom and the other would come out. After he was done, he would go into the bathroom and it would start all over again. The girl thought she found the greatest lover of her life.

The best ribber in the business was Vic Christy. He picked up King Curtis, who had just flown in from Hawaii, at the airport hotel in Los Angeles at 10:00 in the morning for a show at 8:00 that night. Curtis got in the car and they drove away.

They were driving through the valleys and the mountains. Curtis asked, "Do we have time to stop and eat?"

"No," Vic said. "We gotta go. I'm in the first match."

They pulled up to the building about 10 minutes before the show started, after a long day in the car in addition to Curtis flying in from Hawaii. They walked in the building and Vic told Curtis, "I'm going out of town, but someone will take you back to the hotel."

Curtis asked, "How much do I owe you?"

"Never mind," Vic said.

"Well, thank you."

Vic's match ended, and he left the building. Curtis found Steve for his ride. They got in the car and drove about two blocks to the hotel where Curtis and Vic met that morning.

Vic drove through the mountains and the desert, all the way to Vegas and back. That big Hawaiian was sitting there soaking wet because Vic's car didn't have air-conditioning.

I made my own fun on the road. Keep in mind that I didn't go to work until 4:00 in the afternoon and arrived at the building at 7:00. We'd be done by 11:00, so I had all night to party.

Wrestlers always had to be careful where they went. There were a lot of bars filled with guys who thought it was fake and they could beat a wrestler, especially me being a manager and a weasel hiding behind people all my life. People knew that they'd have trouble fighting Hogan, but they could beat me.

Some "fans" were so drunk, they couldn't get up and fight. I would bait them and make fun of them. I'd even order drinks and put them on their tab. The guy would wake up the next morning and think he had a hell of a time with me.

When you're traveling around the country, you can run into all kinds of different people in the business. You can run into big guys like Andre the Giant, and you can run into little people—the midget wrestlers.

I knew this one midget by the name of Fuzzy Cupid. He was in his late forties or fifties (you honestly could not tell), about 38 inches tall; he had a protruding forehead, orange-blond hair, and a goatee to match. He was just a miserable little creature. Blackjack Lanza used to tell him, "You have breath like a dead goat, you surly, tyrant little creature."

He was stuck one night. We were going to Elkhart, Indiana, from Indianapolis, and little Fuzzy didn't have a way to get there. We said, "Come on, Fuzz, we'll take you with." He sat in the backseat, but his breath was so bad, Lanza made him lie in the boot of his Buick convertible. Fuzzy crawled in the boot and lay down like a cocker spaniel as we headed off to Elkhart.

We drove into Kokomo, Indiana, at about 2:00 in the morning. Next to Kokomo was a town called Brazil, which was the summer and winter home for the circus. We needed gas and pulled into a station with Fuzzy fast asleep in the boot. Lanza and I saw the attendant sitting in the station with his "Gomer Pyle" hat on, and we decided we were going to have some fun with him.

"Gomer" was half asleep with his feet up on the table. He must have weighed 400 pounds, but he squeezed himself into a medium shirt. We woke him up to tell him that we had found something.

"What did you find?" "Gomer" asked.

"We found some circus midget down by the river, and he was chewing on some woman's ankle."

He said, "You've got to be kidding."

I said, "No, we captured him and trapped him in the boot of our car."

We desperately wanted to get "Gomer" to wake Fuzz up, because we knew Fuzz, being his miserable self, was going to kill

1
2
3

him for interrupting his nap. He followed us to the car, but what we didn't know was that Fuzzy was wide awake.

The guy walked up to the car, convinced that two strangers had captured a circus freak who had bitten a woman's ankle. As "Gomer" approached the passenger side of the Buick, Fuzzy was getting out of the boot. Fuzz confronted him, pushed the 400-pound attendant aside, and said, "Get the hell out of my way."

The terrified "Gomer" was face to face with the "ankle biter." He ran away screaming. He kept running and running, and we never saw him again. He never came back to the station. We filled our car up with "free" gas and drove away with Fuzzy back in the boot.

There was this young guy who showed up in the promotion, and he'd always bring his girlfriend to spot shows. We'd spot him driving down the road, so we would try to get ahead of him. We'd pop the trunk, and a midget would stand up, playing with himself. We'd do that every few miles until he backed way off.

We never saw him again.

The midgets would always drive with us to Windsor, Ontario. When it came time to pay the toll, we popped the trunk, and Sky Lo Lo would pop up and pay the toll, scaring the hell out of the attendant.

Sky Lo Lo would always wear a fedora-style hat. He would sit at the bar, take it off, and set it on the stool next to him. Inevitably, Pat Patterson would sit on it. Sky would always be in a mood to fight. He would get drunk and then ride his bike home. Usually, he would fall off his bike when he got there. His wife, who was not a midget, would beat the shit out of him for it.

I was driving from Chicago with Guy Mitchell, Gene Kiniski, and Wilbur Snyder. We were all drinking beer, and the weather was snowy. Wilbur couldn't see at all, but he's showing us how you can go 100 miles an hour in the snow as well as you can go 20.

I said, "Yeah, but you can't stop the same."

Gene Kiniski had pictures of his children on the dash, pleading with Wilbur, "Please, please don't do this."

Baron Von Raschke, Pepper Gomez, and I went through Chicago one night in 1973 during the gas crisis. We drove from Fort Wayne to do a television show. I ran out of gas on the Dan Ryan in the hood. I have a 5'10" Mexican with an "Iron Stomach" in the backseat. I have the "Clawmaster" sitting next to me. And the "Weasel" is driving.

We were in trouble.

I said, "Pepper, you stay in the car. Raschke, you and I are going to find a gas station."

We hailed a cab to take us to a gas station to buy a can of gas. We drove for a half hour in the snow. We couldn't find a gas station, so naturally we went to a bar. We picked up a case of beer to drink because we were going to have to sit in the car anyway.

While we were gone, the local police discovered our car and Pepper sitting in the backseat.

The cop asked Pepper, "Why were you sitting in the car?"

He said, "My friends went to get gas."

"But you're on the highway. What if you got rear-ended?"

"That's OK. I don't sell the neck," Pepper said. ("Selling" is wrestling slang referring to when a wrestler reacts to or "sells" what is happening to him—for instance, snapping their head back and acting woozy after a punch.)

The cop had no idea what he meant.

It was at that point that Raschke and I showed up, of course with a case of beer. The police ignored the alcohol and pushed the car off the Dan Ryan and up the off-ramp with their car. Eventually, we all ended up in the parking lot of a closed Clark gas station.

It was about 4:00 in the morning, and we thought we might freeze to death. We started drinking beer until we fell asleep. I woke up at 7:00 and discovered that the sun was up. I looked across the street, and there was an all-night gas station that we didn't see the night before because of the snow.

That's right. The "Weasel," the "Clawmaster," and the "Iron Stomach" drank a case of beer across the street from an open gas station in the parking lot of a closed gas station.

Raschke turned to me and said, "That's why they call you 'the Brain.'"

When I toured Japan in the early seventies, I found out that in some hotels you could get both massages and "special" massages. Having decided to stay in one of those hotels, I told the desk clerk that I wanted a massage. I went back to my room, showered, and waited.

Later, I heard a knock at the door and opened it. There was the bellman from downstairs standing there. But he was with a blind guy who looked to be in his seventies.

I said, "I don't think you understand." Knowing that he didn't speak English, I took my hands and made the motion of a woman's figure.

Realizing the mistake, he said, "Ah, so," and left.

I put some cologne on and waited some more. Twenty minutes later, he came back with a woman—a woman who was 65 years old.

And blind.

I gave him the money. He said, "Ah, so."

I said, "I am."

Some guys would travel with the blades that they used to "whack" themselves with during matches to make themselves bleed. They used the same blade for months. They'd keep them all in a medicine bottle and pick out the one that they were going to use. Mine always went into the toilet after one time.

I would always carry the blade in an inside pocket of my trunks—a blade pocket. I'd reach in, grab it, and rake the guy's eyes. I'd pull my hand back where I kept the blade. When I went down, I'd push the blade up and move my head. Then, I'd grab the guy by the trunks, punch him, and put the blade in there. I'd always tell him to not reach down there or take a piss before he got back to the dressing room.

Some guys were terrified of blading. I remember Wilbur Snyder would whimper when it was time for him to blade. I'd say, "Come on, Willie. Time to whack." He'd whimper. "Willie, come on." He'd whimper some more. "Come on, we've got to go home." He'd carry on. Then, when the blade hit his skin, he'd cry out so loud. The guy in the last row heard it. It didn't hurt. It was like a paper cut.

When you bladed a guy and the blood wasn't coming out good enough, you either told him, "Not enough," you punched him to open it up a little more, or you'd grab his nose and tell him to blow. I used to do it too to get the blood to flow.

I never let anybody cut me, because I didn't know where the blade was or where the other guy had it. You didn't think about AIDS or herpes in those days, or about catching anything.

I worked one night against Dr. X in the AWA. He was wrestling me in a match where he had to defeat me in 10 minutes. I think the finish was that he would beat me in nine minutes. Two minutes into the match, he said, "Get your juice now."

I wasn't paying attention to myself. As I'm whacking myself with the blade, he pulled me up and I hit an artery. Mind you, I'm wearing blue and white boots, pink tights, pink trunks, and a pink singlet. All this with blond hair.

I went back to the dressing room after the match, bleeding heavily. Oliver Humperdink met me in the back. At that time he was still using his real name, John "Red" Sutton. He was an usher at the building and a Santa Claus at the Minneapolis Donaldson's department store. He was just getting into the business. He used to carry my blades for me and place them on a chair when I needed them.

Wally Karbo told him, "Take him to the hospital. That's not going to stop."

So, Humperdink took me to the hospital on a Saturday night at 11:00. Every drunk in St. Paul was in the waiting room. The doctor sewed me up with 13 stitches. He told me not to wash it off because of chlorine in the water. I had to wash around it. I walked into the waiting room where the drunks were sitting, and I was covered in dried blood from head to toe wearing my pink jacket that said "Heenan" on the back.

"Good evening," I said. "I'm Dr. Heenan. We've just lost one in O.R., but as soon as I scrub out, I'll be right out to talk to you."

You could see the drunks file out of the room. They weren't staying.

Chapter 10

WORKING WITH CELEBRITIES

You always have to be careful about celebrities that you bring in to wrestle or work an angle. They can do more damage than good. After all, they're not there to help you. They are there to get themselves over. They live in the town that we're in that night. Or they own a bar or car wash or something.

Still, it was fun to meet famous people, whether it was in the ring or other places.

I was on a plane one day going to New York. George Steinbrenner, owner of the New York Yankees, was on the same plane, and I saw him trying to jam his bag into the overhead.

I yelled at him, "Sit down!"

"Who the hell said that?" he shouted.

"Bobby Heenan, World Wrestling Federation," I said, extending my hand and introducing myself.

He was actually happy to meet me after wondering who was yelling at him. He knew Dusty Rhodes and Vince McMahon. We talked several times on future flights. He even gave me season tickets to spring training and has become a real good friend of mine.

Andy Kaufman was my assistant for one night in Chicago. I was managing Ken Patera in a match against Jerry Lawler, who was feuding with Kaufman at the time. They had just appeared on the David Letterman show, where Lawler slapped Kaufman, who threw coffee on the "King."

Kaufman was real strange. I picked him up at the Air Host, a little dump we stayed at in Chicago. I told him I'd meet him in the lobby at 6:00. At 6:15, he wasn't there, so I went up and knocked on the door. He opened the door. It was real dark in his room.

I asked, "Are you ready?"

He quietly said, "Yeah."

He got in the car and said nothing. We drove to the arena and went inside. It came time to go to the ring. He took his sport coat off and reached into his inside pocket. He had about 50 pens and pencils.

He asked me, "Where should I put this stuff?"

I asked him if he was wearing his jacket to the ring. He said no. I told him to put the pens in his jacket and put it in my bag or on the hook. You didn't have to be bright. Where do you put a jacket? The nail on the wall was not for a picture.

Andy walked to the ring with me. Fans were kind of wild in Chicago. (Still are, for that matter.) He made the mistake, when people were yelling at him, to turn and look at them, leaving his back open to the other fans. All night long he left his back open. I finally took him aside and advised him to put his back to the ring. After the match, I brought him back to the dressing room, he picked up his jacket and pens, and we went back to the hotel. He never said a word, outside of "thank you."

I found out later on that he was sick and knew he was dying at that time. Someone told me that he was likely meditating in his room before the match.

WCW often signed professional football players to wrestle in special matches, including Kevin Greene and Reggie White. I met Greene in Las Vegas before a WCW pay-per-view. The limo pulled up, and I was standing by all the press out back behind Caesar's. Keep in mind, I had never met the guy.

I walked through the people and said, "I've got to meet you. I remember watching your dad, 'Mean Joe.' Boy, could he play."

We shook hands, and he squeezed mine so hard, it hurt my shins.

When I met Reggie White, I said, "I've got every one of your albums."

He said, "That's *Barry* White."

Before Wrestlemania, the WWF booked a few matches where I was handcuffed to Mr. T to prevent me from interfering. That was a little hard, because he didn't know how to work. The fans would cheer, and he would raise his arms in the air. I would have to remind him that I was hooked to the other side of the cuffs.

Another time I was attached to someone else was in Indianapolis. Bruiser had me handcuffed to a race car driver from Indianapolis named Bud Tinglestad. But no one bothered to smarten him up about the wrestling business. When I first met him, all he said was, "You just shut up." I thought he was playing with me. I would get up to go do something during the match, and he would pull me back, almost breaking my wrist.

"Hey, loosen up," I'd say.

Then he hit me in the chest. I punched him. He punched me back. He wasn't a big guy, but I started to realize that this guy wasn't "smart." The referee walked over, and I was yelling, "Tell him. Tell him." I wanted the ref to smarten this guy up.

After the match, I asked him, "Didn't you know what we were doing?"

Bud said, "No, no one ever told me that. I thought it was real."

I screamed, "No!"

"I'm sorry."

"So am I," I said.

"Gee, I wouldn't have done that. I would have had a good time."

"I would have too," I shot back.

I met a Secret Service agent at a show in Washington. He told me, "Anytime you come to Washington, give me a call. I'll take you over to the White House. But it's best to call when the president is out of town because I can show you around more. There's not that many people in the place."

I asked him, "Can you show me the door where Kennedy sneaked Marilyn in?"

He said, "I can show you the door where Clinton leaves."

We all know how *that* ended up.

I had the privilege of meeting Muhammad Ali before his match with Antonio Inoki in 1976. He was boxing in exhibition matches in Chicago. I went out there with Nick Bockwinkel. Ali was going to box Kenny Jay and Buddy Wolfe, who were with the AWA at the time. Before he met with Ali, Verne Gagne told us not to "smarten" up Ali to the wrestling business. The plan was that he was going to knock off Kenny Jay real quick. Verne told Ali to be careful when he was boxing Buddy Wolfe because he opened up easy over the eyes.

Ali said, "OK, I'll hit him a couple of times, so he can back away and cut himself."

Ali was "smart."

We had a brief conversation. "Are you a good guy or a bad guy?" he asked.

I said, "I'm a bad guy."

"Do you guys get a lot of pussy?"

I saw him nine years later at the first Wrestlemania. Even then, Ali was showing signs of Parkinson's disease. He was originally supposed to referee the main event all by himself, but Pat Patterson ended up as the referee in the ring while Ali stood outside. Ali wouldn't have been there for all the spots. He wouldn't have known when to go in and count. It was better to have him on the floor.

I did the Jerry Lewis Labor Day Telethon with Randy Savage, Marty Jannetty, and the Bushwhackers. All Jannetty and the Bushwhackers did was answer phones. Savage and I actually went out there with Jerry.

The producer told the two of us, "You can do anything you want with Jerry, but he has a bad back. He'll play along with anything you want to do."

Jerry introduced Savage. Randy did his whole shtick, "Oooh, yeah. Let's give a big backdrop and a bodyslam for MD."

I think Jerry thought of a wrestler as a guy who looked like a wrestler. Back then, Savage looked like a tough rodeo clown with the cowboy hat and his colorful outfit. Still, Jerry pretended to be scared of him.

They sent me out. I walked up to Jerry and said, "You're not going to believe what this means to me. My heart is beating. You don't know what a pleasure and privilege this is. Could you do that thing with Lamb Chop, that little puppet?"

Lewis shot back, "That's Shari Lewis."

"OK, can you sing 'Great Balls of Fire' for me?"

He said, "That's Jerry *Lee* Lewis."

I asked him, "What do you do here?"

Lewis said, "I'm a Jew in heat."

I appeared on David Letterman's sixth anniversary show when he was with NBC. Before the show, Vince McMahon told me I could do anything I wanted to do. I sat in the audience with my wife, Cindi, Basil DeVito, who was a WWF vice president, his wife, and two former Rockettes. Dave introduced me, and I stood up with a Bobby Heenan action figure. I walked up on stage and gave him the doll.

I asked him, "How did you get all these people here? Did you promise them free cheese?"

He looked shocked and didn't know what to say.

I continued, "Well, I wish you six more good years of marriage."

I left the set and went backstage. Someone from NBC confronted me. "You can't do that. You can't walk onstage."

I said, "But Vince McMahon told me . . ."

"I don't care," he said. "This is scripted. This is timed. You can't have an extra spot on there. Now promise us you won't do that again."

"I won't," I said. "I give you my word as a professional."

"Jesus Christ, Bobby," he said. "Letterman does not like surprises."

"I don't blame him. I thought it was OK."

They taped the second show. I got out there to sit down. This time, the producers had a guy sitting next to me. He opened up his coat a little to reveal a gun. I guess if I started to go onstage again, he would block me or shoot me. Letterman announced me for the second time. I stood up and waved and sat back down. This time, Letterman noticed that I was wearing a black suit with gold on it.

Letterman said, "Nice looking suit. Do you need some Brasso?"

Later on, he was doing a "Stupid Pet Trick." He looked over at me and said, "Is that OK, Heenan?"

He loosened up a bit, but I don't blame him for being upset. I figured out what Vince wanted to do. He wanted to get me locked up in jail. It would have made all the papers. Free publicity for the WWF.

I told him later, "Vince, with my blond hair and bubble butt, I can't do a lot of time."

Sting, Madusa, Roddy Piper, and I did *Politically Incorrect* with Bill Maher. Once again, WCW never plugged that we were going to be on. They didn't even show excerpts of the show after we appeared. Piper got into it with Maher when we arrived at the studio and when we were on the air. The producers wanted him to do some promo for something. To this day, Piper doesn't like anybody that thinks wrestling isn't real. That's his mentality.

For the record, Roddy, wrestling is not real. Thank God. I wouldn't be in this. I would be with Al Bundy selling shoes and looking up women's dresses.

I heard that Maher jerked off before he did the show. So I asked him on the air, "How do you prepare for shows?"

"I masturbate," he said.

"Well, when we're done here, there's no reason to shake hands. We can just say good-bye. We didn't come here to get jerked around."

Rick Rude and I did the Regis Philbin and Kathy Lee Gifford show. Around that time, Rude did the Chippendale gimmick. At the shows, I would call a girl out of the audience—it was all set up—and she would get a kiss from Rick and fall to the mat. He would stand over her, put his hands behind his head, and wiggle his hips. He always had airbrushed trunks with a picture of himself on the back. They were very nice.

Rick wore his trunks, boots, and robe on the show. He told Regis he had a surprise for him. We sat down with him and Kathy Lee Gifford. Regis kept saying, "Take off the robe. I want to see what you have to show me. What do you have under the robe?"

"Wait a minute," I said.

We did a two-segment appearance. Kathy Lee was her typical self—very unfriendly. When we were ready for Rude to take off his robe, they hit Rude's "stripper" music. Rude undid his robe, and on the front of his trunks was a picture of Kathy Lee. He turned around and had Regis on his butt.

He wanted to give Kathy Lee "the kiss." He looked at her and she looked at him. Realizing what was going to happen, she jumped over the couch. Rude jumped over the couch. The set behind her had stairs going up, but once you got to the top, there was nothing there. She ran up the stairs, knowing it was a set. Rude was right behind her.

Kathy Lee turned around and blurted out, "Don't kiss me. Frank is in New Orleans doing the Monday night game, and he's watching."

"I'm not going to kiss you," Rude said. "I just wanted to see how far I could chase you."

Regis watched it all and was happy with everything. I said to him, "Well, Regis. He's up there kissing your cohost. I guess it's just you and me."

I did the Arsenio Hall show twice. The first time, I brought Cindi with me. The producers flew us out first class and put us up in this nice French hotel in West Los Angeles. They even put my name outside the dressing room with a star. After the show was over, they left us a basket in the room with ham, summer sausage, cheeses, mints, and other things. My wife picked up the basket and started to leave.

"Where are you going with that?" I asked.

"It's for us," she said.

"I know, but we don't take it. It would be like the Clampetts coming to town."

She said, "I'm taking it."

I said, "No, you're not. Put it back."

She returned the basket. We went back to the hotel for a few drinks. We got back to our room about 1:00 in the morning, and I was starving. I said, "Boy, I wish you would have brought that basket. There's nothing to eat."

She walked over to her purse and opened it up. She had taken everything out of the basket. Ham, cheese, and everything. I think there was stuff that wasn't even in the basket.

The second time I did the show, I felt like I should apologize for taking the basket. Arsenio said, "No, that's for you. It's a gift." I told him I didn't want him to think we were deadbeats.

The next day, a basket arrived in the mail at my home for my wife. Along with the food, it had an Arsenio Hall doll and a jacket for my daughter.

I told Cindi, "From now on, steal whatever you want."

I also took my wife to the Comedy Awards in Los Angeles. I was invited by George Schlatter because he was a fan of mine and liked my shtick. I was talking to some people while Cindi was having a cigarette.

She started to look around the room and told me, "No one is smoking but me."

"You're right," I said.

"I'm embarrassed. What do I do? There's no ashtrays in this place."

"Here's what you do," I said. "Take a puff, hold it in your mouth, drop the cigarette, and I'll step on it."

"OK," she said.

She took a puff and dropped the cigarette. Instead of stepping on it, I took three steps back and yelled, "What the hell are you doing? Putting out a cigarette on a floor in a nice place like this?"

Everyone was looking at her. All she could do was let a puff of smoke come out of her mouth.

She was furious. Three days in Beverly Hills. No talking. No nothing.

Ray Combs, the host of *Family Feud*, was a good friend of mine. He committed suicide several years ago. He was very frustrated in that he wanted to be Johnny Carson. He wanted to do comedy and felt demeaned doing a game show. But he had six kids to support.

It was fun doing his show. The producers had the WWF versus the World Bodybuilding Federation (WBF). "Team WWF" was me, Sherri Martel, Jimmy Hart, the Mountie, and Brian Knobs. We thought the WBF was just a bunch of muscleheads and we could beat them easily.

Before we did the show, the producers took us to this room to play practice games. Since it was all for charity, I told my team that we should let the WBF win if they were not doing well. We should just drop the ball and let them catch up from time to time.

The producer immediately said, "No, you can't do that. You have to play this. If you win all the games, you win all the games."

I found out the game was a lot harder to play than it was to watch. They would say, "You have three seconds. Give me the number one answer to a kind of dog food." But you're not thinking about the question—you start counting the seconds.

On the show, they asked Sherri, "What is a place where you don't take children?"

I would say porn movie, liquor store, or bar.

Sherri said, "Hawaii."

Combs wanted her to be more specific, "You mean Honolulu?"

She said, "No. No place in Hawaii."

Combs asked the Mountie, "Name me a profession dealing with horses."

The Mountie said, "Horsemen."

He asked Brian Knobs, "Where is a good place to meet women in sports?"

He said, "Football game."

Yeah, there's nothing I like better than a 300-pound woman named Wanda with a big coat on with a cheesehead.

When we played "Fast Money," they placed me in this curtained booth and put headsets on me while Knobs was answering the first set of questions. There was a guard standing there so I wouldn't turn around and see the board.

We needed 200 points to win. The guard tapped me on the shoulder. He says to me, "Good luck; you'll need it."

There were four points on the board, but I got every number one answer except for one.

Knobs was giving these dumb answers. Answers like, "Play the trumpet" for questions like "Name something a dentist would do."

By the end of the taping, we won $4,000 dollars for our charities. The WBF? Those musclehead dummies? They won $38,000. They creamed us. I think they even put us over once so we didn't look bad.

After the tapings, I looked at "Team WWF" and said, "Well, I don't think we should tackle *Jeopardy* right now."

Not long after my appearance on *Family Feud,* Ray Combs opened up a comedy club in Cincinnati, and his agent invited me out to be his guest. Combs had no idea I was going to be there. In the middle of his set, I stood backstage with a hand-held microphone.

"Hey, Combs!" I shouted.

He stopped his show and looked around.

"Hey, Combs!"

"Who is that?"

I walked out onstage. We hugged, and he introduced me to the crowd.

"Do five minutes," he whispered to me.

I turned to the audience but couldn't see anyone because of the lights. Don't get me wrong. I can make people laugh. I can make my friends laugh. I can make anyone laugh.

But on that stage, I froze.

I didn't have any material, and I didn't know these people. I just didn't feel comfortable. I honestly didn't know what to say. I finally blurted out, "There's not enough money," and I walked offstage.

On top of the talk shows and game shows, I even made an appearance in prime time, but no one told me I was. John Studd and I appeared in an episode of *The A-Team*. We got to the Los Angeles arena that night. Mr. T was in the crowd. Studd was wrestling Hogan that night, and we were told to go have our normal match with T at ringside.

"Whatever he does, Bobby, just go along with it. He's working for us," I was told.

But I didn't know they were filming for a television show. So we were not aware that whatever the viewers saw on that episode would be shown on television.

In 1994, Jimmy Hart called me and told me that these producers were looking for two guys to be announcers in a movie they were filming. Gene Okerlund and I got the parts of announcers in a movie called *Timemaster*. I played a guy named "Bob." Okerlund played a guy named "Howard." We played the announcers of a futuristic video game. James Glickenhaus, the director, makes a lot of movies for video and put his 14-year-old kid in the lead.

I've never received a residual off it, and I've never known anybody who has ever seen it. More people watch the video cameras at Wal-Mart than have seen *Timemaster*.

I even went to the premiére in Los Angeles. I brought out my mother-in-law, wife, and daughter. I rented a limo, but everyone else in the movie drove their own cars. In addition to what I spent on that, I had to pay $1,050 to join the Screen Actors Guild. They paid me only $1,000 for the movie. Again, that's why they call me "the Brain."

One of the greatest honors of my life came in 1998. I was selected to the "All Madden Team" by John Madden. Every year, he picks guys from the NFL for his team. For some reason, he selected me as a manager. And there are no managers in football, just coaches. I got a beautiful, cast-iron trophy with "All

Madden Team" on the front and every player and position Madden picked on the back. At the bottom, it said, "Manager: Bobby 'the Brain' Heenan."

The funny thing was that I never met him. He was just a fan.

Not long after that, I was standing outside the Marriott in Philadelphia, and I saw the Madden Cruiser. I approached the security guard in front of the bus and asked him, "Could you tell him that Bobby Heenan is outside and I'd just like to meet him?"

The guard walked in and came out a minute later, "Go on in."

I walked into the cruiser. There were 10 televisions going. Jars were open with spoons and forks all over the place. Socks were lying about. It looked like a locker room at the Y.

"How are you doing, Bobby?" he asked.

"Well, I don't want to take too much of your time."

"Not at all. I've always liked you. You're funny," he said.

We sat and talked about football and other things. I never asked him why he picked me that year. I just thanked him for the honor of the award.

By the way, if you want to see the trophy, it's at Tim's Pawn Shop on the corner of Third and Main . . . just kidding.

Chapter 11

FAMILY AND FANS

Being "the Brain" was always easy for me to do. But who is "the Brain"?

"The Brain" is not smart. He's a manager of wrestlers and a flimflam man. He's the kind of guy that if you invite him for the weekend, he'll stay for a month. He'll go through your drawers while you're not home, just to see if he can find anything on you that he can use later. If you go out to dinner with him, he'll claim that he left his wallet in his other jacket or other pants. Or he'd claim that he sent a $500 money order to Guam to take care of that orphanage full of kids.

"The Brain" used to say, "I'd love to have this guy to manage, boy could I rip . . . I mean, could I make this guy money." For example, he'd invest all of Blackjack Lanza's money into a fertilizer farm and say he thought it would do better.

He tells everyone that he has Rolls Royces in Beverly Hills but rides his bike to the mailbox every day. He doesn't even live in Beverly Hills, but very close to it. He has a gold Rolex, but it's not real gold, nor is it a real Rolex.

"The Brain" will cheat and lie. He'll be everyone's friend, but he'll backstab them, always smiling to their faces. If you make him mad, he'll tell you what he thinks, knowing he has a way out—the Bill Clinton of wrestling. He's truly a weasel. He's kind of a combination of a dangerous used car salesman and a movie agent who does nothing but porn films.

In the WWF, I had opportunities to really develop the "Brain" gimmick. The WWF decided to have me do a photo shoot out in Beverly Hills for their magazine to show where "the Brain" lived. We went from house to house and all we saw were Rolls Royces. That just didn't seem right. We drove by one place and saw an Edsel in a driveway. It was perfect.

Working up some tears, I told the lady at the house, "Excuse me. My uncle had an Edsel just like that, and he was killed in it. I was wondering if we could take some pictures of it."

"Oh, please help yourself," she said.

We took pictures throughout her house for about three hours.

If you really want to know how "the Brain" works and how smug he can be, I was in Japan to buy a silk screen. My wife wanted this specific type. There was a guy in Japan named George Silk who sold them. He had a reputation as a real hard guy to bargain with. But the boys told me that if I got him a bottle of whiskey and got him drunk, he would forget everything and I could get everything for almost nothing.

So, "the Brain" went in to see George Silk. "The Brain" talked to him for about an hour as George brought out every silk screen he had. They were all starting to look alike.

I said, "Let's have a bottle of whiskey and think about this."

I got the bottle out and started pouring. I was watching him sell. "The Brain" poured him another. "The Brain" had another. By the end of the day, we made our deal. I paid him the money, and he promised to ship them home to me.

I called my wife later, "I'm so proud of myself. I got the silk screen you wanted and I got it real cheap. And I got that other silk screen you wanted too." I described the screen to her and she said, "I didn't want that one."

George Silk had gotten "the Brain" drunk and sold me two silk screens, convincing me that I needed it. I thought I paid $300 for one. I paid $1,000 for two. And they weren't even the ones she wanted.

And what would "the Brain" be without his "Family"? I called any group I managed "The Bobby Heenan Family." I never used the term "stable" or anything like that. I picked "Family" because of what was going on with Charles Manson at the time.

The Assassins, Joe Tomaso and Guy Mitchell, were the first tag team I managed. Guy is still a real good friend of mine. He once wrestled as my brother, Guy Heenan, in Terra Haute, Indiana. I honestly don't remember it, but others have reminded me of it. Joe is a tough little guy from Canada who used to wrestle down south as the Bat.

I hit it off with Blackjack Lanza the first day I met him. It was just one of those things. We made each other laugh and became the best of friends. Every time I was out of town for Thanksgiving, Jack always had me over for dinner with his family.

Harley Race is a terrific guy. We had a lot of laughs. I managed Harley in the AWA for about a month or so and then again in the WWF when he was "the King." But I never managed him at his peak, when he was the NWA champion.

Baron Von Raschke is a jewel. I always hoped my daughter would marry a guy like him, and I hope all her kids are like him.

He's just a decent man. And he's the best worker in the world because he made people mad, yet he does not have one mean bone in his body.

Whether he drank one beer or one hundred, it was the same effect. He was sipping on some Boone's Farm wine once when we were walking out of a hotel. It was icy on that day, and Baron stepped on a patch of ice while taking a drink out of the bottle. He flipped in the air and landed on his back. I thought he was dead.

Baron got up and brushed himself off. He took one look at the bottle of Boone's Farm and said, "Wow, what a kick!"

It was fun to manage Ernie Ladd. He wore plaid clothes, suspenders, and a big crown to the ring. He played football in the NFL and had the best stories. He would always sit in the dressing rooms, taping his knees, which had so many scars on them from all the operations he had.

Back then, the promoters would always take their time getting the transportation money to the wrestlers. Ernie would ask for it, but the promoters wanted to add it to his check. Ernie didn't trust them. He wanted his money first.

As he was slowly—and I mean slowly—taping his legs, the promoter would say, "Come on, Ernie. Let's go." It was time for his match.

"I haven't seen my money yet," he'd say without even looking up.

By the time he'd get done taping his knees, they'd be there with his money. He put his money in his sock, laced his boot, and went out to the ring.

The Valiant Brothers were a complete waste of my time.

Blackjack Mulligan, whose real name is Bob Windham, was a big guy, about 6'8" and 300 pounds. He was in Minneapolis as a referee and got a break to go to New York. Vince McMahon Sr. said, "I'm going to make you a cowboy."

When Lanza and I came back from Japan, Mulligan approached Lanza and said, "I hope you don't mind. I'm going to be a cowboy."

"I don't care," said Jack.

"I'm also going to have a black hat," said Mulligan.

"I don't care."

"I'm also going to wear a black glove."

"Anybody can wear black gloves," Lanza informed him.

"They're also going to call me Blackjack Mulligan," Windham said.

"You have the right to use any name you want."

Jack pointed to me. "You want him, too?"

"Nah, I think I can get over by myself," Mulligan said.

"What do you mean?" Jack said. "You stole everything but the name 'Lanza.'"

I managed Nick Bockwinkel and Ray Stevens in 1974. My God, did I learn from them. I learned not to talk to Nick in more than two sentences because he would go on and on and confuse you. If you ask Nick what time it is, he tells you how to build a watch. If I'm going to the electric chair, I want Nick to be the preacher who talks to me. I'll die of old age before I get to the chair. But he means well.

Nick, Ray, and I wrestled a six-man against Verne and Greg Gagne and Jim Brunzell. I turned to Ray and said, "I didn't get the finish. I forgot it."

"I wasn't there when they gave it out," Ray said.

"So, it's just you and me here, and we don't know the finish?"

He said, "Nick knows enough for both of us."

Ray was like Richie Allen, an old pro ballplayer. They said he was nothing but trouble, drinking and carousing all night. But on the baseball field, which they call "between the lines," he was great. Ray was like that. He would stay out all night, and sometimes we couldn't find him for days. But when it came time to be in the ring, he was there.

Bobby Duncum came into the AWA and teamed with Lanza. He was from Texas and played in the minor leagues for the St. Louis Cardinals. He took great bumps and had great acceleration. He is a very nice man who lost his son a couple of years ago. Bobby Duncum Jr. was a wrestler in WCW.

Ken Patera was an athlete and an Olympian. He's a big, tough, strong guy, and he lets everybody know it. He has this personality that he won't take any crap from anyone. He's real loud and boisterous and has caused a lot of his own problems. We've been friends a long time, and he's always been nice to me.

In 1988, we worked an angle in the WWF when he came back from his stay in jail. We even had a "debate" on television. But Vince wouldn't let me call him what I wanted to call him. He had just gotten out of the can, and I was going to have some Danishes and coffee on a nearby table during our debate. "Would you like some, Stickybuns? I mean, would you like some sticky buns?"

Vince said, "Don't do that." I didn't.

Wrestling Patera was like working with the bear. You knew he was strong. Usually, when someone picked me up for a bodyslam, I would help him. Patera would just pick you up with ease like a forklift. He was that powerful. Verne Gagne always said that Patera would have won the Olympic gold medal in weightlifting if he hadn't been out all night trying to attack the German girls the night before.

I managed the Barbarian, who used to look a lot like one of the Road Warriors. When I was with him, he would wear this outfit with reindeer antlers on his head. I never managed a guy with antlers. I stepped in the ring first and sat on the ropes so he could come through. He stepped through the ropes and stood up. The problem was that he hooked me by the balls with the antlers.

I screamed, "Put me down! Put me down!" as he was trying to stand up with me attached to him.

I managed Nikolai Volkoff before he was Nikolai Volkoff. At the time I managed him in the AWA, he was Boris Breznikov. He was a big guy from Yugoslavia, but he was real softhearted and a good family man.

They never used managers in Japan, but I was over there when Antonio Inoki and Giant Baba had a major split. Abdullah the Butcher left Baba and jumped to Inoki. Tiger Jeet Singh left Inoki and went to Baba. Tiger is a Hindu who lives in Toronto. I enjoyed managing him, but not hanging around Japan with him. All he wanted to do was look at cameras all day.

They also made me the manager of the Missing Link, who was Dewey Robertson. He painted his face green and had three dots of hair on his head. He used to grab what hair he had and run it into the post. We were in New York and had to go to Los Angeles the next day. He asked me, "What time does your plane leave in the morning?"

"Around 10:00," I said.

"Mine's at 9:15. If you get there around quarter to nine, that's fine."

"For what?" I asked.

"To get my ticket. My gimmick is that I don't talk."

I told him, "You better start talking tomorrow. I'm only your manager for 10 minutes a night."

"But with my haircut . . ."

"You're in New York," I said. "People will think you had a bad barber. They don't care here. You'll blend in."

Rick Rude wasn't as open to my help. He was jealous of everyone and always scared that someone was getting his shot. He felt that he should have been the champion and always in the main event. That was his mentality.

We were in Buffalo one night and going 20 miles to Niagara Falls. Rude was getting his rental car. I was going to get a cab.

I asked him, "Are you by yourself?"

"Yeah," he said.

"You want company? I'll pay half the car."

He said, "No, I'll go by myself."

That was Rick. He was just all for himself. That's the way he wanted to conduct his life and business.

"Mr. Wonderful" Paul Orndorff was a man who could have had it all. He could have been the big babyface under Hogan. He was an athlete and in great condition. But when he tore his bicep and hurt his neck, he suffered nerve damage and was never the same.

Another member of my family was King Kong Bundy, or "Shamu," as I called him. Steve Hecht from Coliseum Video had a big party in his house in Toronto. He invited Bundy and me to his party, but no one else would come. I thought I'd be nice to the guy and kiss up to him.

"What does Bundy like to eat?" he asked me.

"He loves Cornish hens," I said. Honestly, I didn't know if that was true. I just made it up.

We got to his house. The guy had 75 Cornish hens out with some lunchmeat. Bundy had a bologna sandwich. Hecht got stuck with 75 chickens.

Adrian Adonis was funny. He used to like his wife to take naked pictures of him. Then, he'd take the film to the local Walgreens to have it developed. He'd call the Walgreens to see if his film was in. He'd ask them, "Would you look in there to see if they're the ones from the bar mitzvah?" just to get them to look through the pictures.

I also managed Haku and Tonga, the Islanders, for a while. They weren't hard to deal with at all. They were very kind, docile, nice people. But if you got them drinking, you'd have a problem. One night in a bar, a guy said something derogatory to Haku. Haku reached in his mouth and broke off the guy's bottom teeth with his fingers.

Tully Blanchard got mad at me after he left the WWF in 1989. I saw him at a legends gathering in Philadelphia years later. I asked about Joe, his dad, who was a good friend of mine.

"How's your dad?" I asked.

"Why don't you call him and ask him?" he shot back.

"What are you hot at me about?"

He said, "When I left the WWF, I heard you knocked me on TV."

"I was told to," I answered. "I didn't care if you left or stayed. All I said was the reason I got rid of you was because you were hard to do business with. I couldn't handle you anymore. You were doing your own thing. It was part of the story line."

That was it. He was upset about it.

Curt Hennig is a tremendous athlete. His father, Larry, wrestled as the "Ax." I call Irene, his wife, the "Battle-ax." I've known Curt since he was a kid. Curt was like a Barry Windham or a Ray Stevens. He has that ability to bounce back in the ring. If he does something wrong, he can easily recover.

When McMahon was hyping IcoPro, a bodybuilding supplement, in the WWF, Curt gave his kid some before a football game. The kid ended up not playing because he had the shits for four days and couldn't practice.

Hercules Hernandez was a funny guy, but he was always half asleep or into something bad. We were standing outside the airport in Newark, under a partition, waiting for the rental car. Herc was standing under the partition with a chain that he normally wore to the ring around his neck. He had a piece of tape on one side of his head and a cut on the other. He had the tape on the wrong side. He was wearing a World Gym T-shirt with no arms, a pair of shorts, and shower shoes.

We were standing there with five or six businessmen. Herc noticed there was a button that read, "Push for Heat." That would make the coils warm up the partition in the winter. Herc looked at the businessmen and said, "What happens if you push that for 'heat'? Does a guy come out and pull your tights?"

They had no idea what he was talking about.

I even managed the "Brooklyn Brawler." (I really went up in the world. Kenny Jay must have been sick.) His name is Steve Lombardi, and he actually is from Brooklyn. But he had no idea how to be the "Brooklyn Brawler." He had jeans and a T-shirt that said "Brooklyn Brawler," but they were laundered. I told him, "No, you've got to be dirty."

I had this idiot crawling on top of the furnaces in the Hershey Park Fieldhouse in Pennsylvania. I told him he had to get dirty, not just regular dirty from the ground, but with soot like he was in the bowels of the buildings and alleys. I tried to talk him into carrying a rat with him, but he wouldn't do that. He wasn't going to go anyplace with that gimmick. He could have been "the Brooklyn Rooster" for all anyone cared.

And what would "the Brain" be without his fans?

I called them humanoids. A humanoid is the kind of guy who has a white sock on one foot and a brown one on the other and thinks he has a pair at home just like them. A humanoid has no fingernails and hair cut at an angle. One side is higher than the other. He has where he works on one shirt pocket and his name on the other. Usually, it's two names like Billy Ray or Bobby Earl—something intelligent. In his pocket are 150 pens that don't work. And on his belt around his work pants, he has this round ring with 600 keys on it. Are there 600 people who would give this moron a job, or a key to anything they owned?

He goes home to his rented furniture. He sits between the spring and the cat poop on the couch. He watches his old black and white TV set with aluminum foil around the antenna. As he eats his TV dinner and sips on a lukewarm Busch beer, his wife looks at him and he looks at her. She looks at the TV and says, "Oh, that rasslin' is fake."

I also called fans "ham-and-eggers." A ham-and-egger is the easiest thing to have on a menu—ham and eggs. They are the easiest things to have and the simplest thing in the world.

I never went to places where I was going to be around that many fans. When I had my time off, I went to my own restaurants and clubs and hung out with a different crew, mainly my Indianapolis friends. I didn't hang out with wrestling people. I never had too much trouble. Occasionally, I'd see a few guys who would want to mess with me, but someone would always call security.

But in the ring and out of the ring, I'd see violence and a few weapons.

In the south, every fan carried knives and straight razors— which I have been hit with—for some reason. They would be working with it, whittling or opening up a box. I worked in Jonesboro, Arkansas, in 1965, and the fans would sit there, drinking out of big jugs and holding rifles.

In Cleveland, the fans used to take their steel chairs from the stands, fold them, and toss them like Frisbees at us. I would confront the promoter and say, "Jesus Christ, they're killing us. How about a little protection?"

We couldn't get anywhere with him, so we asked the police, and they told us, "The promoter told us not to mess with the fans because they pay to get in."

Every time some asshole fan threw something, it usually hit someone, but not me. I was in the ring one night in Lafayette, Indiana, when a fan threw a chair in the ring. I learned later on in my career that the first thing to do is grab the chair for three reasons. First, if I didn't, it would bounce and someone else would get hit. Second, I had it to fend off other chairs. Third, if that fan got in the ring, he was all mine.

I saw this chair coming and, at that time, I didn't know the rule about grabbing a chair. I started running backward, looking over my shoulder as if I'm going to catch it like Willie Mays. I shouted, "A chair!"

Someone in the ring yelled, "Catch it!"

I put my hands up, and they went through the rungs. The seat hit me right on the top of the head and knocked the shit out of me. I thought I was knocked out. I had a funny taste in my mouth and I couldn't see. I didn't know that I had to grab the chair, not put my hands up and catch it like a football.

In Winnipeg, I was shot one night in the elbow by a pellet gun. There's an old saying in the business—you don't sell a "potato." If a mark hits you, you never sell it. I was hit right above the elbow, and it felt like someone took a hot needle and stuck it in. After I was hit, someone yelled at me not to move and sell it. I think I had an accident in my trunks.

Then again, fans can also be overly friendly. Jay York, who wrestled as the Alaskan, was 280 pounds and had this big beard. He was working one night, and there was a male fan in the front row wearing women's ski pants, high boots, a mink stole, jewelry, and his hair done up.

The guy ran to ringside, got up on his tiptoes, and shouted to Jay, "Scratch him, Alaskan, you big walrus, you!"

In those days, a lot of people believed wrestling was real. If you were a real no-good, dirty guy in a three-on-one situation, that got heat. You could have heel against heel, and whoever I managed was a bigger heel. Nowadays people don't care. They just like the action.

My first time at Madison Square Garden was scary. I got there at 4:00 in the afternoon, and the fans were packed outside the entrance, pounding on the cars.

I was managing Paul Orndorff one night. As I was sitting at ringside, I noticed this guy sitting at ringside with a sledgehammer. I called the cop over and said, "Get this son of a bitch out of here."

The "fan" said, "I work here. I'm going to take the ring down when it's over."

Not only was it hard getting out of the ring sometimes, it was hard to get out of the building. In the Garden, we'd have to get there early, but there was no place to park inside so we would always take a cab. But, if we were on last, we were in pretty bad shape because there were no cabs waiting outside. The door we came out of was on 33rd, between Broadway and 9th. Both Broadway and 9th had a mess of people because both streets were one-ways.

But there was an ambulance at the Garden. We would each give the driver 10 bucks, and he'd drive us to the Ramada at 49th and 9th where we parked our cars. The guy would make $100 every time. He would turn the lights and sirens on. "Everyone back away. Ambulance," he'd shout.

When I would work in Houston, Texas, this one old lady would always come there and sit ringside. This woman would curse at me like a drunken sailor or a member of a wrestling locker room. I had never heard talk like that in my life. She'd call me every filthy name in the book.

"Miss Texas of 1911" would always spit at me, but one night, her teeth followed the spit. The plate landed in the ring, bounced like a hockey puck, and landed by me. I walked over to where they landed, looked at her teeth, and looked at her. Then, I cocked my right leg as if I was going to stomp her teeth.

Like a heel wrestler begging off from a babyface, the foul-mouthed woman started pleading with me, "Please, please, Bobby. Please, I'm sorry." At least I think that's what she said. It's hard to understand an old woman with all the teeth out of her head. It's like talking to a prune with eyes.

Feeling nice, I kicked her teeth back to the now-kindly old woman. She picked them up, shook them, and put them back in her mouth. She then turned on me and continued to call me every filthy name you can possibly imagine.

And I understood every word.

Sometimes, fans decide to be a little more confrontational. Some people are tough. You just never know. When a fan would jump into the ring, I would try to nail him as quickly as I could. I didn't want to have to rely on the babyface to help me.

The babyface would say, "Let me have him," and then he would "accidentally" elbow the guy in the face or step on his ankle. That is, unless I was working with Brad Rheingans, who decided to hold me for the marks coming in the ring.

When I confronted people as a manager, I used to pick out one guy. Keep in mind, I used to do that. One night in Hammond, Indiana, this huge guy with no neck who had to be an iron worker started walking toward the ring. He shoved the cop away. I yelled at him, "Get in here."

The guy walked up to the ring, grabbed it, and curled it. Blackjack Lanza said, "If he gets in the ring, he's all yours."

I would often wrestle at Buck Lake Ranch in Angola, Indiana. It was like a western ghost town where they lifted a rock at 8:00 and the fans came out from underneath. One night, I was thrown out of the ring. An old mark walked up to me and tried to kick me in the balls. I grabbed his foot and tried to kick *him* in the balls. Just as I was about to connect, our knees cracked together. He limped back to his seat, and I limped back to the ring.

Lanza shouted at me from the ring, "Get in here before you get killed!"

A more memorable night at Buck Lake Ranch resulted in a riot. Blackjack Lanza and I wrestled the Bruiser. The midgets were also on the card. We wrestled on this outdoor stage that was painted like an old western town where they did shows.

As I was sitting on a chair next to the ring, I heard this whizzing sound past my head. Fans were throwing rocks and lighters so hard that they would stick to the back of the set.

Moose Cholak was standing outside eating popcorn. At some point in the match, Bruiser was supposed to be in trouble because of Blackjack Lanza. He would yell, "Help me, Moose!" Moose would run in the ring, make a comeback on Jack, and we'd split. The problem was that Bruiser didn't sell anything that Jack was throwing at him.

Moose didn't want to go in the ring. Bruiser started yelling, "Hey, Moose." Moose looked at the people and yelled, "Let's get him," and waved for all the fans to run to the ring.

The fans rushed the stage and the shit was on. Moose was trying to grab me, and I'm trying to hit marks coming at me. Even Bruiser was trying to step on a mark's foot or ankle, desperate to keep them out of it.

We made our way back to the dressing room. People were outside rioting, and there was no way we could get out of town. The cops were county sheriffs with cowboy hats and blackjacks, but no guns. They finally found a crop duster truck, and we drove away from the arena with the fans waiting in their cars.

My car wasn't parked there. It was parked two miles away at a Phillips 66 station. I got a ride to the arena from one of the boys and always got a ride back. I never wanted my car where the fans could cut my tires. The crop duster truck dropped me off, and I got in my 1968 Chevy Nova with Lanza.

The people were still following us. I drove to the interstate to go back to Indianapolis, and I had the Nova wide open, doing 90 miles per hour with the marks right behind me. Roger Littlebrook, one of the midget wrestlers, pulled up next to me in his car.

"You've got some problems, mate," he yelled.

"I know!" I shouted.

"Go off on the next off-ramp, drive over the road, and get back on the interstate. I'll block the road for you."

I turned off on the next ramp with Littlebrook and about 35 other cars right behind me. I drove across the street and back onto the interstate. Littlebrook got on the ramp, turned his car sideways, and jumped out. This midget, who is 3'1", was ready to fight. The fans stopped, got out of their cars, took one look at him in his fighting stance, and laughed.

Johnny Valentine had a creative way to protect his car. One night, we were wrestling in Chicago. We were looking out the window to see about 10 rough-looking teenagers outside near all the cars.

Johnny yelled, "Don't touch my fucking car, you little bastards!" and walked away.

I looked out the window, and they were standing on the car, jumping up and down on it and kicking in the windows. I yelled for Johnny to come over.

"Johnny, come here. Look at what they're doing to your car."

He smiled, "That's not my car."

I learned that when I parked my car, I would put my bag on the car next to me. I'd shout at the fans to get the hell away from me and not to touch my car. When the night was over, that car would have slashed tires or no tires at all.

I walked out to the ring one night with Lanza in front of me and Mulligan behind me. If a mark grabbed you, you never turned to him, because that would leave your back open to other people. You just kept going. That was the rule. If they didn't knock you down, you kept going.

A little guy charged me once, and Mulligan, who had played for the New York Jets, tried to block him, but the fan got around him. I told Mulligan later, "You should write a book called, *I'm the Reason for Namath's Knees*, because you let everyone get through you."

This guy hit me with a ballpeen hammer on the top of my head. It didn't hurt. But when I brushed my hair back and looked at my hand, it was full of blood.

The police brought the guy into the dressing room and held him up against the wall. They said, "Go ahead."

I took off after him and, just as I cocked my hand to punch him, Dusty Rhodes kicked the guy in the balls. He dropped to the ground, and I hit the cement wall. I told the cops, "Get him out of here before he kills me."

Boston was a violent town. Gorilla Monsoon was refereeing a match between Blackjack Mulligan and Pedro Morales. Mind you, if you take Gorilla's glasses off, he can't see how many people are in a room. A fan jumped into the ring with a stiletto and stabbed Mulligan up the leg. Mulligan reached out for the guy but got cut up the arm. Monsoon, blind as a bat, grabbed the guy and threw him out of the ring without knowing that the guy cut anybody.

We took Mulligan to the hospital to get sewn up, but his cut became infected. The "fan" had dipped the knife in pig fat. It took 100 stitches to close up that leg.

The Boston fans would throw frozen hard-boiled eggs in the ring. They could pick you off at 500 yards. The management put a plastic shield around the ring. The fans got more creative, with one of them throwing a trumpet in the ring. They put a screen net over the ring, but no one could outsmart the Boston fans. They started throwing big, 20-penny nails.

But nails, trumpets, eggs, and ballpeen hammers were nothing compared to what happened to me in 1975.

I was managing at the Chicago Amphitheater when a fan actually shot at me with a gun. Verne Gagne, the AWA champion at the time, was wrestling Nick Bockwinkel. The match came to the finish, and I was outside the ring. Nick picked up Verne, slammed him, and covered him. The referee counted: one, two . . . On two, Verne put his foot over the ropes to break the count. Naturally, the referee didn't see it and made the three count.

The people thought there was a new champion. I acted as if there was a new champion. Nick and I jumped up and we hugged each other. I was on the apron. He was in the ring. Suddenly, I heard these two "pops." In those days, people used to break plastic cups with their feet all the time, so I didn't think much of it.

The referee saw Verne's foot on the rope, and he called for the match to continue. We didn't notice what was going on. Verne dropkicked Nick in the back and into me. I fell to the floor. Nick landed on his back, and Verne covered him for the pin.

After the match ended, Nick and I started to walk back to the dressing room and there was no heat. No one was booing. Everyone was real quiet. We got to the dressing room and Ray Stevens was waiting at the door.

"Are you all right?" he asked.

I was confused. "What do you mean?"

He told us five people were shot.

Apparently, when I jumped up to the ring apron after Nick "pinned" Verne, this fan weighing about 250 pounds and wearing a fur coat said, "I'll get him down." He had a gun, put his hand on the shoulder of this kid sitting next to him, fired the gun, and deafened the kid. He shot only twice, but the bullets went through five people (they all recovered). The bullets never made it to ringside, just to the people near the ring.

No one testified against him. He even came to the matches after that, but he never did anything after the shooting. It was awhile before I was involved in finishes or anything in Chicago. I was really concerned. I would come to the ring, but I wouldn't trip anybody or jump up to the apron. I was just there. That experience scared me.

Hosting "Cauliflower Alley" with Mike Tenay.

Photo by Michael Lano (wrealano@aol.com).

Reminiscing with "Playboy" Buddy Rose.

Photo by Michael Lano (wrealano@aol.com).

In front of the WCW "Nitro" fans.

Interviewing WWF champion Bret the "Hit Man" Hart with Gene Okerlund.
Photo by Michael Lano (wrealano@aol.com).

Presenting a posthumous "Thank You" award to the late WWF referee
Joey Marella at the Cauliflower Alley Club.
Photo by Michael Lano (wrealano@aol.com).

Ringside with Gene Okerlund.

Photo by Michael Lano (wrealano@aol.com).

With the late Gorilla Monsoon, my longtime pal
and broadcast colleague.

Photo by Michael Lano (wrealano@aol.com).

Donning the headset with famous WCW announcers Mike Tenay (left) and Tony Schiavone (center).

Photo by Michael Lano (wrealano@aol.com).

Cutting up with Gorilla Monsoon.

Photo by Michael Lano (wrealano@aol.com).

With good pal Pat Patterson, who
once managed. I was quite pleased
with this EAC plaque, which I
received in 1996.
Photo by Michael Lano (wrealano@aol.com).

Chapter 12

BRAIN REFLECTIONS

The three biggest thrills of my life and career were my debut match against "Prince" Pullins, managing Andre the Giant at Wrestlemania 3, and wrestling at Comiskey Park in Chicago during the eighties. I teamed with the Original Sheik and we wrestled Bruiser and Bobo Brazil.

I remember saying in the ring that night at Comiskey, "I used to carry all their jackets. Sheik would give me five bucks to wash his car. Bruiser used to give me five bucks to wrestle for the year. And Bobo would have given me 50 if I would have asked him."

It's hard to pick a favorite wrestler whom I managed, but the ones I had the most fun with were Blackjack Lanza and Baron Von Raschke. I was in my twenties then, and everything was new to me. My idols in this business were always Buddy Rogers and Ray Stevens. I got to know Rogers and wrestle him in 1968. I managed, teamed, and wrestled Ray.

Today, managers are few and far between. Years ago, a lot of guys couldn't talk—that's why they had managers. Like Bob Orton Jr., who is a great athlete but stutters. Some guys couldn't come up with anything to say, so it was good for them to have a manager.

Verne Gagne put me with Nick Bockwinkel, but Nick didn't need me because he could talk. I was a way to save the matches and add more possibilities to the finish. If Nick would have come out with Jimmy Hart yelling through his megaphone, I don't think that would have worked because they wouldn't look like they belonged together.

The reason that promotions like the WWF don't have managers anymore is that no one knows how to manage. They think that they can go out there and yell and scream and say, "Tonight, he's going down." Like no one has ever used that before.

No one knows how to develop their character. Wrestlers used to be able to develop a character, even changing their own nationality. Sheik Adnan al-Kaissie was a wrestler from Oklahoma State University and a native Iraqi. He wrestled for years as Billy White Wolf, an Indian. Another "Indian" named White Owl, out of Detroit, was actually black. When I was in Japan, Carlos Colon worked as an Indian, and he's Puerto Rican. Little Beaver wrestled as an Indian, and he was French Canadian. Chief Jay Strongbow's real name is Joe Scarpa, and he's Italian.

I always said I was from Beverly Hills. I never said Los Angeles or Hollywood because if you ever go to those places, there's a lot of garbage. Beverly Hills is where the money is. I got my character established. I yelled and screamed when the time was right. If someone yells and screams all the time, then when the time is actually right, there's nothing to yell and scream about.

Managers can't get over because no one can get over anymore. It's all been done. There is no emphasis put on a manager. If it wasn't for a manager, the business would have been dead. There wouldn't have been finishes. The wrestlers would always have to beat each other or get disqualified. That's the only thing you could do. With a manager, you have three guys involved and different possibilities for finishes.

Every manager wants to wear sunglasses. But when they wear sunglasses, no one can see their eyes or expressions. Everybody wants to have a beard and long hair. But then they look like the guy who takes tickets.

No one knows how to beg off. No one knows how to sneak. You never do anything where the referee catches you, because the referee doesn't draw you a dime. No one says, "Get the kids, Helen, we're going down to the auditorium. Freddy is refereeing tonight." Besides, the promotions like the WWF feel that there is no need for managers anyway.

Vince McMahon used to have a dress code. I don't know if he has one now. But WCW never did. I remember when I was a kid, I'd watch a guy and I'd look at his feet for nice shoes and his hands for nice jewelry. Fans needed to see guys like Buddy Rogers and Ric Flair wearing nice suits and think, "God, I want to be one of those guys because they make money." If you look professional, you usually are, or close to it.

Today, wrestlers walk around wearing jeans with the ass ripped out or Zubaz and a shirt that says "Gold's Gym." They're the world champion, dragging the belt around. They forget that wrestlers are perceived by a lot of people as buffoons and garbage and now they've confirmed this perception. It's all in how they present themselves.

I never liked a guy carrying a belt over his shoulder or dragging it. I used to tell guys, "If you win a Super Bowl ring, you don't take it out of your pocket and show it. You wear it. And you look better standing out there with the belt around your waist. It frees up your hands to talk."

I used to tell the guys who wore the fanny packs, "You want to meet some women tonight?"

They'd say, "Yeah."

"Well, you're not going to do it that way. Put that inside your pants."

Today, the wrestlers run to the ring and take the belt or their jacket off before they get to the ring. What those dummies don't know is that they might not be on camera. Stay in the ring until the bell rings, and *then* take your stuff off.

Why wear a beautiful robe to the ring when no one sees you? To keep warm? You open up your robe. The match starts. "Whoa," you say. You take the belt off, fold it, and give it to the timekeeper. Then, there's always some goon ready to take your robe back to the ring. "Wait a minute," you say. You fold that robe carefully because you want people to believe that you paid $100,000 for it. (Flair spent $10,000 to $20,000 at least on his robes.) Then, you look like a pro. And you have to live the part 24 hours a day.

Monsoon used to have a jacket he'd wear on the way to the ring. He'd carefully take it off, fold it real nice, put it down on the mat, and kick it.

Wrestling got over so well because of the Dumont Network, which is now ABC. Wrestling had an audience, a crowd, and lights. All they had to do was bring in one camera. That's why it got over.

"Gorgeous" George, the first real wrestling star, was an accident. Another guy was going to be "Gorgeous" George, but he broke his leg, so they made George Wagner "Gorgeous" George in Los Angeles.

Something's wrong, though. Baseball players and athletes don't get any TV residuals because it's a sports show. You only get residuals when you have a written or scripted show. Wrestling is just that. We never got one dime, not one residual. For some reason, the actors union doesn't care about us and has never delved into it.

My God, we've been on TV longer than *Gunsmoke*, or anything, and we should have gotten something. We never did. It's because there is no union.

Anytime a wrestler would talk about putting together a wrestling union, a promoter would blackball him. They didn't want you to start doing that. If you were making five grand a week for one guy and you didn't like it, you could try to make five grand somewhere else. But the promoters made it so you couldn't just pick up and move. You had an apartment and a lease. They had you. I even knew of a tag team where each member had one-year contracts, but those were negotiated six months apart. One always needed the other.

I saw Lou Thesz go to a one-hour broadway—which is the wrestling term for a time-limit draw—with a broken ankle wrestling the Bruiser. Today, a guy would take off eight years to recover. In those days, you just got in the car and continued to the next town to work. If you didn't, you didn't have a job.

I have worked with a groin pull, broken collarbone, and sprained ankle, which is worse than a break. I used to get a bucket of boiling water and a bucket of ice water. I'd put my ankle in the ice until I couldn't take it anymore. Then I'd put it in the hot water. I did that for an hour twice a day so I could get the circulation going and at least walk.

I've never experienced winning or losing in my life at a major level. I won and lost at Little League, but that was it. I never went to the NCAA championship. I never went for that putt for $100,000. I never went for a World Series ring. And I never went to high school, so I never played on a team.

I don't know the agony of defeat. I've never been defeated. I know the agony of a bad paycheck, and I know the good feeling of getting more money than I thought I would, which didn't happen that often.

I was out there to entertain. There are Shakespearean actors like Lawrence Olivier, comic actors like Robin Williams, and athletic actors, which is what I was. Nothing less. Nothing more. There are some wrestlers like Verne Gagne, who was a very tough man, good wrestler, and great shooter. But there is no shooting that draws you money in professional wrestling. If there was, he would have been in it and would have won it all.

But he would have never met me.

I have a wonderful education just from traveling and being around people who are bright. A lot of people think wrestlers aren't smart enough to put their underwear on the right way; they have to have a code—yellow in front, brown in back. Johnny Case was superintendent of Antioch schools, Angelo Poffo was a graduate of DePaul, Ken Patera was an Olympian who went to Brigham Young, Verne Gagne and Jim Brunzell went to the University of Minnesota, Baron Von Raschke went to the University of Nebraska and taught, and Blackjack Lanza was a sociology teacher.

They are educated people, not a bunch of buffoons and morons, even if they dressed and looked like it. And they're good-hearted people with families. Sure, they're off-the-wall people. But we never had that in the Congress or Senate, now did we? You know how women know that sex is over with Ted Kennedy? When the dome light goes on. You know why he wears wool underwear? To keep his ankles warm.

You get my point.

To be a "macho man," you don't slap a woman around and wear 12 chains. A true man is a guy that does the best he can to feed his family and not infringe on anyone's privacy. That's a good man to me.

But it doesn't hurt to marry a woman who has a Lotto ticket and a can of whipped cream and owns a liquor store.

Some people are very bitter about the business and the way it is run right now. Things change. You adapt or get out. You think about the times you had, the money you made, and the fun you had. If you think about everything negative, your whole life will be negative, and that's the way you will be.

They say it was better in the good old days. No, it wasn't. They make more money now these days than we did in the "old days." It was more fun in those days because it was easier. I could sit in an armlock for a half hour with Bruno Sammartino. Now wrestlers go through tables or fly off a scaffold.

It's not wrestling anymore. It's sports entertainment.

A lot of guys go out there and take those bumps off the top of a cage or a building because they can't work. That's the truth. If they could work, they wouldn't have to do that. Falling off a cage wouldn't hurt me. My trunks would be so full of shit halfway down, I'd land in a nice, big, soft spot.

It's a different crowd now watching wrestling, and it affects how the wrestlers perform.

Now guys get nervous if they miss a spot because they have their whole match laid out. They will go back to the beginning and start their match over again. When I started, we'd ask, "What do you want to do tonight." "Oh, let's work the arm or work the leg." You never wanted to do what the other guy did. We were always taught not to use another guy's finisher or use that move for a high spot.

There are no places left for a guy to hone his craft. In the old days, there were full-time territories—George Shire in San Francisco, Gene LeBelle in Los Angeles, Stu Hart in Calgary, Gene Kiniski in Vancouver, Joe Dusek in Omaha, Fritz Von Erich in Dallas, Joe Blanchard in San Antonio, the Funks in Amarillo, and Paul Boesch in Houston. Verne Gagne had Minnesota, Illinois, Wisconsin, Denver, San Francisco, Winnipeg, and Ottawa. Dick the Bruiser had Indianapolis. Nick Gulas had Tennessee, and the Jarretts had Tennessee, Alabama, and Kentucky. Bill Watts had Oklahoma, Arkansas, and Louisiana.

The Sheik had Michigan and Ohio. Vince McMahon Sr. ran from Bangor, Maine, to Charlotte, North Carolina. Frank Tunney was in Toronto. Johnny Rougeau promoted Montreal. Emil DuPree had Halifax in the summer. Eddie Graham had Florida. The Crocketts had Charlotte. Ray and Ann Gunkell and Jim Barnett had Atlanta.

Now you have Stamford, Connecticut, and the WWF. That's it.

Promotions won't make it now because there is no TV outside of the WWF. They'll just get local guys, put paint and funny little outfits on them, and pay them 50 bucks. The "stars" want guaranteed money, first-class travel, everything paid, and they want to go over. But they shouldn't. I never wanted to go over. You have to pick someone up.

A guy once asked me if wrestling was fake. I said, "You know, I used to think so. But if it was, wouldn't they let me win at least once?"

I beat Kenny Jay. Then again, he beat me too. He said in the locker room after that match, "Do I have to go another 20 years now?"

With my gimmick, I worked with Bruiser and Crusher in tag matches. I could work single matches only coming off an angle, not going after a title. A guy like Buck Zumhofe was perfect for me because of his size and that radio. 1-2-3 Kid would have been perfect for me. I wish I had a Rey Misterio or Eddie Guerrero. What I could have done with them.

But I never was a full-time wrestler. I never went into a territory as a wrestler. In Indiana, I started as a manager. Same as St. Louis and Minneapolis and the other territories.

I wrestled in specialty bouts, including midget matches. Bruiser and Little Bruiser against Blackjack Lanza and me. Or sometimes it was a six-man with Bruiser, Crusher, and Little Bruiser. It was funny. If we were in Indiana, the midget was Little Bruiser. If we were in Milwaukee, we'd call him Little Crusher.

There is an old wrestling joke that I tell and hear from time to time. It sums up the business as I know it.

There was a guy who went to the promoter and wanted to be a wrestler. The promoter said, "You don't look tough enough, kid."

The kid said, "But I want to be a wrestler."

"Go clean my office," said the promoter. The kid cleaned his office. The promoter took the kid down to the gym and stretched the kid.

"He won't be back," the promoter boasted.

The kid came back the next day. The promoter asked him, "What do you want?"

"I want to be a wrestler."

"Go wash and wax my car," ordered the promoter.

The kid washed and waxed his car. The promoter took him down to the gym and stretched him.

"Give me a hand job," said the promoter.

The kid gave him a hand job and left. The promoter was sure he wouldn't come back the next day.

The kid came back. "I want to be a wrestler," he claimed.

The promoter said, "Wash all the windows in my office." The kid did it and the promoter took him down to the gym again and stretched him.

"Give me a blow job," the promoter ordered.

The kid said, "I don't want to be a babyface."

Chapter 13

I JUST WANTED TO SEE HIS FACE

Mary Brunzell suggested the title for this chapter, so I dedicate it to Mary and her husband, Jim.

My dad and mom had split when I was less than a year old. It never bothered me not having a father—maybe when we had a "father and son" thing at school and I had nobody to invite. I was raised by my mother and grandmother, and my aunt would live with us periodically.

I never thought about looking up my father. What I thought was that my grandmother, who was like Schultz from *Hogan's Heroes*, ran the guy out. It was never important to me. But many years ago, I found out there were these companies that searched for lost relatives. I asked my wife to write this company and see if they could find out anything about my father and what happened to him. My mother never talked about him. Didn't tell me a thing. No pictures or anything.

We heard back from them with his name, where he worked, and all this information. But I wanted to see a picture. I found out he lived in Las Vegas. In 1997, I was out there to work Halloween Havoc. Cindi and I spent the weekend at Mike Tenay's cabin in Utah. When we left for Vegas, we decided to look up the address and see who lived there.

We drove to the other side of the strip in Vegas. It was a nice neighborhood. We found the house and parked in front of it.

"Let's just sit here and watch to see who comes in or out," I told Cindi. "But if there's a kid on the porch playing a banjo, we're getting out of here."

So I waited. It was probably two minutes, but it felt like hours. I couldn't wait. We drove up to the driveway. I asked Cindi to knock on the door and tell whoever answered the door that we were lost and were trying to find Ferm Street, something I just made up.

This woman came to the door. She had glasses and grayish hair and kind of looked like she could be a sister. I didn't really know. I told Cindi to put her butt up against the hood of the car, so whoever was facing her had to look at me. I had a camera nearby, and as the woman was talking to Cindi, I picked it up, but I immediately dropped it. I picked it up again and it started making this whirring sound. I couldn't figure out how to fix it, so I threw the thing down.

The lady said, "I don't know where Ferm Street is. Let me get my husband."

She walked into the house, and then she and her husband walked out. He looked like me, but he was too young to be my father. He walked past the car and saw me and kept walking. He stopped and turned back, looking at me for just a second. He walked into the garage and came back out with a street map and laid it across the hood of the car, trying to find the street for Cindi, but he just couldn't.

As Cindi was getting back in the car, they said, "We wish we could help you. We wish there was more we could do."

She got in the car and I told her, "They seem like nice people. I'm going to go in."

Cindi said, "Let's go to Denny's first and have breakfast and talk about it."

"Cindi, I'm this close. After 53 years, I'm not going to choke on a bone at Denny's or get hit by a car."

"I'll be right behind you," she said.

I got out of the car, walked up to the house, and knocked on the door. The woman came to the door.

"Excuse me, ma'am," I said. "May I see you and your husband please?"

She stared at me for a moment. She called out, "Jim."

Later on, Dottie, the woman I was speaking to, told me that she was concerned that the car had broken down and, since we're all Heenans, we can't fix anything. My idea of repairing something is opening up the phone book and calling for someone.

Jim walked out. He was wearing a Notre Dame T-shirt and the Notre Dame football game had just started.

"I have reason to believe that you and I are brothers," I said.

"Come on in," he said.

I walked into the house. I was nervous. The most nervous I've ever been in my life. I showed him my birth certificate and where my father signed it. I also told him that my father's job in Chicago was as a printer who printed labels for Al Capone and racing forms. He would perform in bars with cymbals on his knees and a banjo. And if a guy was down on his luck, he'd give him his suit.

I sat there for an hour and told him everything I knew. I showed him my pictures and passport. Not once did he say, "Wait a minute, no way." He just sat there and listened.

When I was done, Jim stood up, said, "Welcome to the family," and hugged me.

I asked him for a picture of my father. He showed me a photo of my father with a cowboy outfit—hat, gun, and everything. He looked like Blackjack Lanza in his seventies.

"You can have it," he said.

Cindi and I went back to the MGM Grand. The phone rang the next morning. It was Jim.

"I haven't slept all night," he said. "I called your other brother in Florida."

I had an older brother, John, who lived six miles from me, that I never knew. He's 10 years older than me. He's from Chicago, like they all are. He's retired now and enjoying his family and grandchildren. Jim is a security cop at the Hilton in Las Vegas. He also was in Air Force security on Air Force One with Presidents Johnson and Nixon. My younger brother, Bob, of all names, is an educator and a former priest.

Now all the kids ask him at school, "Where's your brother?"

He answers with, "You have to pay me."

It turned out walking up to that door was the best thing I ever did. I now have three brothers. My father died in May of 1990 in Las Vegas, and my sister had passed away as well. My brother Bob took me over to our father's grave. I put my hand on it and spoke to my father for the first time.

"I'm not mad at you. I'm not mad at you at all," I said to him.

When I worked at the Showboat in Las Vegas, about a mile from them, my name would be on the marquee. I asked them if they ever put two and two together.

They said that people would ask them if they were related to Bobby Heenan, but they always said no. They just didn't watch wrestling. Now, John wears a Bobby Heenan T-shirt and challenges people around town. I have nieces, nephews, aunts, and uncles. I'm a godparent to one of my niece's children. My brothers and I talk every month. They're a great addition to my life. I'm proud of all of them, and they seem to be proud of me.

I remember as we were leaving that driveway in Las Vegas, my wife said, "Isn't this great?"

"Yeah, it's a ball," I said. "An hour ago we were on our way to Denny's. Now I have to buy 85 Christmas gifts."

EPILOGUE

Around March of 2001, I was having pain in the side of my jaw right behind my ear. I had lost a tooth there and I thought my jaw had moved or something. I let it go for a while.

Meanwhile, in the late spring, it really started to bother me. Someone told me that I had TMJ or something else in the jawbone area. I went to the doctor to get it checked and he told me I had to go to an oral surgeon. The oral surgeon told me that I had to go to my dentist and have a mouthpiece made to correct the problem.

I was doing all this back and forth when I started to notice that my speech was getting slurred and my food tasted metallic and funny. My dentist said, "Where are the X rays from the oral surgeon?" I told him he didn't take any. My dentist called the surgeon, who told him that the machine was broken on that day.

I was misdiagnosed for quite a while. Finally, Dr. Gene Balis, who did a 7½ hour operation on my neck, told me to go see Dr.

Douglas Klotch. That doctor x-rayed me to make sure that I didn't have a brain tumor. When he didn't find that, he x-rayed me again and saw that I had a growth on the back of the tongue and throat on the right side.

The doctor told me I had throat cancer.

I was already standing and started walking in a big circle in his office. I got real cold and real sweaty at the same time. I looked at Cindi, who was in there with me, and said, "I have to sit down."

A nurse took me into this room, laid me on the table, and put my feet up. After about 10 minutes, I was okay.

The first thing that occurred to me was to ask the doctor, "How long do I have?" It was like *Family Feud* all over again. Just trying to think of how much time I had. It's the truth.

The second thing I thought of was: "Am I going to lose my hair?"

In the end, Dr. Klotch told me I needed six weeks of radiation and chemotherapy. He gave me an 80 percent chance of recovery and told me not to worry.

He really is a good doctor. He told me that I was really healthy. I asked him if there was anything I should do. He said, "Yeah, don't buy any LPs, and pay me in cash."

But I was very concerned, because my daughter Jessica was getting married around the same time. I was just told that I had cancer and, on top of everything else, Christmas was coming. I didn't want her to know that I was diagnosed with cancer until after the wedding. But she was home when the doctor called to make the arrangements for my chemo. She found out.

Jessica told me, "Dad, you're tough. You've been through worse. Mom had cancer and beat it. You'll get better. You have an 80 percent chance."

I heard from all my friends. I was surprised by the people that did call and the ones that didn't call. I guess that's how you find out who your friends are sometimes.

The week after I found out that I had cancer, I called Jim Brunzell in Minneapolis. We've always been good friends and always kept in touch about three to four times a year. I told him what was wrong and we talked for a bit.

About a week or so later, I got a phone call from none other than Jesse Ventura, the governor of Minnesota. He had spoken to Brunzell and wanted to give me some encouragement. We talked for about a half hour. He wished me the best. I figured I'd never hear from Jesse and began to wonder who I would hear from next. The only person I had called was Brunzell.

A half hour later, the phone rang again and it was Greg Gagne. He had talked to Brunzell too. He wanted to wish me good luck. I never expected to hear from him. The very next day, I was gone. When I came home, my wife told me that Verne Gagne had called me.

I said, "I'm sure he has. He's called me a lot of things."

She said, "No, he called. He heard that you were sick and wanted to wish you a speedy recovery."

Angelo Mosca called me. Harley Race called me. Pepper Gomez, who lives out in San Francisco, called me a couple of times. Nick Bockwinkel, Hawk, Jack Lanza, Baron Von Raschke, Hillbilly Jim, George the "Animal" Steele, and the Crusher called. Even David McClane from WOW called me. I would never have expected to hear from some of those people at all.

One day I was sitting upstairs, just going through some mail, and the doorbell rang. I thought to myself, "I don't feel like seeing anybody." I walked downstairs and looked out the window. I saw Mike Graham (Eddie Graham's son) with Verne Gagne.

I thought, "Oh hell, he's finally come to get me." So, I grabbed a coat, wrapped it around my arm, and grabbed a knife and a broken bottle. Not really. I opened the door and said, "Come on in."

I greeted Mike and looked at Verne and said, "How are you?" extending my hand.

"Give me a hug," Verne said.

Mike lives down the road from me and Verne was in town on business. He wanted to see me and Mike told him that he knew where I lived. After a little while, Mike had to leave, and I asked Verne to stay. For the next couple of hours, we drank beer and talked about old times and how they changed. We told Wally Karbo stories and stuff like that. When he needed to leave, I gave him a ride to where he was staying.

We shook hands and I told him how nice it was that he had stopped by. He told me what an asset I had been to the business. That made me feel good—to see Verne come over and call. He usually doesn't do that for anybody.

It always seems that it's the people you would never expect who come around and do something like that.

We got nice letters from people. At first, I kept things quiet. After a while, though, I figured there was no sense in hiding it anymore.

Your life changes when you're diagnosed with cancer. Traffic doesn't mean anything anymore. I don't want to give the guy in the bulldozer the finger because it just doesn't matter. Just like I told my wife before our honeymoon: if I get there late, start without me.

As I write this, I am in my second week after my six weeks of treatment. I can swallow a lot better and my speech has improved. It still feels like I have Mr. Ed's tongue.

Getting cancer really changed my perspective on life. At Christmas time, my sister-in-law was visiting. We have four cats. One of the cats was underneath the tree. She walked up to me and said, "The cat is by the tree."

I said, "You get him; I've got cancer."

She thought that I was worried about a cat! They had just told me a week before that I had cancer and she wanted me to climb up a tree with the balls and the lights and chase a cat out. That was my Christmas with her.

But it's the truth.

I owe my life to Dr. Balis, Dr. Klotch, and Dr. Harvey Greenberg, my oncologist, not to mention the staff at Moffitt South Outpatient Clinic at Tampa General. They were great. They answered all my questions and didn't pass anything off on someone else. They knew what I was there for. No one cared who I was. Ken, the assistant to Dr. Greenberg, confessed to me later on that he was a big WWF fan and that he watched me when he was a kid growing up. Other staff members did that as well.

Throughout the whole treatment, I knew there was nothing I could do but play the hand that I was dealt. And if "the Brain" could cheat and grab some spare change while in the waiting room, so much the better. That's what he would do. "I'll watch your wallet while you go to the bathroom," he'd say. "I'll watch your Ensure for you."

Seriously, if it weren't for them, I would have ended up with some proctologist with a thermometer behind his ear, wondering where his pencil was.

I'm not going to retire. In fact, I'm looking forward to doing personal appearances and I may even start a singing career. The WCW couldn't shut me up. I'm sure as hell not going to let cancer do it.

Just remember, the Brain has not left the building yet. And he didn't lose his hair, but he was able to grab a couple of wallets and a few cases of Ensure.

INDEX